Women in Health Management

Writings on health and health management have long been concerned with the great figures that have preserved, protected or extended life. From Hippocrates and Galen to Vesalius, Lister, Mengele, Pasteur, Jenner and Fleming, these writings have celebrated individuals whose knowledge and practice has treated our ills and sought to better manage our care. For the most part, this has been a history of 'great men' [sic]. There are honourable mentions for a small number of women such as Elizabeth Blackwell or Florence Nightingale but, by and large, one would be forgiven for assuming that the management of health has nearly always been the preserve of men. The contribution of women is largely absent – written out.

This book contributes to the process of writing women back into our shared history and understanding of health and its management. Its chapters detail how women have been the main healers for communities across the globe for over four millennia. It considers the manner in which 'wise women' who used their knowledge of herbs, ritual and healing were excluded from emerging medical professions, while their good works were written over and written out of local histories through their marginalisation and repositioning. More positively, it brings to our attention inspiring women who have shaped the ways in which we develop and deliver health in its broadest sense. Drawing on the work of women from Kenya, Nigeria, Hawaii, Türkiye, USA, Ireland and the UK, and from disciplines that span medicine, social work, mental health, health promotion, occupational therapy, midwifery, pharmacology and traditional healing, the women considered in this volume advance our understanding of alternative ways of developing, delivering and managing health. This includes organising services for areas of neglected health (e.g. women's health, health prevention, rural populations), tackling contentious health issues (e.g. female genital mutilation, management of mental disorders) and the care of health providers themselves (e.g. providing space for women to practice, managing the mental well-being of healthcare workers). This book also shows how the work of these women went beyond health management to influence political and societal change.

Robert McMurray is a Professor and Chair of Organisational Studies and the Associate Dean for Education at the Sheffield University Management School, UK.

Éidín Ní Shé is a Senior Lecturer at the Royal College of Surgeons Graduate School of Healthcare Management, Ireland.

Routledge Studies in Health Management
Edited by Ewan Ferlie

The healthcare sector is now of major significance, economically, scientifically and societally. In many countries, healthcare organisations are experiencing major pressures to change and restructure, while cost containment efforts have been accentuated by global economic crisis. Users are demanding higher service quality, and healthcare professions are experiencing significant reorganisation while operating under increased demands from an ageing population.

Critically analytic, politically informed, discursive and theoretically grounded, rather than narrowly technical or positivistic, the series seeks to analyse current healthcare organisations. Reflecting the intense focus of policy and academic interest, it moves beyond the day-to-day debate to consider the broader implications of international organisational and management research and different theoretical framings.

Innovating Healthcare
The Role of Political, Managerial and Clinical Leadership
John Storey and Richard Holti

Co-production and Japanese Healthcare
Work Environment, Governance, Service Quality and Social Values
Victor A. Pestoff

Management, Organization and Childbirth
Towards a New Model for the Birth Path
Gabriella Piscopo and Margherita Ruberto

Women in Health Management
Global Revolutionaries
Edited by Robert McMurray and Éidín Ní Shé

For more information about this series, please visit: www.routledge.com

Women in Health Management
Global Revolutionaries

Edited by Robert McMurray and Éidín Ní Shé

Routledge
Taylor & Francis Group
NEW YORK AND LONDON

First published 2026
by Routledge
605 Third Avenue, New York, NY 10158

and by Routledge
4 Park Square, Milton Park, Abingdon, Oxon, OX14 4RN

Routledge is an imprint of the Taylor & Francis Group, an informa business

ISBN: 978-1-032-89825-4 (hbk)
ISBN: 978-1-032-90223-4 (pbk)
ISBN: 978-1-003-54661-0 (ebk)

DOI: 10.4324/9781003546610

Typeset in Galliard
by Apex CoVantage, LLC

Contents

Contributors

Catherine Brogan commenced her career in health 45 years ago and has 20 years senior management experience in the not-for-profit and public sectors in Ireland and brings key skills in the areas of leadership and planning. Her current role is as Chair of the National Implementation and Monitoring Committee for '*Sharing the Vision*', Irelands Mental Health Policy and is also the Senior Policy Advisor on Co-creation with Mental Health Europe. Catherine believes strongly in the power of co-production and is passionate about recovery and what can be achieved in changing culture within mental health services through the centrality of lived experience being integral to service design and delivery. Included in her portfolio are qualifications in nursing, health promotion, project management, events management, team, executive and mental health and well-being coaching, performance management, QQI in training, delivery and evaluation and certification in charity law. In a voluntary capacity Catherine in 2001 co-founded and co-ordinates Turas Le Cheile a bereavement support service which provides support for those bereaved including those bereaved by suicide. She is also a Board director of H.U.G.G. [Healing Untold Grief Groups].

Dr John-Paul Byrne (JP) is a Lecturer in the Graduate School of Healthcare Management at the Royal College of Surgeons in Ireland (RCSI) University of Medicine and Health Sciences. A sociologist with expertise in qualitative and ethnographic methods, JP's research explores the social structures at the heart of the work–health nexus: how working lives and professional and organisational environments effect well-being ('health' of work) and the processes, structures and cultures that comprise healthcare ('work' of health). He is particularly interested in the role of psychosocial working conditions (e.g. autonomy, work-time, relationships) in shaping the working lives, organisational cultures and well-being of healthcare professionals. JP's research has contributed to generating knowledge across multiple domains, directly through ethnographic research on the healthcare experience and the working lives of hospital doctors, a psychosocial framework for healthcare workers' mental well-being, co-developing methodological advances in ethnographic approaches in health, and informing medical workforce policy in Ireland. He is passionate about the importance of social science in healthcare improvement and the power of research and research-informed teaching, to improve organisational conditions for the betterment of health globally.

Dr Mairead Cahill is an Associate Professor in Occupational Therapy at the University of Limerick, Ireland, and a member of the Ageing Research Centre and Health Research Institute at the University of Limerick, Ireland. Mairead was awarded a BSc (Curr. Occ. Ther.) and MSc from Trinity College, Dublin. She completed her PhD at the University of Limerick in 2022. Prior to taking up an academic position, she worked as an Occupational Therapy Practice Education Co-Ordinator at the University of Limerick for several years. Mairead also gained clinical experience as an occupational therapist in acute and rehabilitation settings in Ireland and the United Kingdom for over a decade before entering academia.

Dr Lorraine Carroll, PhD, is an Assistant Professor/Lecturer in Midwifery at University College Dublin (UCD) School of Nursing, Midwifery and Health Systems. She holds a PhD from Trinity College Dublin (TCD), in addition to a Master's in Research, a Professional Certificate in Healthcare Education (UCD) and a Bachelor of Midwifery Studies from TCD. She was also a recipient of a UCD College Teaching Excellence award in 2020. Her doctoral research included systematic reviews of risk factors for and pregnancy, birth and neonatal outcomes associated with reduced foetal movements in pregnancy and a prospective case-control study. Additional research interests include perineal management and repair, physiological birth, foetal monitoring, the education of midwifery students and the development of maternity care guidelines. Lorraine is a registered midwife, general nurse and tutor with nearly 30 years of clinical practice and over 10 years education and research experience. Prior to moving into university academia, Lorraine gained extensive clinical midwifery and management experience working in a busy labour and birthing unit at the National Maternity Hospital, Dublin.

Dr Mary Curtin is an Assistant Professor in Midwifery at the School of Nursing, Midwifery and Health Systems in University College Dublin and a registered midwife and midwife tutor. She graduated from City University (London) in 2005 with a BSc (Hons) in Midwifery, completed an MSc in Midwifery in 2010, and a Post-Graduate Certificate in Higher Education in 2014. Her doctoral research examined humanisation in pregnancy and childbirth for high-risk women. Mary has worked in all aspects of maternity services including community midwifery services but her practice has often focused on intrapartum care. She has a proven track record of clinical and operational leadership with particular interest in high-risk women and the provision of midwifery care for women at risk and the emotional aspect of birth. She has a strong interest in autonomous midwifery practice in all aspects of maternity services and a strong supporter of a woman's right to have choices in pregnancy and birth.

Dr Mehmet Ali Icbay works in the Department of Business Communication at Vienna University of Economics and Business in Austria. Earlier, he worked at Middle East Technical University, The Ohio State University, Southern Illinois University School of Medicine, the Royal College of Surgeons in Ireland, and Çanakkale Onsekiz Mart University. His research focuses primarily on ethnomethodology, conversation analysis and ethnography. He has been involved in projects supported by US National Institute of Health in 2012 and by the Irish Health Research Board in 2024. He also completed a project on violence against healthcare workers, supported by TÜBİTAK, in 2024. He has published articles in international Q1 journals such as Classroom Discourse, Medicine, Conflict and Survival, and Talk and Text. His recent projects include an ethnographic study on the EMCA Community and research on the role of talk in interactive learning.

Dr Caroline Keegan is an Assistant Professor and Head of Midwifery at University of Galway, having previously worked as Director of the Public Health Nursing programme (UCD) and Associate Professor of Midwifery and in Dundalk Institute of Technology (DKIT) and UCD. Caroline helped establish the first Midwifery Led units (MLU) in Ireland and introduced the first Waterbirth, Community postnatal services, Midwifery satellite clinics and Examination of Newborn programme for midwives in Ireland as a HSE Manager for MLU services. Caroline has represented the HSE as a national expert midwife in research projects and for the Home Birth Service. Caroline has a strong passion for educating the next generation of midwives, humanistic care, providing choice and compassionate midwifery for women, promoting active birth, research, change management and promoting equality through team building. Caroline has presented findings on her research nationally and internationally.

Dr Mary McAuliffe is a historian, lecturer and Director of Gender Studies at University College Dublin. She specialises in Irish women's/gender history, traumas histories of gendered and sexual violence of Ireland's revolutionary period and histories of sexualities. Her most recent publication was a biography of the feminist, trade union activist and revolutionary woman, Margaret Skinnider (UCD Press, 2020). She was the co-editor, with Emilie Pine (UCD) and Miriam Haughton (NUIG) of the work *Commemoration, Gender, and the Postcolonial Carceral State*, published by Manchester University Press in November 2021. Besides academic publications, she plays an active role as a public historian and contributes to documentaries, radio, TV and news media and is active online. Her most important work as a consultant and contributor was the groundbreaking documentary on gendered and sexual violence against women in the Irish War of Independence and Civil War – 'Cogadh ar Mhna/War on Women'.

Professor Robert McMurray holds a Chair in Organisation Studies with a career spanning the universities of Durham, York, Leeds and Sheffield in the UK and the Graduate School of Healthcare Management at RCSI in Ireland. Robert's expertise lies in understanding people and their performance in specific contexts ranging from healthcare to voluntary work, social care, death work, night-time economies, banking and service work. Through top-ranked publications, edited book series, monographs, funded research and popular press, Robert's research has extended our understanding of how emotions, ethics, gender, toxicity, dirt, professionalisation and perceptions impact work, management and organisation. Robert is also recognised for his pedagogic innovation and practice in respect of student led teaching and learning.

Dr Purity Mwendwa is a Research Fellow at the Trinity College Institute of Neuroscience (TCIN) Dublin in Ireland. Her research interests lie in the field of global health and much of her work has focused on reviewing health policies and researching the social determinants of health in the context of Africa and immigrant communities in Ireland and the USA. Her research underpins the notion of inclusion which calls for identifying and addressing the barriers faced by disadvantaged groups in access to resources, services and opportunities. She has particular expertise in qualitative methods and participatory research based on her extensive work engaging diverse communities in research, education and practice development. Her passion is to conduct research that has a wider societal impact in terms of improving the lives of the most vulnerable populations including older people, people with disabilities and mental health challenges. Her current research explores how local communities of people and places can better support people living with dementia and their families in Kenya.

Dr Éidín Ní Shé is a Senior Lecturer at the RCSI Graduate School of Healthcare Management (GSM) in RCSI University of Medicine and Health Sciences. She is the programme director of the MSc in Healthcare

Management. Éidín's teaching experience in higher education spans over 20 years, with experience in both Ireland and Australia. Éidín has a disciplinary focus in co-design and applied health systems research. She has focused on outputting work with policymakers, members of the public, healthcare staff and academics. Her projects in Ireland have included work on developing interprofessional competencies in the care of older people with the national clinical programme, assisted decision-making, frailty pathway co-design and supporting staff in speaking up about safety.

Michael John Norton is an early career researcher currently studying at doctorate level in the Royal College of Surgeons in Ireland. He previously worked for the Health Service Executive [HSE] as an Engagement and Recovery Programme Lead where he had responsibility for the development of peer support, family recovery, as well as the co-production of the next iteration of '*A National Framework for Recovery in Mental Health*.' Additionally, within his role, he also led on the implementation of several '*Sharing the Vision*' recommendations. Michael is an established author with publications relating to peer support, co-production, mental health and recovery. He is also the author of three academic textbooks including: '*Co-Production in Mental Health: Implementing Policy into Practice*', '*Different Diagnoses, Similar Experiences: Narratives of Mental Health, Addiction Recovery and Dual Diagnosis*' and more recently '*Peer Support Work in Mental Health Services: Theory, Research, Policy and Practice*.'

Jennifer O'Mahoney is an occupational therapist based in Co Waterford, Ireland. She graduated with an MSc in Occupational Therapy (Professional Qualification) from the University of Limerick in 2015. As part of her programme of studies, Jennifer wrote a thesis on Irish occupational therapy pioneer Ann Beckett. Jennifer is a member of the Ann Beckett Committee, which oversees the foremost award in Irish occupational therapy, which commemorates Ann Beckett, the first diploma-qualified occupational therapist in Ireland.

Professor Judith Pettigrew, PhD, is Head of the School of Allied Health and Professor of Occupational Therapy at the University of Limerick, Ireland. She is a member of the University of Limerick's Health Research Institute and the Ageing Research Centre. Judi has academic backgrounds in social anthropology, occupational therapy and history. Her enduring research interests are mental health, the history of occupational therapy, gender, the politics of identity and the impact and legacy of political violence. She has published widely. Key outputs include a monograph on the impact of Nepal's civil war on everyday life, cultural practices and well-being. She is currently exploring therapeutic practices in Irish psychiatric hospitals during the early to mid-20th century and analysing the structures that shaped these practices and the dynamics that led to the professionalisation of some practitioners while others were overlooked. Judi is currently working on a monograph on the 'forgotten'. Before joining the University of Limerick in 2009, Judi held positions at the University of Central Lancashire (1998–2007) and Leipzig University (based at Tribhuvan University, Kathmandu) (2007–2008).

Dr Eleni Tzouramani is a Senior Lecturer of Management at the University of the West of Scotland. Her research explores work, identity and spirituality, focusing on how individuals draw on cultural and spiritual resources to integrate aspects of unity into who they are. She has held senior academic roles and contributed to research projects in the UK and internationally.

Dr Aisling Walsh is a Sociologist and Lecturer in the Department of Public Health and Epidemiology, School of Population Health, at RCSI. She has experience of conducting qualitative and mixed-methods health research in Ireland and Africa. Aisling's research interests are in health services and systems research, particularly in the areas of maternal health and disability. She has co-ordinated two global health research networks and has trained researchers in qualitative and mixed-methods research in Africa and Ireland through these roles. She is currently a principal investigator on an HRB Applied Partnership Award to develop health information and education resources for women with epilepsy from preconception to postpartum. She is co-investigator on a number of studies relating to maternal health and disability services in Ireland. She is also co-investigator on projects relating to participatory approaches to population needs assessment in Ireland, evaluation of the Sláinetcare Healthy Communities programme, and exploring the health needs of female Ukrainian refugees in Ireland. Aisling supervises a number of PhD and master's students in RCSI.

Professor Kristin S. Williams is the Director of the FC Manning School of Business at Acadia University, one of the oldest and most respected liberal arts universities in Canada. She is an Associate Professor (Management) at Acadia University and holds a Visiting Researcher appointment at the University of Eastern Finland (Innovation Management). Dr Williams is also the Founder, Managing Director, and Principal Researcher at Prudentia Institute: Youth Knowledge Exchange, home to the award-winning Student Research Lab. She is co-editor in chief at the journal of Culture and Organization and a member of the editorial advisory board at the Journal of Management History. She has received several academic awards and is a recipient of the Queen Elizabeth II's Platinum Jubilee Medal.

Dr Nuran Yıldırım graduated from the Department of Turkish Language and Literature at the Faculty of Letters, Istanbul University in 1970. She completed her doctorate at Istanbul University, Istanbul Faculty of Medicine and received the title of 'M. Sc. Dr.' (Doctor of Medical Sciences) in 1982. She became a professor in the Department of Medical History and Ethics at the same faculty in 1996. After retiring from this position, she joined Bezmiâlem Foundation University in 2016. Dr Yıldırım, whose studies focus on the health histories of the Ottoman Empire and the Early Republic, has published nationally and internationally on topics such as Turkish medical manuscripts, medical education, pharmacy, dentistry, nursing histories, epidemics and infectious diseases, quarantine organisation, women's struggle for existence in health professions, and the history of ethics. Her works include authored books, book chapters, numerous articles and encyclopaedia entries, catalogues of the health history museums and exhibitions she has curated to preserve and promote the material heritage of health history have been published.

1 Introduction

Harming the Healers: Wise Women, Witches and Visionaries

Robert McMurray and Éidín Ní Shé

Introduction

In one form or other women have been at the centre of health and its management throughout human history (Latta, 2017). In each community 'wise women' were recognised as the only people with knowledge of ailments, bodies, herbs and rituals required to treat the ills of people, animals and communities (Yakushko, 2018). As we shall see, from Europe to Africa, and the Middle East to West Asia it was wise women who were the doctors, anatomists, midwives and herbalists of history (Spearing, 2019). It was to these wise women that people turned when ailing or in need of support. Theirs was a specialist knowledge that garnered respect in life and reverence in death. The purpose of this book is to celebrate such women for their delivery and management of health and care from antiquity to the present day.

This book should not be necessary. We should already know the women who cared for our ancestors and shaped lives. However, despite the long involvement of women in health and healing, surprisingly little has been written about their lives, their work or their contributions to well-being. The available histories of medicine and healthcare are histories of men for the most part. There have been tomes written on the 'great men' [sic] of healing from Galen to Flemming. Most of us are aware of Hippocrates or Jenner, but how many of us could name the women who promoted health over the last three millennia? Florence Nightingale, Mary Seacole or Elizabeth Blackwell from the 19th century might come to mind, but what of the innumerable other women who managed the health of our communities? Why are so few women healers known to us?

One explanation is offered by Bourdillon (1988) who notes that history has tended to be written by men, based on public records produced by men, detailing the lives of 'great figures' who also tend to be men. By and large, the lives and oral histories of everyday people, including wise women, are under reported and under-represented (a point considered in Chapter 6 by Aisling Walsh). However, the omission of women is not just consequence

DOI: 10.4324/9781003546610-1

of poor and biased bookkeeping. It is also a consequence of active erasure. In what follows we will consider how the rise of Christianity, the enlightenment and patriarchal structures oppressed women healers, first in the West, and then more widely as non-Western indigenous healers were subjected to European colonisation (Yakushko, 2018). We will explain how and why women were moved from the privileged position of healers descended from goddesses, to one of abjection and persecution as witches serving the devil or, latterly, rendered as inferior emotional being's incapable of grasping modern science (Jessee, 2021).

It is against this backdrop that we work to correct past omissions and challenge gender-based erasure by bring to light and celebrating the contribution that women have always made to healthcare and its management. This is important because, as the chapters of this book demonstrate, women have a track record of seeing and managing healthcare differently. As Ekong (2021:841, citing Halbert, 2006) notes 'women's way of knowing is an alternative to a status quo premised upon an exclusively masculine tradition. Articulating a women's standpoint is therefore a political activity that provides us with a different understanding'. Within healthcare, the results of this 'alternative' have been the development of services for people whose needs would have gone unrecognised and unmet (a theme we return to time and again in subsequent chapters). The re-emergence of women at the forefront of healthcare and medical science has also been crucial to overcoming the male-streaming of medicine and its tendency to base diagnosis, treatment and cure on male bodies and concerns (Benton, 1985) to the detriment of women specifically, and those who deviate from the 'norm' more generally.

Before we celebrate our revolutionary women in Chapters 2 to 11 we begin with a brief history of the rise and fall of wise women as healers. This necessarily brief exposition considers how and why the wise women who healed and cared for our communities were demonised and marginalised by patriarchal systems of power. As the chapter concludes, we consider women who have continued to transform our understanding of health and its management despite the obstacles they face.

Wise Women of Health and Medicine

Until the 15th century, it was women, not men, who possessed the specialist knowledge and skills required to heal (Benton, 1985). Archaeological evidence suggest that for millennia it was women who acted as healers in the societies of Northern Europe. Through a mixture of herbal knowledge, praxis, ritual and metaphysics (magic), they tended to the health needs of their local communities. Knowledge was passed down to generations of women through both familial links and mentoring. This teaching was combined with folklore and empirical observation to form and develop practice.

Wise women treated all strata of society but were particularly important in rural communities where alternative medical provision was scarce. Travelling between communities, they provided personal and accessible care to those who required it. In effect:

> They were the unlicensed doctors and anatomists of western history. They were abortionists, nurses and counsellors. They were pharmacists, cultivating healing herbs and exchanging the secrets of their uses. They were midwives, travelling from home to home and village to village. For centuries women were doctors without degrees . . . They were called 'wise women' by the people.
>
> (Barbara Ehrenreich and Deirdre English (1973) cited in Spearing, 2019:45)

Wise women often blended healing with ritualistic, magical or religious elements that spoke to what were assumed to be the 'otherworldly' or spiritual basis of ill health and ill luck. This included the use of amulets, charms, strings and incantations which addressed the external or supernatural cause of any ill. Spearing (2019) contends that such rituals were also important for giving confidence in a cure. This is not to say treatments or poultices were without efficacy. Ingredients used by wise women have been shown to kill parasitic worms, relieve pain and even tackle modern superbugs (Spearing, 2019).

Wise women were respected and revered. They were called on to find lost items and settle disputes. Their prestige drew on long standing reverence for women deities and goddess such as Ishtar, Freyja, Isis and Eostre (Bourdillon, 1988; Spearing, 2019). They were honoured in death: buried separately with the tools of their trade and objects denoting status (though a tendency for them to be buried at the edge of the cemetery with their bodies weighed down or staked also spoke to a degree of marginality or fear arising from their difference and connections to the spiritual and otherworldly).

Further afield, women practised medicine and nursing in ancient Alexandria and Egypt, while also lecturing in medicine at prestigious schools such as the Salerno, Italy, in the Middle Ages. Evidence exist for women in roles including doctor, midwife, herbalist and death practitioner across the Middle East, Northern African, West Asia and Europe; with suggestions of shamanic involvement as far back as 30,000 years (Yakushko, 2018). Merit-Ptah is widely considered the first named women to have practised medicine as chief physician around 2700 BCE in Egypt (though see Kwiecinski's (2020) critique of the historic-political evidence) while Queen Hatshepsut (1479–1458 BCE) was said to have founded medical schools and encouraged women to pursue medicine. For the most part, however, the women who managed health were local. They were essential members of their communities caring for the ill, infirm and underserved. Their power was derived from their availability, effectiveness and belief systems that linked their work to the creation stories of powerful female deities. As the power of these deities diminished so too did the power and position of wise women.

From Wise Women to Witches: Demonising, Diminishing and Dismissing

Spearing (2019) provides an excellent account of the fall of wise women. Her interpretation links the overthrow of the supreme goddesses, the rise of the Christian church and the actions of paternalistic professions to the marginalisation of women in healthcare. Briefly, the fall of goddesses as creator deities is said to foreshadow the fall of powerful women in societies. From Mesopotamia to Greece and India to North America there are accounts of supreme goddesses who created the world and were known by names such as Tiatmat, Gaia, Nüwa, Spider Grandmother, Coatlicue and Ammavaru. These supreme goddesses were associated with giving live and nature: associations that were passed on to women healers. In some societies wise women were said to be descended from or channelling the power these female creation deities.

As belief in and deference to supreme goddesses was eroded, so was the position and status of powerful women. Spearing (2019) notes that the replacement of these supreme goddesses begins gradually around 3000 BCE as societies moved from agrarian to larger hierarchical and more militarised collectives. Increasingly patriarchal in character, these societies shift towards male deities associated with kingship, war and law. In many cultures the goddesses that once ruled alone are slowly joined by and then usurped by male gods. In this way belief systems encourage societal acceptance of the primacy of men over women. The growth of the Christian church supercharged the process.

From diminution we move to subordination denigration and demonisation rooted in ecclesial writing that spreads misinformation, controversy and prejudice to the detriment of women generally, and wise women in particular, all while asserting the primacy of men. Spearing (2019) locates the root of this campaign in the work of St Augustine and his contention that women, in the form of Eve the temptress, bring evil into the world. Women are positioned as contaminated and unclean vessels mired in carnality. They are a distraction from living a godly life. Moreover, they pass their sin and imperfection to their children. As for wise women, the apparent benefits they brought to local communities were to be explained by collaboration with the devil. This was evidenced by their use of chants, threads, amulets, potions, poultices and binding plats to the body all of which spoke to the black magic practised by those (women) predisposed by their sex and status as a physician to 'cavorting with daemons' (Spearing, 2019:80). Thomas Aquinas developed this theme labelling women as 'defective and misbegotten' because unlike the perfect form of the masculine sex 'the production of women comes from a defect in the active force or from some material indisposition' (Spearing, 2019: xiv). By the 15th century it was not enough just to demonise wise women: they were to be hunted, tortured, drowned and burnt as witches (*sidenote: Spearing roots the linguistic origins witch with the word 'Hwicce' which described a tribe in southwest England where wise women were said to have originated. Hwicce would be corrupted to 'whych' in Middle English and latterly to 'witch'*).

The publication of *Malleus Maleficarum* (*The Hammer of the Witches*) by Heinrich Kramer in 1486 was the accelerant that drove the witch hunts. This publication took the church's rejection of the status and role of women in pre-Christian societies and weaponised it. If magic could be shown to cause physical harm, Kramer reasoned, then women could be tried in court for the damage they wrought (Spearing, 2019). The ritual chanting and charms of wise women, coupled with their apparent power of life and death, made them vulnerable to accusations of dark magic. The lack of licence from state, university or medical profession left room for questions to be raised as to the source of their power, their intentions and competence. For Kramer, the only answer was that they drew their power from the devil. Accordingly, when wise women dealt with children or childbirth it was said that 'for when they do not kill the child, the offer it to the devil' (*Malleus Maleficarum*, 1478, cited in Bourdillon, 1988). Kramer contended that infant death at the hands of these women was never a natural occurrence but rather slaughter by witch-midwives at the behest of the devil (Cleghorn, 2022).

From the 12th to 18th centuries, this hostility reached new heights with the witch trials that saw (wise) women from across Europe and the Americas tried, tortured, drowned, hanged and burnt. During this time, the reaction to women holding knowledge and power was often violent, particularly where they were perceived to threaten patriarchal structures such as the church (Yakushko, 2018). Only men were deemed to be able to heal through divine authority. Bourdillon (1988) goes on to note that women who were outspoken (of devilish tongue) and critical of the status quo were more likely to be accused.

The 'witch-hunts of Europe were so severe that historians estimate that hundreds of thousands of women were tortured, drowned, hung or burned at the stake in a span of three centuries', all during the dawn of the 'age of reason' (Yakushko, 2018:2). Yakushko (2018) also points out that these practices were disseminated by Western colonialism. In occupied territories, women of socials status or authority were ignored by the invaders, while female deities and women's involvement in healing and associated rituals were labelled unnatural, hypersexualised and demonic. From Africa to Latin and North America such practices among native peoples were punished by torture and death. The social authority of women in these societies was effectively crushed under the weight of Western paternalistic society, rules and practices (see Yakushko, 2018 for a fuller account and further reading). Moreover, we witness the vilification of women-healers as witches and charlatans running parallel to the rise of Western empirical sciences and the development of both the academia and professional designations that gave primacy to men when it came to social authority.

Patriarchal Androcentric Medicine

Where religion had prosecuted wise women on the basis of evil (while appropriating and institutionalising much of their knowledge and practice), medicine sidelined them in the name of safety and the presumption that they were mentally and emotionally unfit for such professions (Jessee, 2021). Torture and burning were replaced by exclusion, discrimination and intimidation (Benton, 1985) at the hands of androcentric medicine as male physicians 'jealously guarded the privileges of the growing medical profession' (Bourdillon, 1988:5).

Cleghorn (2022) identifies Aristotle's description of the female body as the 'inverse of the male' as a starting point for marking women as different, faulty, defective and deficient. The point is extended by the 13th-century Italian physician and misogynist Cecco d'Ascoli who wrote on: the inferiority of women's bodies, who by nature were imperfect, stupid, greedy and crazy. Often the religious and medical worlds would combine to mark menstruation as evidence of weakness, impurity, original sin and evil work. In person and practice, women were singled out as dirty and likely to corrupt or taint those with whom they came into contact, particularly (though not exclusively) when menstruating. As such they were said to be unsuited to medical work morally, physically, intellectually and emotionally.

Registration, licensing and exclusion were lobbied for by men of medicine and surgery to restrict traditional (female) health practitioners and those seeking to enter the male-dominated professions. These kinds of attacks served to push women out of health and healing. In Paris, despite testimonies to her effectiveness, Felicie De Almania (Paris, 1300s) was found guilty of illegally practising medicine and excommunicated because it was 'certain that a man approved in the aforesaid art could cure the sick better than any woman' (Bourdillon, 1988:15). In England women who practice medicine professionally were described as 'worthless and presumptive women [who] usurp this profession to themselves and abuse it. Who, possessing neither natural ability, nor professional knowledge, make the greatest possible mistakes, thanks to their stupidity . . .' (John Mirfield, Breviarium Bartholomei: the medical writing of clerk at St Bartholomew's Hospital, c. 1370, cited in Bourdillon, 1988:13).

Despite the absence of evidence, male medical professionals resisted the admission of women to medicine and denigrated female dominated healing professions on the basis that the latter were: quacks, a danger to the public, mental inferiority, suffered the (unclean) disruptions of menstruation, could be harmed by too much education, lacked the temperament to deal with crises and trauma and were not up to the task physically and did not enjoy the confidence of patients (Kelly, 2013; McMurray, 2011). Deeper examination of the evidence suggests that these barriers to entry have mostly been about restricting competition, whether from women doctors in the 1800s, or emerging professions such as Advanced Nurse Practitioners 200 years later (McMurray, 2011, 2015). For example, concerns about the training, diagnostic abilities, prescribing and safety of largely female Advance Nurse Practitioners – as expressed in medical trade magazines and journals – have been found to lack any basis in fact (McMurray, 2011). Moreover, as late as the dawn of the 20th century, regulation and male dominance of medical professions and universities worked against any significant role for women in medicine. Many men of medicine felt that women were better suited to [sic] 'lesser' and 'supportive' professions such as nursing (Benton, 1985).

In England, from the 16th century, the healing work of women was increasingly confined to the home and the informal. It is worth noting that even during this period wise women were still allowed to tend to the pauperised and the plagued. The dirty work of stigmatised bodies was delegated to women: a pattern that would repeat for generations as masculine medicine passed its unwanted work to feminine nursing (McMurray, 2012). However, while the work of wise women with the poor persisted, the increasingly industrial and urbanised landscapes of modernity made it difficult to access or grow the herbs used in traditional treatments (Bourdillon, 1988). By the 1800s the writing and practice of women in the home was in decline, even among upper class women, as men, with the university education largely denied to women, pushed the latter aside (Bourdillon, 1988). Excluded from centres of leaning and power, women were denied knowledge and practice in new areas such as anatomy and pharmacology.

In the 19th century, 'woman physician' was used a derogatory term for those who conducted unlicensed abortions and were likened to the '"Murderess," "hag," "she-devil," "the instrument of the very vilest crime known in the annals of hell"' in popular American literature (Jessee, 2021:253). Jessee argues that this positioning reflected the terrifying threat both women physicians and abortion presented to traditional masculinity. These women were portrayed as foreign contaminating and corrupting forces whose actions were inspired by greed. Real virtuous American women would be at home. This final point feeds into gender narratives that locate a women's place in the home. It conflates her biology and person to assign a single purpose: to reproduce (Cleghorn, 2022). How could a woman be a doctor and avoid neglecting her children? How could she possibly support her husband and provide him with a calm home environment if pre-occupied with medical work? Such neglect of familial and societal duties speaks of selfish women who present a material threat to the patriarchal family ideal (Kelly, 2013).

Do No Harm . . . Unless to Women

Medicine's treatment of women has often been harmful and abusive in professional and personal terms. Professionally, where women succeed in overcoming all the barriers to medical entry, they are frequently subjected to harassment and sexual abuse. From Australia to the UK, women are told they are they are not good enough or strong enough to enter the profession or flourish in male dominated disciplines such as surgery. Even today, they are subjected to sexualised 'banter' and sexual assault with '[n]early two thirds of female surgeons reported being sexually harassed by colleagues, and nearly a third reported being sexually assaulted by a colleague within the last five years' (Cox, 2023, see also *The Working Party on Sexual Misconduct in Surgery*) in what can only be viewed as a damning indictment of the profession and the society of which it is a part.

Where women reach the top of their profession, as in the case of **Professor Dame Clare Gerada** (Chapter 11), there is often gender-based resistance and stereotyping (GP Online, 2022). Professor Gerada notes that it is difficult being one of the few women who lead. She notes that gendered natured of her portrayal as 'outspoken, strident, pushy' speaks to deliberately negative terminology reserved for and intended to undermine women as leaders (as a man these descriptors would likely be replaced by 'visionary, decisive, challenge focused and determined'). Resistance to women leaders also arises in the form of marginalisation and erasure. Chapter 3 recounts the ways in which **Maida Herman Solomon** had to seek to influence policy and professions through her husband (because a women's voice would not be heard), while having her name removed from publications due to her race and gender.

While women have always worked to inform and shape healthcare management the record of their contributions are too often diminished, dismissed, erased or appropriated. For each women this comes at a personal professional cost. However, the refusal to heed and acknowledge women leaders in healthcare has also been to the detriment of all women.

Elinor Cleghorn's (2022) work, titled *Unwell Women: A Journey through Medicine and Myth in a Man-Made World*, provides an intricate account of how women's health has been misunderstood, misdiagnosed and mistreated throughout history. Focusing on the social and cultural construction of medicine, she reveals how medical misogyny has propagated and pathologised the myth of women as inherently weaker, less rational, more emotional and even hysterical in ways that have required (often harmful) male interventions that have ranged from forced surgery to high rates of tranquiliser and antidepression prescribing. The symptoms and pain of women have often been minimised or ignored – being ascribed emotional and psychological causes rather than physical – resulting in delayed diagnosis and poor treatment. This has been exacerbated by the androcentric basis of much medical theory and practice wherein women are (mis)treating as men without penises. Taboos on examining women's bodies from the time of Hippocrates through the Middle Ages and beyond meant that the female body was mysterious, unknown and shameful, much to the detriment of women's health. This extended in modern medicine to the exclusion of women from randomised controlled trials such that medical knowledge and decision-making was based almost wholly on an understanding of male bodies – where the average or typical is a male specimen – again to the detriment of women. The situation is worsened where the intersection of gender, race, class and disability are ignored, resulting in a paucity of targeted treatments for marginalised groups and worsening health outcomes.

From the Middle Ages, medical writing and practice were developed for men by men. When women came under the care of male physicians, their treatment was a product of 'the way men understood women's bodies, functions, illnesses, needs and desires . . . the most fundamental questions of their health and illness were defined by men' (Benton, 1985:30–31). As we have seen, where informed by religious doctrine this could be at best partial and at worst deadly. Cleghorn (2022) observes that it did not have to be this way. As far back as Hippocrates, it has been known that women's bodies and illness needed to be treated differently. Ignoring this fact has resulted in the unnecessary suffering and death of women. Considered thus, the re-emergence of women in health and medicine is not only important in terms of reversing professional oppression but also for widening the scope of bodies, minds and needs treated.

Despite the paternalistic violence perpetrated on women generally and wise women particularly, Yakushko (2018:24) notes that from Latin and North America to Africa 'one of the ways that oppressed peoples around the globe maintained their connections to their pre-colonization cultures was specifically through maintaining indigenous healing traditions'. Under such circumstances, the practices of healing are not just acts of inter-generational care but also of resistance. Moreover Cleghorn (2022) reminds us that feminist writers and campaigners have resisted oppressive androcentric ideas and practices since the 1960s as they relate to healthcare specifically and also in the socio-cultural, legal and artistic reclaiming of women's bodies. The

#MeToo movement is a recent example of the continued need to stand against individual and systemic violence inflicted on women and their bodies. It speaks to a reclaiming and agency. Accordingly, it is worth taking a moment to note some of the women who have served as healthcare visionaries and pioneers.

Visionaries and Pioneers

Despite persecution, marginalisation and exclusion, women have fought for the right to practice, deliver and manage healthcare. When it comes to healthcare – including non-traditional, non-Indigenous medicine – women now make up over 70% of the workers. In Africa 80% of the population depends on traditional medicine which, again, is largely the work of women (Ekong, 2021). In addition to the women who deliver and manage healthcare daily, there are also those who pioneer new services for neglected populations and make breakthroughs in healing and health.

If we take just the last millennia, we can identify Trotula de Ruggiero (1050–1097) a pioneering physician associated with the Salerno school in Italy (which was unusual in its admittance of women). She furthered the fields of gynaecology, obstetrics and women's health. Her influence was spread through three texts (*Conditions of Women*, *On treatments for Women*, and *Women's Cosmetics*) known collectively as the *Trotula* (though there is some contention over authorship, see Benton, 1985). Her work provided comprehensive insights into reproduction, pregnancy and birth and was notable for its patient-centred emphasis on pain management, hygiene and comfort. These texts also suggest that women should be trained in medicine not least because they are better placed to treat other women in terms of accounting for societal norms. In 1674, Hannah Wolley published the *Pharmacopolium Muliebris Sexus* on diet and medicine for women (Bourdillon, 1988). In the early 1700s observations of the work of wise women in Türkiye who inoculated people against smallpox (by giving a mild version of the virus) was brought to England by Lady Mary Worley Montagu (Bourdillon, 1988), half a century before the acclaimed work of Jenner.

In terms of the delivery of healthcare, the works of Mary Seacole and Florence Nightingale have long been recognised for the organisation of wards and the raising of standards. Overcoming prejudice rooted in race and gender Mary Seacole paid for her own passage to the Crimean war to establish 'The British Hotel' to tend to the wounded and diseased. For her part, Nightingale sees women as both the cause and cure of much that is wrong with the nation's hospitals noting that 'women, and the best women, are woefully deficient in sanitary knowledge; although it is to women that we must look, first and last, for its application' (Nightingale, 1860:location 1373–1375).

Her writing stood as a treaty on disease, hygiene and sanitation. She identifies nursing as an occupation whose knowledge and work are central to the effective organisation or care and the betterment of the patient. Yet, in so doing, she tended to reinforce the hierarchically inferior position of nursing as an occupation based on 'knowledge which everyone ought to have' while the doctor is privy to 'medical knowledge, which only a profession can have' (Florence Nightingale, 1860:preface). In this sense, Nightingale reinforced the gender hierarchy of roles and occupations 'to produce nurses who are servants of medicine, surgery and hygiene, and not of physicians and surgeons' (Holliday & Parker, 1997:487) and implicitly promoted a masculine logic of organising (Davies, 1995; Abbott & Meerabeau, 1998; McMurray, 2012).

Elisabeth Blackwell trained in the USA to become a BMA-registered doctor in the UK in 1859; she was also a prolific writer and lecturer (Jesse, 2021). Thereafter rules were changed to ensure only those education in British universities could become doctors in England and, at that time, women were not allowed to study in British universities (Bourdillon, 1988). Elizabeth Garrett Anderson practised as a nurse and attended lectures but was prevented from becoming a doctor in Britain. In response, she set up her own dispensary for women. This 'loophole' to practice was soon closed as apothecaries were required to work in a recognised medical school (from which women were excluded). To qualify Elizabeth had to travel to Paris to pass her medical examination (Bourdillon, 1988). At every step there were personal–professional barriers erected in opposition to her gender as she and those who followed, such as Sohpia Blake and Edith Pechy, were subjected to abuse, harassment and exclusion. In response, Blake founded the London School of Medicine for Women in 1874 while still campaigning for women to be entitled to qualify as doctors in Britain (Kelly, 2013). Enabling acts and access to universities would come during the late 19th century, with the King and Queen's College of Physicians in Ireland (KQCPI) permitting women who had taken their medical degrees abroad to take its licence examinations from 1877 and the Royal College of Surgeons in Ireland admitting women from the late 1880s (Kelly, 2013).

By the late 1800s women were admitted to universities in Europe and the USA and to the profession, though the preference was to guide them towards lesser but still worth occupations such nursing: as handmaidens to medicine (McMurray, 2011). **Safiye Ali** (Chapter 2) felt a sense of comradeship that transcended gender during her training as a doctor in Germany in the 1920s and was recognised as Türkiye's first female doctor of the new republic. Even here, lack of trust in a 'woman' doctor meant that clients were scarce, while allegations of dishonesty from male colleagues limited her contributions and good works.

Then, there are Nobel Prize winners. As the only person to receive the Nobel Prize twice (1903 and 1911) in different categories Marie Curie's discovery of polonium and radium paved the way for radiotherapy. She also promoted the use of x-rays in medicine. Gerty Cori (Nobel Prize 1947) uncovered the process of cellular energy storage and release, extending our understanding of metabolic processes, enzymes and disease. Dorothy Crowfoot Hodgkin (Nobel Prize 1964) is celebrated for groundbreaking use of x-ray crystallography to see molecules in penicillin, vitamin B12 and insulin to aid the development of lifesaving medicines for diseases such as diabetes. Battling orthodox science Barbara McClintock (Nobel Prize 1983) waited 30 years for her discovery of gene transposition to be accepted with its implications for biology and medicine. Gertrude Elion (Nobel Prize 1988) revolutionised our approaches to drug development ushering in a new era of antiviral therapy. Françoise Barré-Sinoussi's (Nobel Prize 2008) work led to tests and ultimately treatments for HIV while also campaigning for greater access to treatments. While not possessing a medical degree or doctorate Tu Youyou (Nobel Prize 2015) extracted a compound used in traditional Chinese medicine for the treatment of malaria. She was the first test subject for the resulting drug and has saved millions of lives. In short, throughout history, there have been an abundance of women who have advanced healthcare and its management. We simply need to write and read more about them. To that end, we have ten compelling chapters on women who have shaped health and its management around the world.

Book Chapters

We begin with the remarkable life of *Safiye Ali* (Chapter 2) Türkiye's first female physician who, as political activist, who fought for women's rights and social reform. Her role in the formation of the republic contributed to the codification of women's rights including suffrage, equal pay, and access to professional careers. Foreshadowing a recurring theme within the book, we learn how Safiye Ali worked to redress the neglect of women and women and infant health, developing public health provision to the children of the poor, comprised of direct treatment, nutritional provision, case specific record keeping and education. In terms of practice and organisation her work pointed up the necessity of considering the relations between medical, social, economic, cultural and political determinants of well-being. Her enduring contribution was to demonstrate the ways in which treatment must go alongside, education, prevention, resources and rights if people – particularly women and children – are to thrive. On this basis Safiye Ali continues to be an inspiration to women in Türkiye and, we hope, beyond: the very epitome of a health revolutionary.

In Chapter 3, Kristin S. Williams brings to life, the works and achievements of **Maida Herman Solomon** (1891–1988) a pioneer of clinical social work. As an educator, researcher, practitioner and advocate, Solomon was in the vanguard of those who established and shaped clinical social work as discipline. She was at forefront of developments in clinical record keeping, research and evaluations of social efficacy. Her work with a wide range of associations, committees, clubs, boards and foundations spoke to a contribution to health and its management that went well beyond her profession. Yet, as William's explains, an intersection of biases centred around gender, race and discipline combined to ensure that her contributions were neither adequately recorded nor lauded. As a counterpoint, in this chapter, we see just how much is owed to a Jewish woman who challenged disciplinary boundaries (while insisting that women be named – be visible – in written work) and focused on the delivery of evidence-based provision for perennially unfashionable/stigmatised people and illnesses. We come to understand the work and writing of a woman who considered health and its management in its widest sense; as a practice 'dedicated to improving well-being, using ecological, clinical and pharmacology interventions at multiple levels of society (individual, family, community)'.

The theme of improving society is taken up in Chapter 4 and its insightful unfolding of the pioneering story of **St Ultan's Hospital** for Sick Infants in Dublin. The hospital was founded in 1919 by a remarkable group of women doctors and social activists. McAuliffe highlights the hospital's unique position as a secular, female-run institution in a predominantly Catholic Ireland. She explores the backgrounds of key including women including Dr Kathleen Lynn, tracing their involvement in suffrage and social activism. The chapter underscores St Ultan's innovative medical practices and its role as a radical, feminist space where women doctors could set their own agendas. It also addresses the challenges the hospital faced, notably from the Catholic Church, and its enduring legacy in advocating for secular, female-led healthcare. McAuliffe's work offers a compelling look at the intersection of medicine, politics and gender in early 20th-century Ireland.

In Chapter 5, we stay in Dublin to appreciate the life of **Ada Shillman** (1859–1933), an immigrant Jewish woman and pioneering midwife in Ireland. Not only did she establish services for childbirth and children, she also championed a much-respected individualised midwifery centred on philosophy and practice. Ada is a good example of the way in which women are required to work against marginalisation, difference and stigma to meet their own needs and those of their communities. Her informal use of means testing, community-based practice, record keeping, networking and collaboration all speak to an effective approach to the management and organisation of care. We also learn – in echo of the history of women in healthcare – of the ways in which her individualised and community-based approaches to midwifery were steadily overridden by the medicalisation and institutionalisation of childbirth in the course of the 20th century. This could frame Ada as a forgotten revolutionary: shaping healthcare locally and temporarily. Curtin et al. reject such a frame noting instead that Ada Shillman should be seen as in the vanguard of effective maternity care and management; it has taken nearly 100 years to produce the evidence needed to support her past practice and, in so doing, point the way to the future.

A riveting Chapter 6 transports us to Nigeria as Aisling Walsh delves into the life **Elizabeth Abimbola Awoliyi**: Nigeria's first female medical doctor, obstetrician and gynaecologist. Awoliyi dedicated her career to improving health standards and services for expectant mothers and improved birth rates in Nigeria. We learn how she broke into a male-dominated western field overcoming race and gender-based discrimination to refocus colonial obsessions with curative medicine towards more preventative public health for the great benefit of women and children. Improvements in areas such a child death rates, material health and contraception uptake are all associated with her practice, though she is not necessarily credited. Within the British colonial context of mid-20th-century Nigeria, local black women such as Dr Awoliyi did not merit naming or celebrating in the official record, though their deeds may be mentioned in the local press. We also learn that she trained local workforces and campaigned for their improved working conditions before and after Nigeria's independence; and chaired the National Council of Women's Societies (NCWS) advocating for women's rights and empowerment, including education for girls and women's suffrage (something we see echoed in Chapter 2 on Safiye Ali). Despite the lack of recognition, she stands as a trailblazer and a beacon for women practising and leading medicine.

The work of **Edwina Jeruto Kwallah** is considered in Chapter 7. As a campaigner against gender-based violence, Edwina works within the Maasai communities in Kenya to fight against child marriage and female genital mutilation by creating a space, through Cara projects, where girls at risk of these practices can find solace, support and growth. Purity Mwendwa's account of gender-based violence and female genital mutilation remind us that such issues are often rooted in the cultural, social and economic imperatives of place. We also come to appreciate the gendered nature of such practices rooted in patriarchal cultures of control. The work of Edwina stands in opposition to such control. It embodies an approach to healthcare management rooted in making a difference to people's lives on the ground. Based in a specific geography, culture and time and it is nonetheless possible to trace the echoes of millennia of wise women who work with their communities to make a difference where it matters, while also engaging in attempts to shape wider discourses from the bottom up.

In Chapter 8, we shift gear and methodology through an autoethnographic account of the life and leadership of **Catherine Brogan**. In this chapter, working with co-author Michael John Norton, Catherine considers how her gender informed her experiences and approach to healthcare generally and healthcare leadership specifically. This chapter considers her development and advocacy of a personal recovery model for mental health. The importance of listening and attending to others on their own terms and how this in turn can facilitate positive change is a major theme. We learn how Catherine develops this approach in the form of co-production with clients to better tailor mental healthcare. Catherine's impact ranges from individuals to organisations and the national stage, all underpinned by the aim of advancing mental health provision and the voice of patients in Ireland and beyond. We also come to appreciate how better health and healthcare management is a collaborative rather than individual effort. Finally, this chapter points up the need for more women to talk about, share and celebrate their contributions to healthcare and its management if we are to better appreciate the difference they make.

In a compelling Chapter 9, Judith Pettigrew, Mairead Cahill and Jennifer O'Mahoney illuminate the remarkable story of **Ann Beckett**, the first diploma-qualified occupational therapist in the Irish Free State. The authors trace Beckett's journey, from her training at Dorset House under the influential Elizabeth Casson, to her pioneering work in establishing occupational therapy in Ireland. Beckett's approach, shaped by Casson's social reform ethos, emphasised community, participation and client-centred care. This chapter details her significant contributions to various Dublin hospitals and clinics, her role in founding the Association of Occupational Therapists of Ireland, and her innovative use of assistive technology. We see how her personal experience with disability profoundly influenced her practice, fostering an environment of empathy and empowerment. This chapter not only celebrates Beckett's legacy but also highlights the enduring impact of her pioneering spirit on contemporary occupational therapy and healthcare practices.

In an enlightening Chapter 10, Eleni Tzouramani introduces us to the transformative work of **Morrnah Nalamaku Simeona**, a Hawaiian Kahuna Lapa'au who modernised the traditional practice of Ho'oponopono. Tzouramani explores how Morrnah's updated method, Self I-Dentity through Ho'oponopono (SITH), shifts healthcare paradigms by focusing on 'cleaning' subconscious memories to address problems. Here, we consider health, connectedness and relationality in their broadest senses and what they might offer beyond the narrower confines of modern medicine and healthcare. This chapter unpacks Morrnah's life, her cultural background and the influences that shaped her innovative approach. It positions her work within broader debates in healthcare, critiquing conventional models for their reductionist and hierarchical nature. Tzouramani highlights how Morrnah's ontology of unity integrates physical, emotional, relational, and spiritual dimensions, challenging paternalistic structures and promoting co-creative healing. Ultimately, this chapter reveals how Morrnah's legacy reimagines healthcare as a participatory inclusive practice grounded in interconnectedness, offering a powerful alternative to fragmented and expert-driven systems.

Chapter 11 brings us to the present day and the contributions of **Professor Dame Clare Gerada** to the organisation of the medical general practice and the care of its workers. Byrne considers how much Gerada's work has been directed at deconstructing the myth of medic as superhero. Her work and writing draw our attention to the potentially detrimental effects of fetishising self-sacrifice, professional omnipotence and pride, for both the future of the profession and the individual well-being of its members. Her work calls on us to put the human back into healthcare, not only in the ways that the profession views itself but also in our collective approaches to managing our medical workforces such that management and resourcing of our health systems is not predicated on the acceptance of overwork and burnout. Through her leadership, writing and practice Dame Gerada challenges us to manage in ways that care for our carers. As with so many of the women considered in this book, she helps us to see healthcare and its management differently.

In the final chapter, we draw out some of the cross-cutting themes and lessons from our women health revolutionaries, while reaffirming their position in the historical account. This is important because, as Yakushko (2018) notes, women's struggle for equality, self-determination and agency is challenging precisely because women are denied a historical account: history has been made by men for men from a patriarchal standpoint. This been to the detriment of women specifically and societies more generally. It has meant that different ways of seeing, managing, practising curing and caring have been marginalised, excluded and lost. If we are to manage health better, for all people, and in recognition of difference, there is a need to embrace the diversity of talents and experiences that can inform health and healing. There is a need for more inclusive research and practice that acknowledges the impact and potential of intersectionality. Much more needs to be done to ensure that women's health is taken seriously and that women as healers achieve equality in professional, societal and economic terms. One path to this is greater recognition of women's expertise, voice and difference making. The chapters of that book contribute to such recognition.

References

Abbott, P., and Meerabeau, L. (1998) Professionals, professionalization and the caring professions. In Abbott, P., and Meerabeau, L. (eds) *The sociology of the caring professions*. London: UCL Press.

Benton, J. F. (1985) Trotula, women's problems, and the professionalization of medicine in the middle ages. *Bulletin of the History of Medicine*, 59(1), 30–53.

Bourdillon, H. (1988) *Women as healers: A history of women and medicine*. Cambridge University Press.
Cleghorn, E. (2022) *Unwell women: A journey through medicine and myth in a man-made world*. Weidenfeld & Nicolson.
Cox, B. (2023) The sexual abuse of female surgeons comes as no surprise to me: I quit rather than endure the misogyny. *The Guardian*, 13 September. https://www.theguardian.com/commentisfree/2023/sep/13/sexual-abuse-female-surgeons-quit-misogyny-women-healthcare. Accessed 17.02.2025.
Davies, C. (1995) *Gender and the professional predicament in nursing*. Buckingham: Open University Press.
Ekong, O. E. (2021) Coalescing intellectual property incentives, gender inclusiveness and environmental sustainability for female traditional healers in Nigeria. *African Journal of Science, Technology, Innovation and Development*, 13(7), 839–850. https://doi.org/10.1080/20421338.2021.1889758.
GP Online (2022) *'My mental health suffered': RCGP president describes impact of online abuse*. https://www.gponline.com/my-mental-health-suffered-rcgp-president-describes-impact-online-abuse/article/1740863. Accessed 03.11.2024.
Holliday, M., and Parker, E. (1997) Florence Nightingale, feminism and nursing. *Journal of Advanced Nursing*, 26, 483–488.
Jessee, M. J. (2021) 'Cutting up dead babies': The literary legacy of the woman physician as abortionist. *Women's Studies*, 50(3), 253–272. https://doi.org/10.1080/00497878.2020.1824915.
Kelly, L. (2013) 'The turning point in the whole struggle': The admission of women to the King and Queen's college of physicians in Ireland. *Women's History Review*, 22(1), 97–125. https://doi.org/10.1080/09612025.2012.724916.
Kwiecinski, J. M. (2020) Merit Ptah, 'the first woman physician': Crafting of a feminist history with an ancient Egyptian setting. *Journal of the History of Medicine and Allied Sciences*, 75(1), 83–106.
Latta, S. (2017) *Bold women of medicine*. Chicago: Chicago Review Press.
McMurray, R. (2011) The struggle to professionalize: An ethnographic account of the occupational position of advanced nurse practitioners. *Human Relations*, 64(6), 801–822.
McMurray, R. (2012) Embracing dirt in nursing matters. In Simpson, R., Slutskaya, N., Lewis, P., and Höpfl, H. (eds) *Doing dirty work: Concepts and identities*. London: Palgrave-Macmillan.
McMurray, R. (2015) Care as politics: Ethics as violence. In Pullen, A., and Rhodes, C. (eds) *The Routledge companion to ethics, politics and organization*. Oxon: Routledge.
Nightingale, F. (1860) *Notes on nursing: What it is and what it is not* (Kindle Edition). London: Harrison.
Spearing, S. (2019) *A history of women in medicine*. Yorkshire: Pen and Sward Books Ltd.
The Working Party on Sexual Misconduct in Surgery. https://www.wpsms.org.uk/about-us.
Yakushko, O. (2018) Witches, charlatans, and old wives: Critical perspectives on history of women's indigenous knowledge. *Women & Therapy*, 41(1–2), 18–29. https://doi.org/10.1080/02703149.2017.1323474.

2 Safiye Ali

The First Female Physician in Türkiye

Nuran Yıldırım and Mehmet Ali Icbay

Introduction

Safiye Ali's contributions to the medical field in Türkiye, particularly in maternal and child health, were groundbreaking at a time when women's roles in healthcare were minimal. Born in 1894, Safiye Ali's pioneering efforts in early Republican Türkiye laid the foundation for women in health management and challenged the mainstream medical practices dominated by men (see Figure 2.1 for her headshot photo). This chapter will explore how Safiye Ali's approach to healthcare reform – focused on prevention, public health education and advocacy – added a new dimension to health management. Her contributions, which were often overlooked in historical narratives, offer critical insights for contemporary healthcare managers on how women's leadership can reshape healthcare systems.

This chapter begins by exploring the life story of Safiye Ali, focusing on the unique social and political circumstances that shaped her entry into medicine. Safiye Ali emerged as a pioneer during a transformative period in Turkish history, where women's roles were being redefined, yet the medical field remained overwhelmingly male-dominated. The chapter then discusses her groundbreaking efforts to revolutionise maternal and child healthcare in Türkiye, highlighting her contributions to public health. Central to this discussion is her key project, Milk Drop (*Süt Damlası*), a public health initiative that exemplifies her commitment to improving the health and well-being of the nation's children and mothers through preventive care and community education. Following this, the chapter examines the significant challenges Safiye Ali faced as a female physician navigating a patriarchal society and professional environment. It also highlights her resilience in advocating for public health

Note on images and image files:
Nuray Yıldırım notes that all of the photos in the chapter belong to her personal archive and she has the rights to said photos. For the diploma photo, she also has right to use it: Nuray Yıldırım paid Turkish Association of History to have the rights for that photo.

DOI: 10.4324/9781003546610-2

Figure 2.1. Safiye Ali.
Copyright: Yıldırım, 2012.

education despite these obstacles. A critical section is devoted to Safiye Ali's feminist legacy in healthcare, where her role as a trailblazer in advocating for women's rights, both within the medical profession and beyond, is explored in depth. The influence she wielded as a female physician is then assessed, considering how her work reshaped healthcare practices and paved the way for future generations of women in medicine. Finally, the chapter concludes by reflecting on Safiye Ali's later years and the enduring impact of her legacy in public health and healthcare management. Her contributions not only transformed maternal and child health but also redefined the role of women in healthcare, leaving a lasting imprint on the field both in Türkiye and internationally.

Early Life and Education

Hatice Safiye Ali was born on 2 February 1894, into an elite Ottoman family (Yıldırım, 2012, pp. 87–90). Her birth date, varying in some sources, is taken from a document filled out by Safiye Ali herself. Her father, *Ali Kırat Paşa* from Tripoli, Libya, was an aide-de-camp to Sultan Abdulaziz and Sultan Abdulhamid II. Her mother, *Emine Hasene (Hasna) Hanım*, was the daughter of *Hacı Emin Paşa*, the *Şeyhülharem* (a title given to distinguished scholars who taught in Mecca and Medina). As the daughter of an elite Ottoman family, she completed her middle and high school education at American Girls' College in Arnavutköy, Istanbul (Çolak, 2007, pp. 577–590). The college's principal, Mary Mills Patrick (1850–1940), an educator and feminist who advocated for the intellectual development of women, was instrumental in shaping Safiye Ali's ambitions to enter the medical field, a domain traditionally reserved for men (see Figure 2.2) ('Hayatta muvaffak olmuş Türk kadınları', 1928, p. 12).

Following her ambitions, Safiye Ali secured a scholarship from the Ottoman Ministry of Education to pursue medical studies abroad in 1916. Safiye Ali attended the Faculty of Medicine in Würzburg Julius-Maximilians University in Germany, where she studied medicine during World War I. There is limited information about the time she spent in Germany. However, information about her student years at Würzburg University is obtained from the documents in the Ottoman Archive of the Presidential State Archives. The Inspector of Ottoman Students, Ali Haydar Bey, reported to the Ministry of Education that Safiye Ali, despite not knowing German, began taking German language courses simultaneously with her medical education and quickly learned the language (Presidential State Archives, Ottoman Archive, 1916).

Figure 2.2. Turkish female students at American Girls' College in Arnavutköy, Istanbul. Safiye Ali on the far left.

In the same archive, a document completed in Safiye Ali's handwriting on 1 July 1918, titled the *Inspection Form of the Ottoman Student Delegation Abroad*, contains information about her date of birth, family and education prior to her arrival in Germany. She also noted that since she began medical school in 1916, the Ministry of Education had been sending her 350–400 marks monthly and provided the address of the boarding house where she stayed (Yıldırım, 2012, pp. 87–90). Also, in five letters she wrote to Inspector of Ottoman Students, Ali Haydar Bey, during 1918–1919, she spoke about her courses, how her professors allowed her to take the Physikum examination (a prerequisite for medical studies) despite being initially barred from it as an American College graduate, and how she excelled by achieving the top rank in this exam. She also mentioned the difficulties of maintaining communication with her mother due to the harsh conditions of World War I and her desire to elevate the status of Turkish women. In response, Ali Haydar Bey wrote four letters to Safiye Ali, frequently asking about her academic progress and expressing that if she succeeded in earning the title of the first Turkish woman doctor educated in Europe, she would serve as a role model for the advancement of Turkish women (Yıldırım, 2012, pp. 91–110).

From the transcription documents in her university file, it is evident that she took a total of 68 courses, seminars and internships from the summer semester of 1916 to the winter semester of 1920–1921, which, for that time, shows how hardworking of a student she was (Universität Würzburg, 2021). During her time at the Faculty of Medicine, she spent two and a half years studying anatomy, zoology, botany, physics, organic chemistry and inorganic chemistry. Following this, she gained experience by working as an assistant in clinics, took weeks-long exams in various fields and, in practical exams, diagnosed and treated patients assigned to her by professors. After conducting research at the medical faculties of Leipzig University and Heidelberg University, she completed her five-year medical education and successfully passed her doctoral examination at Würzburg University, earning her diploma.

During her studies, Safiye Ali prepared two theses. Her first thesis, on the nutrition of young children with sour milk, was based on her research involving 120 children (Memleketimizin ilk kadın tabibesi, 1921). Her second thesis was her graduation dissertation titled *Über Pachymeningitis haemorrhagica interna im Säuglingsalter* ('On Internal Haemorrhagic Pachymeningitis in Infancy'). With this thesis, she earned her Doctor of Medicine diploma in May 1921 (see Figure 2.3 for her diploma). In the same year, after passing the state medical examination – a prerequisite for practising medicine in Germany – she obtained her licence to practice medicine (Yıldırım, 2012, p. 19).

After she had completed her degree in Germany, Safiye Ali turned back to Istanbul, stayed there for six weeks and then returned to Germany to specialise further. She completed a one-year specialisation in gynaecology and a two-year specialisation in paediatrics at her alma mater, in the Faculty

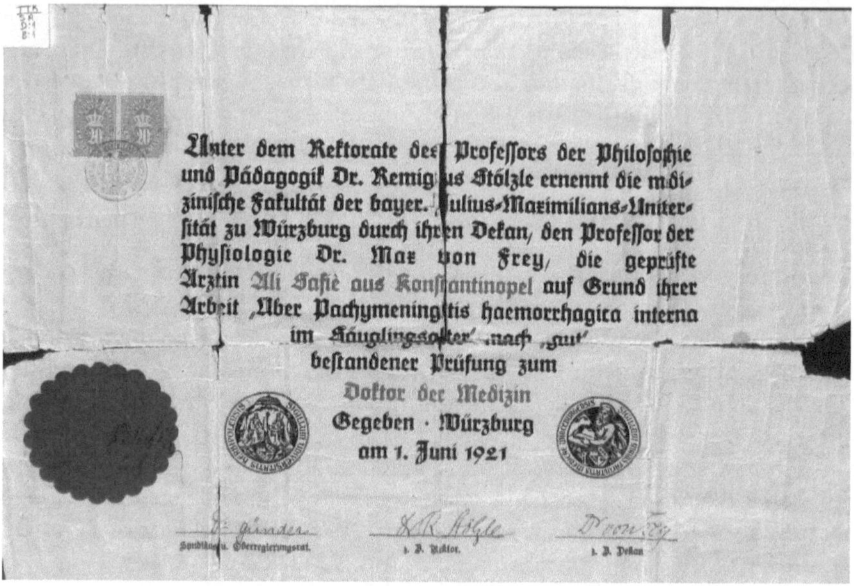
Unter dem Rektorate des Professors der Philosophie und Pädagogik Dr. Remigius Stölzle ernennt die medizinische Fakultät der bayer. Julius-Maximilians-Universität zu Würzburg durch ihren Dekan, den Professor der Physiologie Dr. Max von Frey, die geprüfte Ärztin Ali Safiè aus Konstantinopel auf Grund ihrer Arbeit ‚Über Pachymeningitis haemorrhagica interna im Säuglingsalter' nach ‚gut' bestandener Prüfung zum

Doktor der Medizin

Gegeben · Würzburg
am 1. Juni 1921

Syndikus u. Oberregierungsrat.

Figure 2.3. Safiye Ali's medical diploma from University of Würzburg Julius-Maximilians. Copyright: The Turkish Historical Society, n.d.

of Medicine at Würzburg Julius-Maximilians University ('Hayatta muvaffak olmuş Türk kadınları', 1928, 13). Safiye Ali described her years as a medical student in Germany as the best period of her life. She was particularly impressed by the friendships and camaraderie that transcended gender distinctions at the university and the ease with which she was treated, even though she was a foreign woman. She also received the strongest support from her husband ('Hayatta muvaffak olmuş Türk kadınları', 1928, p. 13). When she returned to Istanbul, she married Dr Ferdinand Krekeler at the German Embassy on 28 November 1924 (Universität Würzburg, 2021).

When Safiye Ali completed her specialisation and returned to Istanbul, she found herself in a nation that had undergone profound political and social transformation. The Turkish War of Independence (1919–1923), a critical period in Türkiye's history, had recently concluded. This war was fought under the leadership of Mustafa Kemal Atatürk, who galvanised the Turkish people against occupying forces and the remnants of the Ottoman Sultanate following World War I. The war's success led to the abolition of the Ottoman Empire, which had ruled for over 600 years, and the establishment of the Republic of Türkiye on 29 October 1923. This marked the beginning of a secular, modern and reform-oriented state. Istanbul, previously the capital of the Ottoman Empire, became a cultural and historical hub while Ankara was chosen as the new capital of the Republic. During this period of transition, significant reforms were implemented, affecting nearly every aspect of Turkish society, including education, healthcare, women's rights and the legal system. The era saw the introduction of secular laws, the Latin alphabet replacing Arabic script, and significant efforts towards modernising and westernising Türkiye (Aslan, 2002).

Safiye Ali in Istanbul

For Safiye Ali, returning to Istanbul meant stepping into a society in flux. The newly founded Republic was focused on building a progressive and egalitarian future, providing opportunities for individuals like her to contribute to the nation's development. In this period of new initiatives, Safiye Ali, who had gone to Europe as the daughter of an Ottoman pasha, turned back to Türkiye as the first female doctor of the Republic (Şuûn, 1923, p. 367). She first obtained permission to practice medicine in Istanbul in June 1923 (Yıldırım, 2012, p. 27). Then, together with her husband, Dr Ferdinand Krekeler, she announced through newspaper advertisements that they had opened a private practice (*Akşam*, 1924, p. 4).

The establishment of the Turkish Republic created new opportunities for women, yet there was significant resistance to the idea of a female doctor. With the enactment of the Turkish Civil Code on 17 February 1926, legal equality between men and women was formally recognised. However, achieving this equality in practice was neither immediate nor universal. For example, Safiye Ali's name appeared as 'Mr Safiye Ali' in a trade almanac (Malul Gaziler Büyük Ticaret Salnamesi, 1928, p. 996). Also, in an interview, she mentioned how wealthy women distrusted her because she was a woman and how some patients said, 'She's a female doctor, so we can pay her less'. In response, she declared that she would treat those without money for free but demanded the same fees as her male colleagues. She became a confidant to her impoverished female patients ('Hayatta muvaffak olmuş Türk kadınları', 1928, pp. 12–13).

While she received support from some experienced and renowned male colleagues, such as Dr Besim Ömer Pasha (Akalın, 1862–1940), others did not trust her simply because she was a woman. Nevertheless, she persevered, simultaneously serving as the physician for the German and American embassies in Istanbul and teaching gynaecology and obstetrics at the Department of Medicine at Constantinople Woman's College. This made her the first female faculty member to teach in a medical school in Türkiye. She quickly gained recognition, and her practice became busy with patients (Yıldırım, 2012, pp. 20, 29–34).

Small Children's Clinic in Women's Centre of the Red Crescent Society

The first public health action that Safiye Ali was involved was her work in *Hilal-i Ahmer Cemiyeti Hanımlar Merkezi Küçük Çocuklar Muayenehanesi* (Small Children's Clinic in Women's Center of the Red Crescent Society). In this clinic, she reached out to poor families, took preventive measures to prevent children from falling ill due to malnutrition, treated sick children, and educated mothers on childcare. Mothers with weak or sick children who had been weaned after reaching one year of age could apply to the Small Children's Clinic. Safiye Ali would weigh and examine the children brought to the clinic every Wednesday. Each child, identified as needing nutrition, was given an ID and health booklet, and their name, address and family's social status were recorded. The mother was given a note on how to feed the child according to their weight and advised to return the following week. In the meantime, a nurse was sent to investigate the family's living conditions to determine if they were genuinely in need, and the visiting nurses taught mothers simple health rules that could be applied even in poverty (Yıldırım, 2012, pp. 35–37).

Between 1 August 1923 and 31 December 1924, the development of 9,360 children was monitored in the clinic, 391 children were treated by providing medication, the health status of 150 children was monitored by visiting nurses in their homes, and 20 children were hospitalised. In addition to health services, the clinic distributed various foods according to the ages, weights and health conditions of 36,500 children, as well as winter clothing, underwear and swaddling. This centre was a sanitary children's charity, providing both health services and assistance. When the Women's Center was dissolved by joining the Turkish Red Crescent Society, Small Children's Clinic was closed on 25 January 1925 (Yıldırım, 2012, pp. 35–37).

The Milk Drop Project

One of Safiye Ali's key contributions was her role in *Süt Damlası* (Milk Drop) project. Milk Drop was the first charity institution established by Westerners dedicated to Muslim-Turkish children. The French Red Cross Women's Society, with the help of the French High Commissioner for the East, and Istanbul Ambassador Gen. Maurice Cesar Joseph Pelle (1863–1924), established a childcare institution called Milk Drop-Small Children's Clinic to assist poor Turkish children in 1921 during the occupation of Istanbul. After the armistice, the French Women's Society donated Milk Drop to the Child Protection Society in April 1925. The key purpose of its establishment was not treatment, but to teach and promote how to care for children and protect their health (Yıldırım, 2012, pp. 38–39).

The institution began to develop when Safiye Ali assumed the role of its doctor and started volunteering twice a week. Initially consisting of three rooms and a milk kitchen, it transformed into a small example of its counterparts in civilised countries through Safiye Ali's selfless efforts and contributions to the care and health of children, particularly those from poor families (Süt Damlası, 1926, p. 276). In the clinic, assistance was initially provided to mothers of twins and children whose mothers had died. After examination, each child was given pasteurised milk according to their digestive capacity. Secondly, children with insufficient breast milk were kept under observation for 15 days and assisted if necessary. The third group included children who had been weaned and were starting to eat something other than milk for the first time. These children were given pasteurised milk, phosphatin and similar food items. Twice a week, 70–90 children from outside the institution were also examined and treated, necessary medications were provided, and their mothers were given advice (see Figure 2.4 for a photo taken at the clinic). In 1924, there were 45 registered children ('Anneleri çocuklarına rabt eden müesseseler', 1926, p. 15)

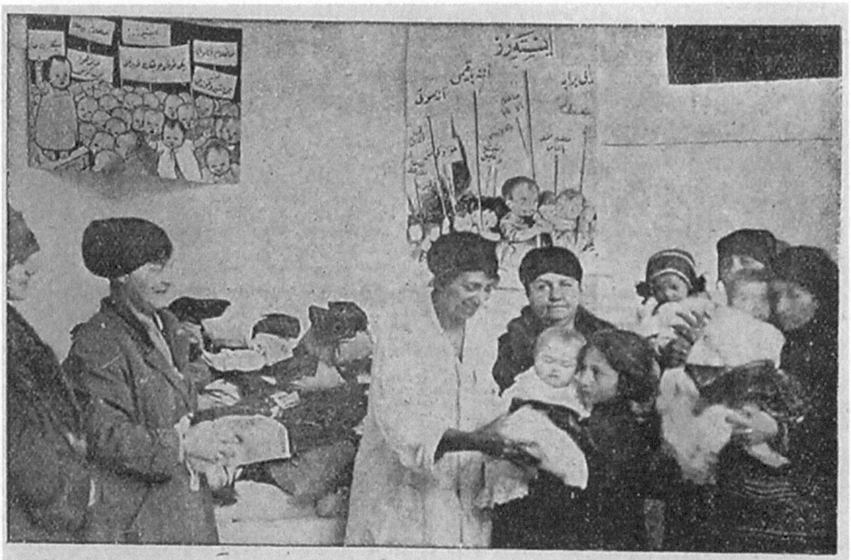

Figure 2.4. Safiye Ali at Milk Drop clinic.

During Safiye Ali's directorship, visiting nurse services, sunbathing and artificial sunbathing (ultraviolet) were introduced at Milk Drop. Children played with toys like buckets and spades, laughing and sunbathing on the fine sands brought from Florya beach in Istanbul. Sunlight and ultraviolet rays were particularly effective in children suffering from bone diseases (rickets), joint and skin tuberculosis. At Milk Drop, Safiye Ali organised a 'Children's Museum', where photos, posters and all kinds of tools and equipment used in childcare were displayed to explain their benefits and risks to mothers. She provided mothers with information and advice on child health through ideal childcare posters she brought from Germany. In addition, she published a book titled *Small Children's Clinic and Milk Drop*, compiling information from German, French and English books and incorporating her experiences at Milk Drop (Yıldırım, 2012, pp. 38–44).

Challenges in a Male-Dominated Field

Despite her success in public health initiatives, Safiye Ali faced significant challenges in the male-dominated medical field. Her leadership in Milk Drop was undermined by accusations of mismanagement, including false allegations that she was stealing milk meant for children ('Himaye-i etfale böyle birden bire ne oldu?' 1927, pp. 1–2). These challenges eventually led to her resignation from the project, stating that some of her male colleagues were envious of the success she had achieved as a female doctor in such a short time (Yıldırım, 2012, pp. 45–50).

However, her resignation sparked a new movement in Turkish society. On 20 February 1927, Safiye Ali, who had resigned, went to the Milk Drop clinic to hand over her duties. About 60 women waiting to have their children examined began pleading, 'Don't leave us', and, holding their children in their arms, they marched to *Himaye-i Etfal Cemiyeti* (Turkish Association for Protection of Children) Headquarters in Cağaloğlu, Istanbul, shouting, 'We want our doctor!' This march was the first protest held by women in Turkish history (see Figure 2.5 for the photo taken at the march). Later, Safiye Ali was accused of inciting the mothers and organising this demonstration against her male colleagues, with whom she had a disagreement. Safiye Ali, finding this accusation absurd, said that the issue was a matter of gender, and that some of her male colleagues were jealous of the success she had achieved in a short time as a female doctor. She stated that she had firmly resigned ('Himaye-i etfale böyle birden bire ne oldu?' 1927, pp. 1–2).

After some time, Safiye Ali noticed certain individuals lingering around her house and learned they were gathering information about the residents. One night, a person who came to her house late at night told her brother-in-law, who answered the door, 'Someone is waiting for Ms. Safiye

Figure 2.5. The protest by women.

Copyright: Himaye-i etfale böyle birden bire ne oldu?' 1927, pp. 1–2.

at the corner, saying there is a patient', which raised suspicions, and she did not go. A while later, another person came with a note, saying, 'Please come to Pera Palace, Room 19, at 4:00 PM', with an illegible signature. She reported the situation to the authorities ('Bu ne? Safiye Ali Hanım', 1927, p. 1). The suspicious incidents indicate that Safiye Ali, as a prominent and pioneering figure, may have been subjected to surveillance or threats, potentially due to her groundbreaking role as the first female physician in Türkiye, her activism or her involvement in social reforms.

By resigning from Milk Drop, Safiye Ali also ended her membership in *Anneler Birliği* (Mothers' Union). She was a member of the administrative board of the Mothers' Union, a branch of Milk Drop that provided prenatal care. Mothers' Union met once a week at Milk Drop, encouraging poor mothers to bring their children to the Small Children's Clinic every 15 days until they were two years old, visiting them in their homes to ensure their health, preparing baskets, cradles, and laundry, encouraging breastfeeding, and providing pasteurised milk from Milk Drop to those with insufficient milk (Yıldırım, 2012, pp. 51–52).

Despite the resignation, Safliye Ali remained active in advocating women's rights in the early years of Turkish Republic. She was elected to the steering committee to present the opinions of Istanbul women on the issues in the

Family Law Decree being debated in the Turkish Grand National Assembly in 1924. At this meeting, it was requested that the polygamy and divorce provisions based on Islamic law be removed. The committee members prepared both the programme of the *Türk Kadınlar Birliği* (Turkish Women's Union) according to their expertise and dealt with family law issues such as divorce and polygamy. Later in 1924, the statute of the Turkish Women's Union was approved, and under the leadership of Nezihe Muhiddin, Safiye Ali was appointed as the president of the Health Commission. The 1925 activity programme developed protective policies for women and children, focused on combating prostitution, protecting women's rights in divorce and prioritising facilitating women's employment (Yıldırım, 2012, pp. 53–54).

The Turkish Women's Union decided to participate in the 1927 general elections on behalf of *Cumhuriyet Halk Partisi* (Republican People's Party) to enter parliament and defend the women's cause. The candidates for parliament included Nezihe Muhiddin, Dr Safiye Ali, Dr Hayrünnisa and Mrs. Azize Hanım, Mustafa Paşazade's wife. Safiye Ali's active efforts as a candidate for parliament were influenced by her work as the president of the Health Commission and her direct involvement in maternal–child health. In a statement to newspapers, Dr Safiye Ali expressed her desire to represent the interests of children in the Turkish Grand National Assembly, emphasising that women would eventually become parliamentarians, even if not immediately (Turkish women seek vote', 1927, p. 7).

In addition to her clinical work, Safiye Ali was a strong advocate for public health education. She believed that the key to improving health outcomes was not just treating illness but preventing it through education and community engagement. Safiye Ali worked with organisations such as Society for the Protection of Children and the Turkish Red Crescent to promote public health initiatives focused on education and prevention (Yıldırım, 2012, p. 30). Her work with these organisations highlighted the intersection of healthcare and social services. Safiye Ali advocated for a healthcare model that went beyond the clinic, addressing the social determinants of health such as poverty, nutrition and education. This approach challenged the curative-focused models of mainstream medicine and demonstrated the importance of integrating healthcare with broader social services.

In the first five years of the Republic, Safiye Ali represented Türkiye and Turkish women, as a symbol of the Republic's advancements, at three international congresses related to her profession. She first attended a congress organised by the Medical Women's International Association (MWIA) in London in the summer of 1924. The congress focused on the services that female doctors could provide to humanity. In the fall of 1924, she attended the Budapest Congress organised by the International Save the Children Union as a delegate of the Red Crescent Society with Besim Ömer Pasha. In 1928, she represented Türkiye at the congress of the International Women

Doctors' Association, held this time in Bologna. During these congresses, held during the ongoing global economic crisis following World War I, she drew attention to the high rates of diseases and mortality among children in Istanbul due to malnutrition, emphasised the urgent need for international assistance due to general poverty caused by the economic depression, and highlighted the freedoms brought to Turkish women by the new Republican regime that the world was closely watching. Safiye Ali's speeches were highly praised (Besim Ömer, 1924, pp. 3–8, 19).

After the congress in Bologna, she and her husband went to Germany in 1928. They settled in Dortmund and opened a private practice. A few years later, World War II began. Having witnessed World War I as a medical student, this time she was in the middle of World War II as a doctor. Due to the War, all the city's doctors were on the front lines. As her husband was unable to go to the front due to a foot injury, they both tirelessly helped patients. In the summer of 1938, she noticed a lump under her left breast. When the lump grew, she underwent surgery to remove her left breast. In the spring of 1940, she underwent a second operation to clean under her left arm, and a cancer diagnosis was made. These were the darkest days of World War II. Despite the swelling and pain in her left arm, she continued to help patients. However, Safiye Ali's illness was advancing. She passed away on 5 July 1952, and was buried after a ceremony held on 9 July 1952, in the large hall of Dortmund Central Cemetery (Türk Tarih Kurumu, n.d., SA.2.1.3–2).

Safiye Ali's husband, Ferdi Krekeler, was a citizen of the Türkiye (Türk Tarih Kurumu, n.d., SA.D.1B.3). Instead of going to Türkiye, which had not entered World War II, they chose to stay in Dortmund and rush to the aid of those injured and sick in shelters under air raids. After her death, an article titled *A Great Turkish Woman Has Died* was published in Rheinische Post, where Safiye Ali, who was heroised as the 'Turkish shelter doctor', was described as 'a true Muslim Turkish woman who remained faithful to the beliefs of her people and to science' (Kahraman, 2022).

Safiye Ali's Feminist Legacy in Healthcare

Safiye Ali's contributions to healthcare were inseparable from her feminist activism, making her a pioneer not only in medicine but also in advocating for gender equality in Türkiye. As a leading member of the Turkish Women's Union, she campaigned tirelessly for women's rights, focusing on suffrage, equal pay, access to professional careers and improved healthcare for women and children (Yıldırım, 2012, p. 53). Safiye Ali viewed healthcare as a fundamental pillar for achieving gender equality, emphasising that women's health and empowerment were intrinsically linked.

Through her work in healthcare, Safiye Ali bridged the gap between medical practice and social reform. She established one of the first medical practices in Istanbul dedicated to providing care for women, particularly those who were unable to seek treatment from male doctors due to cultural restrictions. Her practice addressed critical issues such as maternal and child health, nutrition, and the provision of essential medical services to underprivileged families. By running programmes such as the 'Süt Damlası' (Milk Drop), she pioneered modern childcare practices, teaching mothers how to care for themselves and their children. This effort not only improved health outcomes but also empowered women by equipping them with knowledge and skills to manage their families' health. Also, her efforts extended to social services, where she provided food, clothing, and medical supplies to impoverished families, particularly during periods of economic hardship after World War I. Safiye Ali believed in integrating healthcare with broader social support systems, a perspective that was revolutionary for her time and remains influential in feminist approaches to healthcare management today.

In 1927, Safiye Ali became one of the first women to run for parliamentary office in Türkiye, a bold move that underscored her commitment to political representation for women. Although her candidacy was ultimately unsuccessful, it symbolised a shift in the perception of women's roles in public life and politics. She believed that political representation was crucial for enacting healthcare reforms and advancing women's rights. Her speeches and public appearances often highlighted the connection between healthcare, education, and gender equality, advocating for systemic changes that would benefit women and children across the country ('Himaye-i etfale böyle birden bire ne oldu?', 1927, pp. 1–2).

Safiye Ali also represented Türkiye on the international stage, attending conferences such as the 1924 Budapest Congress of the International Save the Children Union and meetings of the MWIA. In these forums, she highlighted the Republic's commitment to women's advancement, demonstrating how healthcare could serve as a vehicle for showcasing gender equality. Her international advocacy brought attention to the critical role of women in medicine and healthcare reform, inspiring both domestic and global audiences.

Safiye Ali's work laid the foundation for feminist healthcare management practices that prioritise women's health and integrate social services into medical care. She demonstrated that healthcare is not only about treating illnesses but also about addressing the broader social, economic and political systems that shape health outcomes. Her holistic approach continues to resonate, providing a model for modern feminist healthcare initiatives. Safiye Ali's legacy remains a testament to how one individual can challenge societal norms, advocate for change and redefine the boundaries of healthcare and gender equality (Toros, 1993).

Global Influence and Contemporary Lessons

Safiye Ali's pioneering work offers invaluable lessons for contemporary healthcare management, illustrating the interconnectedness of health, social reform and gender equality. Her emphasis on preventive care, public health education and community engagement aligns with modern principles of healthcare management and demonstrates her ahead-of-her-time understanding of holistic health systems. By focusing on maternal and child health, she highlighted the critical role of healthcare in nation-building and the empowerment of women, creating a template that remains relevant in public health discourse today (Besim Ömer, 1924, pp. 31–33, 36, 44).

Safiye Ali recognised the importance of addressing the social determinants of health – economic status, education and community well-being – as integral to healthcare outcomes. Through initiatives such as the 'Süt Damlası' (Milk Drop), she not only addressed immediate medical concerns but also educated mothers on nutrition, hygiene and childcare, effectively merging healthcare with preventive education. Her approach anticipated contemporary frameworks that emphasise integrating healthcare with social services to tackle root causes of health disparities (Yıldırım, 2012, p. 78). In her work with impoverished families, she provided essential services, including food, clothing, and medical care, ensuring that healthcare was accessible to marginalised communities. This focus on equity and access continues to resonate with global healthcare initiatives, such as the World Health Organization's emphasis on universal health coverage and community-based care.

A significant aspect of Safiye Ali's legacy is her role as a trailblazer for women in healthcare management. Despite her groundbreaking work, her contributions were often overshadowed by her male counterparts, reflecting a persistent marginalisation of women's achievements in medicine and public health. Safiye Ali challenged this trend through her leadership and visibility in both national and international forums. Her participation in international congresses, such as the 1924 Budapest Congress of the International Save the Children Union and the Medical Women's International Association, emphasised her commitment to representing Türkiye's progress on gender equality while emphasising the critical role of women in healthcare leadership. She demonstrated that women's unique perspectives, particularly in addressing maternal and child health, are indispensable to effective healthcare management (Toros, 1993).

Safiye Ali's career exemplifies the political dimensions of healthcare management. Her work showed that achieving systemic change requires active engagement with policymakers and public institutions. As one of the first women in Türkiye to run for parliamentary office, she recognised the necessity of representation in driving healthcare reforms. While her candidacy in 1927 was unsuccessful, it symbolised her belief in the power of political advocacy to shape healthcare systems and advance gender equality. Also, her advocacy extended beyond Türkiye. By representing the nation on international platforms, she bridged global and local perspectives, advocating for healthcare models that prioritise community well-being, preventive care and the inclusion of women in leadership roles. These efforts positioned her not only as a national icon but also as a global pioneer in linking healthcare with social justice and gender equality.

Safiye Ali's legacy offers a profound lesson: effective healthcare management is inseparable from the broader social, political and economic systems in which it operates. Her work demonstrated that healthcare is not only about treating illness but also about addressing inequities and empowering communities. In today's context, her integrated approach to health services, preventive education and social advocacy serves as a model for addressing contemporary challenges such as health disparities, maternal and child health and gender inequity in leadership.

Conclusion: Safiye Ali's Revolutionary Contributions to Health Management

Safiye Ali's life and work revolutionised healthcare management in Türkiye by challenging male-dominated medical practices and introducing a model of healthcare that prioritised prevention, education and community engagement. Her contributions to maternal and child health, her feminist activism, and her advocacy for public health reforms continue to offer valuable lessons for contemporary healthcare management.

Safiye Ali's work demonstrates that healthcare management must address not only the clinical aspects of care but also the social, political and economic systems that shape health outcomes. By recognising the unique needs of women and children, and by advocating for systemic change, Safiye Ali showed how women in healthcare management can drive transformative progress. Her legacy continues to inspire health professionals today to think beyond the clinic and engage with the broader social determinants of health.

References

Akşam. (1924, January 12). 4.

Anneleri çocuklarına rabt eden müesseseler. (1926). *Aylık Mecmua*, 3, 25.

Aslan, B. (2002). Saltanatın kaldırılmasının İstanbul'daki yankıları. *Belleten Türk Tarih Kurumu*, 66(245), 95–122.

Besim Ömer. (1924). *Etfâle muâvenet beynelmilel ittihâdı*. Istanbul: Ahmed İhsan ve Şürekası Matbaası.

Bu ne? Safiye Ali Hanım esrarengiz mektuplar alıyor: Zabıtaya müracaat etti. (1927, April 14). *Milliyet*, 1.

Çolak, O. M. (2007). Libya'dan Üsküdar'a bir padişah yaveri: Ali Kırat Paşa (1840–1903) ve ailesi. In C. Yılmaz (Ed.), *Üsküdar Sempozyumu IV: Bildiriler II* (pp. 577–590). Istanbul: Üsküdar Belediyesi.
Hayatta muvaffak olmuş Türk kadınları: İlk kadın doktorumuz Safiye Ali Hanım. (1928). *Resimli Ay (Kânunusâni)*, 4, 11–13, 40, 47.
Himaye-i etfale böyle birden bire ne oldu? (1927, February 21). *Milliyet*, 1–2.
Kahraman, B. (2022). *Safiye Ali-Krekeler: Die erste Ärztin der Türkei in Dortmund.* https://www.frauenruhrgeschichte.de/frg_biografie/safiye-ali-krekeler/.
Malul Gaziler Büyük Ticaret Salnamesi. (1928). Istanbul: Malul Gaziler Neşriyat Kolektif Şirketi.
Memleketimizin ilk kadın tabibesi. (1921, July 13). *Hakimiyet-i Milliye*, 2.
Presidential State Archives, Ottoman Archive. (1916, July 20). MF. ALY. 94/34, Lef. 12.
Süt Damlası. (1926, September 16). *Servet-i Fünun*, 1570–1596, 276.
Şuûn. (1923, June). *Darülfünun Tıp Fakültesi Mecmuası*, 5, 6, 367.
Toros, T. (1993, July). Dr. Safiye Ali: Turkey's first woman doctor. *Skylife*, 11, 123.
Türk Tarih Kurumu. (n.d.). SA.2.1.3–2.
Turkish women seek vote. (1927, June 20). *New York Times*, 7.
Universität Würzburg. (2021, March 9). *Eine Vorreiterin für Frauen in der Medizin.* https://www.uni-wuerzburg.de/aktuelles/einblick/single/news/eine-vorreiterin-fuer-frauen-in-der-medizin.
Yıldırım, N. (2012). *Türkiye'nin ilk kadın doktoru Safiye Ali.* Istanbul: Tarih Vakfi Yurt Yayınları.

3 Health Revolutionary, Maida Herman Solomon

Pioneer in the Field of Clinical Social Work

Kristin S. Williams

Introduction

Maida Herman Solomon (1891–1988) was an educator, researcher, practitioner and advocate. Her contributions to the development and practice of clinical social work spanned over 60 years. Her contributions include (1) authoring and implementing graduate programming which continues to be the taken for granted training in the field, (2) penning some of the most seminal works and advancing theory, (3) introducing academic and scientific approaches which saw the field professionalise and adopt new standards and (4) helping to change the way that society thinks about mental health and sexual health. A confluence of factors contributes to her marginalisation and neglect, and these include (1) her gender, (2) her ethnicity, (3) the feminised field of social work and (4) the stigmatised focus for her research and practice.

Solomon was one of the first clinical social workers, originally a field called psychiatric social work (Sugarman Evans, 2009). Despite common practice in the 1950s, Solomon did not support the extended hospitalisation of patients with serious mental disorders. Many thought her approaches the *vanguard of progress.* She was devoted to helping patients develop positive mental health strategies, by combining the approaches of social work, with psychiatric rehabilitation and psychopharmacology (Sugarman Evans, 2003). Her efforts brought those struggling with mental illness 'back to the mainstream of humanity' and reduced the associated stigma of mental illness (p. 17). However, Solomon is not a visible actor in the history of the field. Despite her facilitating a significant shift in the way mental illness was viewed by both professionals and the public, she has been largely overlooked. Solomon's contributions as a pioneer in clinical social work and in social work research had both empirical and intellectual implications and led to significant progress in treatment and training (Lyday & Solomon, 1928; Solomon, 2004).

This chapter sets out to bring Solomon's contributions to clinical social work into present discourse in management and organisational studies, and to foster recognition for Solomon in her own field of social work,

DOI: 10.4324/9781003546610-3

as forerunner in a developing profession. In this chapter, I explore Solomon's key contributions along with the reasons that I believe she has been overlooked. I take a distinctly feminist approach to help redress Solomon's marginalisation. I consider feminism an ongoing political project and I regard feminism as ontology and epistemology. Writing which stems from this political project is thus polemical, akin to political statements, argumentation and poltical discourse which is fundamentally linked to human experience (Powell, 2017). Polemics offer a tool for argumentation when other forms of intellectual approaches fail (Flannery, 2001; Long, 2011; Williams, 2024). Polemics also acknowledge that present discourse is limited by certain power relations and durable, gendered practices (Flannery, 2001). I use polemics to engage in a form of feminist history writing (Wallach Scott, 2011, 2020). As a polemicist, writing has become my way to advocate, to embrace various genres and styles of writing, to be persuasive and to be present, authentic and embodied in the way that I write. In this chapter, I have adopted Ferguson's (1986) autobiography as polemic. Autobiography as polemic calls attention to silenced and unconventional women.

To develop an understanding of Solomon as a health revolutionary, I drew on Solomon's own writings, writings of her biographers and historical texts associated with the field of social work. This includes Solomon's oral memoirs which were published in part by John B. Gussman (Gussman, 2004). Anne Sugarman Evans also taped several interviews with Solomon between 1934 and 1957 and later penned her own book on Solomon (Sugarman Evans, 2003). Some of Sugerman's research is housed at the Schlesinger Library, Radcliffe Institute, Harvard University (Sugarman Evans, 1978), and at the Jewish Women's Archive (Sugarman Evans, 2009). Simmons University Archives also houses information about Solomon (*Maida Solomon Papers, 1934–1979*, 1979), including her involvement in the suffrage movement (Social Work Faculty, 1914). There is a collection of papers held at Harvard Library (*Maida Solomon Papers, 1901–1988*, 1988) and these are part of the Schlesinger Library, Radcliffe Institute's collection on American women. This collection is devoted to the history of women in the US.[1] Also, Solomon's book which examines over a hundred cases and the social effects of syphilis on family and community (authored with husband, Harry Solomon) and entitled *Syphilis of the Innocent* (1922) has been digitised and is available via the Library of Congress (Solomon & Solomon, 1922).

Psychiatric Social Work

In North America, today's social workers serve as core healthcare professionals, practising in public health settings and drawing on 'a century of experience in combining clinical, intermediate and population approaches for greater health impact' (Ruth & Marshall, 2017, p. S236). However, social work's interdisciplinary roots – combining a dedication to improving well-being, using ecological, clinical and pharmacology interventions at multiple levels of society (individual, family, community) – are underexplored (Ruth & Marshall, 2017). Public health and social work are related and overlapping fields that both developed in the early 1900s. One of the reasons that the development of these fields overlapped was because of the health-related issues which required collaboration between medical and social/community practitioners (Ruth & Marshall, 2017). One such issue was venereal disease control and sexual health and Maida Solomon and her husband, Harry Solomon took a keen interest in both the treatment of syphilis and what was then called, the social hygiene movement – an early health promotion campaign (Sugarman Evans, 2003).

Social work drew its inspiration from two movements: (1) the community-oriented settlement house movement which often focused on poverty, child labour, overcrowding and immigration and (2) charity work, which sought to alleviate dependence on society for aid (Ruth & Marshall, 2017). Solomon began her involvement in social work inspired by her family's philanthropic engagements, most notably with the Hebrew Benevolent Association and Hecht Neighbourhood House. Both organisations were devoted to helping Jewish men and women, immigrants and the poor (Louis Kristein at the dedication of Hecht Neighbourhood house, 1936, as cited in Sugarman Evans, 2003).

Social work has two main historical methodological approaches and Solomon was interested in both (1) the casework approach to address individual psychological needs of individuals and families and (2) the more macro cause-based structural reforms to improve community well-being (Ruth & Marshall, 2017). In addition, the discipline also saw a distinction between medical social work and psychiatric social work, and Solomon's career trajectory saw her spend considerable time trying to bridge the treatment of psychological problems in both hospital and in community (Ruth & Marshall, 2017). In other words, Solomon defied the trends set by her developing field.

During Solomon's time, social work as a discipline was developing quickly. She was part of the *progressive era* when social work first became a recognised profession; a process starting in the early 1900s. This period corresponds to US federal and state development focused on social welfare. Reforms considered interventions for the poor and for children. New legislation worked in tandem with community groups and state and federally sponsored research initiatives. Various social work specialties were established, including psychiatric social work (Herrick & Stuart, 2004). By the 1960s, social work was considered an established profession (Herrick & Stuart, 2004).

If you reference one of today's core readings, the *Encyclopedia of Social Work* (2008), currently in its 20th edition, you will find just one reference to

Solomon in the History Section, which reads 'In Europe, a fascist takeover of the German government led to the emigration of many, including leading social workers like Maida Solomon, to the United States and elsewhere' (Mizrahi & Davis, 2008). Not only is this short statement entirely insufficient in scope, but it is factually inaccurate. Solomon was born in Boston on 9 March 1891 (*Maida Solomon Papers, 1934–1979*, 1979).

The National Association of Social Work[2] published a history of social work which includes when the first classes in social work were taught (in the summer of 1898 at Columbia University). Key contributors to the development of the field and the so-called famous social workers are also included. These include Jane Adams (established settlement houses in Chicago in the early 1900s), Frances Perkins (social worker and first Secretary of Labour) (Williams & Mills, 2017), Whitney M Young Jr (Dean for the Atlantic School of Social Work), Harry Hopkins (Works Progress Administration) and Dorothy Height (National Council of Negro Women). Oddly, there is no mention of Solomon, despite writing the curriculum for the present-day graduate training. Similarly, literature which discusses the beginnings of psychiatric social work also excludes Solomon (see Gabriel, 2005).

This silence and Solomon's novel engagement with the field are the key points to draw from this introduction to clinical social work. A clue to her relative obscurity may be that she not only bore a stigmatising identity as a Jewish woman, but she also studied and practised in an area of social work that continues to be stigmatised today, namely mental illness and venereal disease. For example, Charles and Bentley (2016) suggest that the history of mental health and the history of social work can be best understood by acknowledging the role of stigma and the practices which promote and perpetuate stigma over humanising care (Charles & Bentley, 2016). Indeed, Solomon spearheaded humanising care and progressive thinking, and it may have been enough of a reason to have neglected her.

Maida Herman Solomon

> Having deeply imbibed that spirit, she carried with her, and acted upon, the idea of a profession as in need of being formed, well past the time when her own profession – social work with a new psychiatric and modern slant – was ostensibly already formed. This enabled her to have a signal impact on its development, decade after decade, for over 60 years.
>
> (Judy Radner, as cited in Gussman, 2004, p. 4)

Maida Solomon attended Boston's Girls Latin School, graduating in 1908. She then went to Smith's College (Sugarman Evans, 2003, 2009). After four years at Smith, she graduated in 1912 and was later recognised with Smith College Medal and the Day-Garret Award from its School of Social

Work (Sugarman Evans, 2009). She continued her education at Simmons College (then Simmons Female College), graduating with a Bachelor of Science degree in 1914. She also worked as a research assistant at this time at Civic Service House, a Boston Settlement House (*Maida Solomon Papers, 1901–1988*, 1988) and she enrolled in Portia School of Law and took classes in the evening. It was also at this time that she also became involved in the women's suffrage movement in Boston. She joined the Massachusetts Women's Suffrage Association in 1911 (Sugarman Evans, 2009). She married Harry Solomon in 1916 and followed him into his work at the Boston Psychopathic Hospital (renamed the Massachusetts Mental Health Centre some years later). Here she began research on neurosyphilis. Very quickly, she was working and training in an emerging field, integrating theory with practice in a clinical setting and writing about it at the same time (Sugarman Evans, 2009).

She had four children between 1918 and 1928 (Peter, Joseph, Babett and Eric), but the couple had agreed from the start to be a two-career family. As I noted in my earlier comments about the trajectory of Solomon's career, she combined hospital-based social work and research with community activism and education and she was ultimately recruited to Simmons College School of Social work to build a curriculum of social work (serving as an educator in that role until 1934) (Sugarman Evans, 2003, 2009). Her work in curriculum development helped to transition Simmons undergraduate programme into a two-year graduate programme with a master of science degree (Sugarman Evans, 2003, 2009).

Perhaps unsurprisingly, Solomon was incredibly active throughout her life in a variety of causes. The biography listed in the Maida Solomon Papers (*Maida Solomon Papers, 1901–1988*, 1988) reads in part:

> She was a member of the Board (from 1926) and vice-president (1955) of Hecht House, a Jewish settlement house for girls founded by the Hebrew Ladies' Sewing Society which merged with the Young Men's Hebrew Association in 1959 and closed in 1970. She was a member of the Union Park Forum, a Jewish speakers' forum and of the Monday Lunch Club, an informal gathering of social workers. She was a charter member of the American Association of Psychiatric Social Workers (AAPSW), was its first president, 1926–1928, and served on its education subcommittee, conducting a national survey of PSW curricula, and chairing its Advisory Committee to the American Red Cross, 1940–1945. She was also active in the AAPSW's successor organization, the National Association of Social Workers. She was the first chair of the Social Service Committee of Beth Israel Hospital, 1928–1938, vice-president of the Massachusetts Society for Social Health, member of the board of the Massachusetts

Association for Mental Health, chair of the Budget Committee of the Boston Community Fund, member of the Citizens' Committee of the Boston Community Survey, and on the board of Rutland Corner House, a half-way house.

Solomon retired at the age of 65 in 1957 from Simmons College as Professor Emerita (Social Work Faculty, 1914). However, that official retirement lasted only a few days, because she continued to work well into her 90s as a consultant for Massachusetts Mental Health Centre supervising a number of projects, volunteers and treatments (*Maida Solomon Papers, 1901–1988*, 1988).

Solomon had a warm energy. Friends have described her as having immense 'personal charm, clear and authentic authority and [a] store of boundless health and energy' (Helen Z. Reinherz, 2004, as cited in Gussman, 2004, p. 6). Others have said she was 'eternally youthful in spirit and outlook, always the student learning and growing' (Milton Greenblat, 1979, as cited in Sugarman Evans, 2003, p. 102).

Understanding Solomon's Contributions in Context

Professionalising the Field

Solomon was instrumental in 'establishing social work at large as a profession with a psychotherapeutic component, founded on rigours academic training and methods' (Judy Radner, 2004 as cited in Gussman, 2004, p 4.). She believed in engaging 'the [social] workers as the researchers' to study their own work (Judy Radner, 2004 as cited in Gussman, 2004, p. 2). At first called a 'research psychiatric social worker' (Solomon, *The Oral Memoir of Maida Solomon*,[3] as cited in Gussman, 2004, p. 21), she was oriented at that time to the syphilis movement, with an interest in neurosyphilis.

As a social worker professional, she began a practice of listing the positive and negative elements of each case and making a plan of progress for each patient. This approach and the documentation of regular written summaries 'led directly to the practice today of writing up something and having it in a record (p. 23) [. . .] It meant that you got a detailed social, physical, personal, family, legal history from patients, family and agencies' (Solomon, *The Oral Memoir of Maida Solomon*,[4] as cited in Gussman, 2004, p. 23). Research was introduced to help evaluate the work and research 'studies were part of [the] [. . .] vision for psychiatric social work' (p. 24) from the start.

Solomon worked in a period where 'professionalization and standardization of academic disciplines through American universities' was underway (Sugarman Evans, 2003, p. 81). It was the 'progressive-era concept of basing professions on science, and by extension research' (Judy Radner,

2004, as cited in Gussman, 2004). Solomon was also involved in knowledge mobilisation and began a practice of 'develop[ing] psychiatric and mental health material so that the psychiatric social worker could take the knowledge gained in the classroom into the practice of the agency setting' (Sugarman Evans, 2003, p. 76). She considered herself one of 'a very small group of consummate social work professionals who not only "invented" the field of psychiatric social work, but also oversaw its definition, its development of standards, and its integration with the other institutions of modern American medicine and education – in short, its professionalism' (Sugarman Evans, 2003, p. 75). Solomon was also keen to push up the standards of training social work students at every opportunity and this led to her involvement in developing graduate training (Solomon as cited in Sugarman Evans, 2003).

Feminised Field of Social Work

Solomon had the occasion to supervise many women across a range of research projects. They often referred to themselves as 'Maida's Girls' and later as 'Maida Solomon's Research Associates' (Helen Z Reinherz, 2004, as cited in Gussman, 2004, p. 5). In social work, there was a substantial presence of women practitioners; however, psychiatry remained a man's field. One of Solomon's chronicles notes that 'women psychiatrists were either relegated to the profession's lower echelons or nervously tolerated, at what appears to have been great personal costs, at its high ranks' (Elizabeth Lunbeck, 1994, as cited in Gussman, 2004, p. 40). Also, psychiatry was considered a science, and science was masculine whereas 'social work was considered sentiment and sentiment was feminine' (Elizabeth Lunbeck, 1994, as cited in Gussman, 2004, p. 40).

In the literature, it is acknowledged that social work is a largely female field, drawing from its roots, the unpaid work of women through charity (Dahle, 2012). From the onset, it was therefore challenging to consider social work a profession as theories on professions tended to view professions as being clearly bounded and are largely masculinist (Dahle, 2012). Social work has difficult-to-define boundaries and was very closely linked to women's suffrage (Jones et al., 2019). In the early 1900s, it is important to consider that women were taking up social reform and social casework long before we called it social work. However, this speaks to what Solomon was attempting to do (unconsciously or consciously), by 'performing' the social worker role as more business-like and professional, essentially making it more palatable and *malestream* (Dahle, 2012). Even today, women represent the numerical majority in social work, whereas the more high-status, well-paid positions are occupied by men (Jones et al., 2019).

Gender Barriers

In terms of the field, Solomon saw 'distinctions in the way careers were conceived and the way educational institutions prepared people for them' (Sugarman Evans, 2003, p. 81). She felt that 'there were no overt [negative] feelings; however, some may have felt that men would immediately get the "big jobs" of leadership right away. Men moved easily into administrative jobs' (Solomon as cited in Sugarman Evans, 2003, p. 81). With her husband Harry Solomon acting as an advocate and a support, Solomon was enabled to 'continue to contribute her talents as a teacher and researcher'. She is cited as saying that 'he [often] voiced his opinion [on my behalf]' (Gussman, 2004, pp. 90–91). Many of her chroniclers gloss over the barriers that I think must have been very real and tangible for Solomon. Clearly, she surmounted many of them and tried hard to reduce barriers for others. Though work related sexual harassment has gained attention in the last 50 years, legal procedures date back to the early 1900s (Madsen & Nielsen, 2023). Though Solomon did not overtly focus on it in either her own writings or oral memoirs, she would have inevitably experienced it.

Advocating for Recognition

In 1914, Solomon had been working at Civic Service House and assisting Philip Davis on research he was doing on adolescence. When the research was ready for publication Davis put Solomon's name on the project as 'In collaboration with . . .'. The head of the project said, 'your name cannot be down as one of the co-editors or co-authors or co-anything because we don't want another Jewish[5] name (Davis was Jewish) and we don't want a woman' (p. 51). After that, Solomon insisted that every 'female psychiatric social worker put their names and titles (and dates) on everything they wrote' (Betty Ann Lifson, as cited in Sugarman Evans, 2003, p. 51). Betty Ann Lifson recalls 'up until this time, female social workers were apt to have written chapters for books and articles or parts of articles to which they would not sign their name to and would stand by passively to see their work published under the byline of some male physician or psychologist or sociologist with maybe a footnote thanking them for their "help"' (Betty Ann Lifson, as cited in Sugarman Evans, 2003, p. 51). Solomon is owed tremendous credit for advocating women to receive recognition for their contributions. In a recent study published in *Nature*, it was reported that women are still less likely to receive authorship credit for the work they do (Ross et al., 2022). Jane Lane, a co-author of the report, stated in *Gender Watch* that the 'the gap is strong, persistent and independent of the research field' (Lane, 2022, p. 2).

Opening Pathways for Women

Solomon had 'the idea that [she] could work at whatever [she] wanted to' [and over time] '[she] became more and more accepted as a Jewish, professional American Woman' (Solomon, as cited in Sugarman Evans, 2003, p. 35). Solomon created pathways for other women to follow in her footsteps. At Simmons, she stayed in touch with a group of 475 graduates and helped to build a supportive network of largely women, who were emerging professionals in the field. In 1942 she was appointed the head of the Department of Psychiatric Social Work and her work included establishing field positions, directing field work supervision and helping graduates find employment (*Maida Solomon Papers, 1934–1979*, 1979).

In addition, Solomon created 'part-time employment opportunities for a large number of professionally trained social workers [. . .] and developed significant roles for volunteers' (Sugarman Evans, 2003, p. 60). Solomon required her students to 'devote some time to voluntary service [. . .] to upgrade the concept and practice of volunteerism [to a] professional level' and to give graduates an edge (Robert Rutherford, 1952, as cited in Sugarman Evans, 2003, p. 80). She was committed to helping 'many young, trained, professional social workers to combine their careers with marriage and children'. This was facilitated through a part time employment strategy of her own design. She felt that this was the best way to help women develop professional careers outside of the home (Sugarman Evans, 2003).

Her Pedagogy

Solomon's contribution to the teaching of social work is evident in the legacy of her development of the first graduate training for social workers. In terms of her approach to teaching, she felt that social work education was relying too much on 'learning by doing' and that 'was not an education, but an "apprenticeship"' (p. 84). She promoted practice-informed theory and theory-informed practice (Sugarman Evans, 2003). Her approach to education was to prepare students with a 'firm, rich grounding in the best thinking practice in the mental health field (Robert Rutherford, 1988, as cited in Sugarman Evans, 2003, p. 85). Solomon's praxis orientation is still the approach today. For example, Shaikh and colleagues (Shaikh et al., 2022) promote theory informed social work practice as the most comprehensive teaching and learning tool for social workers. This suggests that Solomon should not only be recognised for developing critical graduate curriculum but also as a key player who initiated principles of teaching that are still valued today.

Published Works

Quite remarkably, Maida published 28 books and papers, and this did not include the teaching aids, curriculum and other resources she also generated.

Her published works include *Syphilis of the Innocent* (Solomon & Solomon, 1922), *The Field of Social Work* (Davis & Solomon, 1915), *Prevention of Hospitalization* (Greenblatt et al., 1963) and *Drug and Social Therapy in Chronic Schizophrenia* (Greenblatt et al., 1965). A review of this last book, penned by S. Mouchly Small, states that 'this study should be convincing to almost everyone of the value of combined drug and social therapy' (Small, 1965). A review of the *Prevention of Hospitalization* by Annie Laurie Crawford concludes that 'it should be required reference reading for all students in the health professions' (Crawford, 1964). *Syphilis of the Innocent* involved writing up 'one hundred and fifty-five cases' (Solomon, as cited in Gussman, 2004, p. 27) with financing from the 'United States Interdepartmental Social Hygiene Board' (p. 26). She also wrote other defining works of the field. These works included but were not limited to an article for *Smith Quarterly*, entitled *Qualifications for Psychiatric Social Work*, which was specifically about working with syphilitics. She also wrote *Qualifications for Training for Social Work* in one of the first social work reference books, *The Field of Social Service*. In so doing, she was specifically inspired to address popular misunderstanding of the facts of disease, permitted by a societal conspiracy of silence (Solomon as cited in Gussman, 2004, p. 37).

Stigmatised Specialty

The area of social work that Solomon studied and practised in was in and of itself stigmatised. She was interested in studying mental illness and sexual health and specifically venereal disease. Management and organisational studies propensity to ignore feminised professions is well acknowledged, but social work ignoring aspects of its own historical practice is interesting. For example, Temkin (1994) talks about the experience of turn-of-the-century nurses. In her article, venereal disease is considered a 'medical secret', often affecting women. Nursing practice focused on sex workers or women with unfaithful husbands (Temkin, 1994). In other words, these were complex social problems that were not discussed openly and the discourse was often about women's relative incapacity (Temkin, 1994). Venereal disease (specifically syphilis) was synonymous with 'female delinquency' (Brice, 2005). Women engaging with these social problems were deemed feminists, and this chaffed against societal values (Brice, 2005). A feminist in the 1900s was a vilified identity. It is easy to see why Solomon (who was openly a suffragette and worked hard to raise critical consciousness around sexual health) was easy to ignore.

Social Hygiene Movement

The social hygiene movement was partly about modifying sexual behaviour and it 'took up a variety of causes, from promoting sex education, [. . .] to arguing for women's rights [. . .]'. Solomon was concerned less with 'morality and more focused on combatting syphilis, and promoting more openness about sex' (Gussman, 2004, p. 38). She was the vice president of the Massachusetts Society for Social Hygiene from 1928 to 1956 (Gussman, 2004). The movement was inspired by the concern that people had very limited knowledge about sexual health. And though the movement was not strictly concerned with syphilis, sex education was a strategy to talk openly about sex (Solomon as cited in Gussman, 2004). The social hygiene movement was certainly contentious at the time, and it represented some thinking which is clearly out of date now, but it was in many respects at the forefront of progressive thought about sexual health and education. Social hygiene as a movement grew alongside social work and ultimately led to various school campaigns about menstruation, sexually transmitted disease and drug use. However, this movement is critiqued for is discursive production of childhood sexuality and the foundational assumptions about hetero normativity (Egan & Hawkes, 2010).

Conclusion

> Educator, researcher, leader in the establishment of the mental health professions [. . .]. To recount the significant points in your career is to describe the establishment of your profession
>
> (Jill K. Conway, 1979, as cited in Gussman, 2004, p. 109)

Solomon's praxis orientation (integrating theory and embodied engagement in a clinical environment) enabled her to immediately put into action what she learned, and it kept her at the cusp of new insights and opportunities in the field. I believe that this is why she was such an active contributor to knowledge formation and field development for over 60 years. However, it does not explain why she is not more broadly known. With various collections at Simmons and Radcliffe (with personal papers and oral memoirs), along with two books and several of her own publications still searchable today, you would think that she would be more than a footnote in the *Encyclopedia of Social Work* (and a factually incorrect one at that). She was an educator, a researcher, a practitioner and an advocate. In all of these spheres, she was exceptional. As an educator, she reframed pedagogical practice from *learning by doing* to a *thinking practice* approach. She also authored and implemented the graduate curriculum which continues to be the taken for granted training in the field. As a researcher, she penned some of the most seminal works in an emerging field and she was prolific in her contributions. As a practitioner, she introduced academic approaches that saw the field professionalised and adopt new standards. As an advocate, she helped to change the way that society thought about mental health and sexual health.

In short, she was instrumental in the establishment of social work as an organised profession, shaping its practices, research, management and delivery.

In this chapter, I have introduced you to Maida Herman Solomon. This chapter builds on an ongoing historical analysis I have been conducting into Maida Solomon and coincides with a paper published recently in the *Journal of Management History* (Williams, 2024). I think that Solomon ought to be an inspiring part of our management and organisational history. At the very least, she ought to be an inspiring part of the history of the field of clinical social work. Ultimately, I believe there are a confluence of factors which contribute to Solomon's neglect, including her gender, her Jewish identity and the feminisation of social work. It is also the stigmatised area of work in which Solomon focused her research, teaching and practice, namely that of mental health and sexual health. It is time to bring Maida Solomon from the periphery to the fore as the health revolutionary that she was.

Notes

1 To find the collection and learn more, visit Harvard Radcliffe Institute, Radcliffe Institute for Advanced Study, Harvard University, Schlesinger Library. https://www.radcliffe.harvard.edu/schlesinger-library.
2 https://www.socialworkers.org/News/Facts/Social-Work-History.
3 The Oral Memoir of Maida Herman Solomon is published in part in Gussman (2004) and Sugarman Evans (2003). The Oral Memoirs can be found under Mrs. Maida Herman Solomon Oral Memoir. William E. Weiner Oral History Library, American Jewish Committee, New York Public Library.
4 The Oral Memoir of Maida Herman Solomon is published in part in Gussman (2004) and Sugarman Evans (2003). The Oral Memoirs can be found under Mrs. Maida Herman Solomon Oral Memoir. William E. Weiner Oral History Library, American Jewish Committee, New York Public Library.
5 Maida was 'not formally religious', but she 'supported many Jewish organizations' (Rabbi H. Bruce Ehrmann as cited in (Gussman, 2004, p. 107). She 'resisted formal religious education' (Gussman, 2004).

References

Brice, T. S. (2005). 'Disease and delinquency know no color': Syphilis and African American female delinquency. *Affilia – Journal of Women and Social Work*, *20*(3), 300–315. https://doi.org/10.1177/0886109905277753

Charles, J. L. K., & Bentley, K. J. (2016). Stigma as an organizing framework for understanding the early history of community mental health and psychiatric social work. *Social Work in Mental Health*, *14*(2), 149–173. https://doi.org/10.1080/15332985.2014.964448

Crawford, A. L. (1964). The prevention of hospitalization; treatment without admission for psychiatric patients by Maida Solomon [book review]. *The American Journal of Nursing*, *64*(9), 174.

Dahle, R. (2012). Social work: A history of gender and class in the profession. *Ephemera*, *12*(3), 309–326. www.ephemeraweb.org

Davis, P., & Solomon, M. H. (1915). *The field of social service*. Small, Maylard & Co.
Egan, R. D., & Hawkes, G. (2010). Childhood sexuality, normalization and the social hygiene movement in the Anglophone West, 1900–1935. *Social History of Medicine*, *23*(1), 56–78. https://doi.org/10.1093/shm/hkp062
Ferguson, M. (1986). Feminist polemic: British women's writings in English from the late renaissance to the French revolution. *Women's Studies International Forum*, *9*(3), 451–464.
Flannery, K. T. (2001). The passion of conviction: Reclaiming polemic for a reading of second-wave feminism. *Rhetoric Review*, *20*(1–2), 113–129.
Gabriel, J. M. (2005). Mass-producing the individual: Mary C. Jarrett, Elmer E. Southard, and the industrial origins of psychiatric social work. *Bulletin of the History of Medicine*, *79*(3), 430–458. https://doi.org/10.1353/bhm.2005.0098
Greenblatt, M., Moore, R. F., & Solomon, M. H. (1963). *The prevention of hospitalization: Threamtment without admission for pyschiaric patients*. Grune & Stratton, Inc.
Greenblatt, M., Solomon, M. H., & Sugarman Evans, A. (1965). *Drug and social therapy in chronic schizophrenia*. Charles C Thomas Publisher.
Gussman, J. B. (Ed.). (2004). *Carrying a banner for psychiatric social work*. Old Heidelberg Press.
Herrick, J. M., & Stuart, P. H. (2004). *Encyclopedia of social welfare history in North America* (1st ed.). Sage Publications, Incorporated. https://doi.org/10.4135/9781412952521
Jones, M., Mlcek, S. H. E., Healy, J. P., & Bridges, D. (2019). Gender dynamics in social work practice and education: A critical literature review. *Australian Social Work*, *72*(1), 62–74. https://doi.org/10.1080/0312407X.2018.1524919
Lane, J. (2022). Study finds that women do not receive the credit they deserve in scientific research. Retrieved at https://wiareport.com/2022/07/study-finds-that-women-do-not-receive-the-credit-they-deserve-in-scientific-research/#:~:text=The%20results%20showed%20that%20women,that%20they%20both%20worked%20on.
Long, I. (2011). Writing gaullist feminism: Francoise parturier's open letters 1968–1974. *Modern and Contemporary France*, *19*(3), 313–327. https://doi.org/10.1080/09639489.2011.588794
Lyday, J. F., & Solomon, M. H. (1928). *The problem of the supply of psychiatric social workers for state hospitals. American Journal of Psychiatry*, *84*(4): 629–638.
Madsen, I. E. H., & Nielsen, M. B. D. (2023). Work-related sexual and gender harassment: conceptual challenges and the need for evidence-based prevention. *Scandinavian Journal of Work, Environment and Health*, *49*(7), 449–452. https://doi.org/10.5271/sjweh.4121
Maida Solomon Papers, 1901–1988. (1988). Harvard University, Schlesinger Library, Radcliffe Institute. https://hollisarchives.lib.harvard.edu/repositories/8/resources/6660
Maida Solomon Papers, 1934–1979. (1979). Simmons College Archives. https://beatleyweb.simmons.edu/collectionguides/ManuscriptsCollection/MS021.html
Mizrahi, T., & Davis, L. (Eds.). (2008). *Encyclopedia of social work*. Oxford University Press. Retrieved 11 Jun. 2025, from https://www.oxfordreference.com/view/10.1093/acref/9780195306613.001.0001/acref-9780195306613.
Powell, A. (2017). Writing polemic as history: The apocalyptic implications of elias of cortona, hugh of digne, and gerardo segarelli in salimbene's cronica. *Franciscan Studies*, *75*(May), 343–384. https://doi.org/10.1353/frc.2017.0013

Ross, M. B., Glennon, B. M., Murciano-Goroff, R., Berkes, E. G., Weinberg, B. A., & Lane, J. I. (2022). Women are credited less in science than men. *Nature*, *608*(7921), 135–145. https://doi.org/10.1038/s41586-022-04966-w

Ruth, B. J., & Marshall, J. W. (2017). A history of social work in public health. *American Journal of Public Health*, *107*(S3), S236–S242. https://doi.org/10.2105/AJPH.2017.304005

Shaikh, S. S., LeFrançois, B. A., & Macías, T. (2022). *Critical social work praxis*. Fernwood Publishing.

Small, S. M. (1965). Drug and social therapy in chronic schizophrenia, Maida Solomon [book review]. *International Journal of Social Pyschiatry*, *13*(3), 240. https://doi.org/10.1002/ss.37119811606

Social Work Faculty. (1914). Maida Solomon 14, faculty, social work. In *Suffrage at Simmmons*. Simmons University Archives. https://beatleyweb.simmons.edu/suffrage/items/show/82

Solomon, H. C., & Solomon, M. H. (1922). *Syphilis of the innocent: A study of the social effects of syphilis on the family and the community, with 152 illustrative cases*. United States Interdepartmental Social Hygiene Board. https://doi.org/10.1007/978-981-16-3634-9_5

Solomon, M. H. (2004). *Carrying a Banner for Psychiatric Social Work: Essays, Perspectives, and Maida Herman Solomon's Oral Memoir*. Regent Press.

Sugarman Evans, A. (1978). *Taped interviews with Maida Herman Solomon re Simmons college school of social work, 1934–57*. Schlesinger Library, Radcliffe Institute for Advance Study, Harvard University.

Sugarman Evans, A. (2003). *A woman ahead of her time: Maida Herman Solomon, mental health visionary*. Tabby Manse Inc., Coastal Villages Press.

Sugarman Evans, A. (2009). *Maida Herman Solomon*. Jewish Women's Archive. https://jwa.org/encyclopedia/article/solomon-maida-herman

Temkin, E. (1994). Turn-of-the-century nursing perspectives on venereal disease. *Image: The Journal of Nursing Scholarship*, *26*(3), 207–211. https://doi.org/10.1111/j.1547-5069.1994.tb00315.x

Wallach Scott, J. (2011). *The fantasy of feminist history*. Duke University Press.

Wallach Scott, J. (2020). *On the judgement of history*. Columbia University Press.

Williams, K. (2024). Elizabeth Gaskell: An overlooked political economist and proto theorist in the field of industrial relations. *Gender, Work and Organization*, *31*(2), 576–593. https://doi.org/10.1111/gwao.13089.

Williams, K. S. (2024). Maida Herman Solomon (1891–1988): An invisible forerunner in the field of clinical social work. *Journal of Management History*. https://doi.org/10.1108/JMH-06-2024-0083

Williams, K. S., & Mills, A. J. (2017). Frances Perkins: Gender, context and history in the neglect of a management theorist. *Journal of Management History*, *23*(1), 32–50. https://doi.org/10.1108/JMH-09-2016-0055

4 St Ultan's Hospital for Sick Infants

Drs Kathleen Lynn, Elizabeth Tennant, Katherine Maguire, Ella Webb and Dorothy Stopford Price

Mary McAuliffe

Introduction

St Ultan's Hospital for Sick Infants, Dublin, was founded in 1919 by a group of women doctors and social activists who were concerned with the excessive infant and maternal mortality rates among the poorest city dwellers, especially those living in Dublin's notorious inner-city tenements. At that time, Ireland was deep in turmoil due to the War of Independence, fought to gain independence from Britain. Many of the supporters of St Ultan's were, like its main co-founder, Kathleen Lynn, involved as republican militants in that fight. Interestingly, while Lynn and many of the nursing staff and civilian supporters were republicans, among the women doctors who worked in St Ultan's were those who opposed the fight for freedom. The fact that the women could overlook these very divergent political views and work together for the good of the poor of Dublin speaks volumes for their character and commitment to their work. Among these women doctors first associated with St Ultan's were Drs Kathleen Lynn, Katherine Maguire, Elizabeth Tennent, Ella Webb and Dorthy Stopford Price.

Through its existence, St Ultan's employed mainly female doctors, and this chapter seeks to understand St Ultan's as a hospital for children an innovative medical space, and a radical, feminist space where medical women could and did set their own professional and ideological agendas. St Ultan's was also a secular, mainly Protestant female space which has comparisons with British, rather than Irish, hospitals. In 19th-century Britain, women founded and ran hospitals, mainly in response to difficulties in getting medical training in mainstream hospitals and exclusions from appointments post training. These women-run hospitals were spaces where they 'could be assured both of a regular income and of gaining postgraduate experience' (Geddes, 2010). One of the first of these women run hospitals in Britain was the New Hospital for Women, established by Elizabeth Garrett Anderson in

DOI: 10.4324/9781003546610-4

1872. Importantly these hospitals provided training for young women doctors, allowed women medics to care for women and children, and promoted professional success for medical women (Elston, 2001).

Women, Charity, Philanthropy and Hospital Care in 19th-Century Ireland

In Ireland there was not the same need for women run hospitals as women were educated in male spaces, while hospitals were founded and administered by civilian women, mainly Protestant, from the late 18th century and by Catholic Orders of religious sisters from the mid-19th century. There had been a huge growth in the conventual movement among Catholic women in 19th century, especially for those who felt called to a life of service among the poor. The rise of religious vocations among women was extraordinary, rising from just 120 nuns in Ireland in 1800, to 8,000 by 1901, making up more than a 'quarter of the professional adult women workers' in the 1901 census (Luddy, 1995) Charitable good works, suitable to the nurturing and caring nature of women, were an acceptable path for educated women seeking an outlet for their intelligence, ability and vocation. Among middle class Catholic women, there was a proliferation of vocations to a religious life, and many new congregations sprung up to cater for this need. Most female congregations established were active orders, working in education, nursing, asylum care, prison care and visiting and in the setting-up of hospitals. Examples include St Vincent's Hospital which was founded on St. Stephen's Green in 1834 by Mother Mary Aikenhead, founder of the Catholic Religious Sisters of Charity, the Mercy Hospital in Cork (1857) and the Mater Misercordiae Hospital in Dublin (1861), both founded by the Catholic Sisters of Mercy.

These foundations, whether by lay women or religious women, were part of the important role women played in philanthropy from the 19th century. These philanthropic roles were, as Luddy argued, 'an acceptable framework for public action' by women, specially the more conservative, Catholic women (Luddy, 1995). Religious life offered Catholic women opportunities other than marriage, motherhood and domesticity, providing a 'respectable alternative to family life or the spectre of 'spinsterhood' (Raftery and Delaney, 2022). A life in a religious Order would offer a woman the chance 'to assume leadership, founding and managing hospitals and networks of schools' (Raftery and Delaney, 2022). The Englishwoman, Fanny Taylor, later Mother Mary Magdalen, founder of an English Catholic religious congregation, the Poor Servants of the Mother of God (SMG), was very aware of the nursing work of the Sisters of Mercy. She visited Ireland in 1864–1865, publishing her travel memoir *Irish Homes and Irish Hearts* in 1867, in which she noted the dedicated work of these religious women (McAuliffe, 2013). Taylor had served, as a nurse, with both Florence Nightingale and the Irish Sisters of Mercy in the Crimea in 1856. Her memoir of that time, *Eastern Hospitals and English Nurses,* indicated she was much more impressed with the care offered by the Irish sisters than by Nightingale (Taylor, 1856). A decade later, in Ireland, she found that similar nursing and hospital services offered by the various female congregations including the Mercy Order again met with her approval and exacting standards. She drew inspiration from the Irish nuns when setting up her own Order in 1869, to provide care, including nursing and hospital care, particularly among the emigrant Irish in London and other English cities.

Within the Irish hospitals run by religious sisters the Sisters were 'responsible for nursing, hygiene, and hospital management'; however, they operated with a strict Catholic ethos and under the governance of the local Catholic male hierarchy. The secular medical and religious hierarchies did 'recognize a role for women as doctors and the need for women doctors to treat women patients'; however, in general, Catholic religious hospitals were staffed mainly by male doctors (Kelly, 2017). As Maria Luddy has argued, while nuns played a very significant role in the provision of nursing and in setting up of hospitals, by 1900, 'Protestant and non-Conformist women' had also 'a pattern of establishing voluntary associations for a variety of causes' (Luddy, 1996). There was, also, more evidently among lay Protestant women than among Catholic women, strong links between those involved in philanthropic works and more radical politics, particularly the campaigns for female suffrage. Again, as Luddy argues philanthropy has a major impact in 'shaping public and political activities, particularly those of women' (Luddy, 1996). These women often used the argument that 'the vote was a means to an end – the spiritual and moral regeneration of society – which they were already attempting to implement through their charitable work' (Luddy, 1996). While only a minority of women involved in philanthropy were active suffrage campaigners, this link between women's public and political roles and healthcare was established from the late 19th century, most particularly among Protestant women.

The presence of women, whether involved in suffrage organisations, on health committees on local Boards of Guardians (from the 1890s) or on committees which campaigned for better sanitation, constituted 'political radicalism' (Ó hÓgartaigh, 2017). For example, prior to the founding of St Ultan's and early in her career, a time when she still considered herself a 'soft unionist', Kathleen Lynn was interested in sanitation and its impact on health, attending meetings and discussions by the Dublin Sanitary Association. She would have known from the Association that Ireland 'was fifty years behind in matters of public health compared to England' (McAuliffe and Wheelock, 2024). Another of St Ultan's doctors, Ella Webb, recognised that that many diseases were caused by poverty, including bad sanitation and housing, and malnutrition and worked among the tenement poor, while Katherine Maguire, one of the early doctors in St Ultan's had delivered a number of papers to the Alexandra Guild, which delivered social housing and charitable good works in the tenements of Dublin, including one on 'The Social Conditions of the Dublin Poor' on the occasion of its launch (McAuliffe and Wheelock, 2024).

The First Women Doctors in St Ultan's: Lynn, Webb, Tennant and Maguire

In looking at the lives of the four of the five women doctors associated with the founding and running of St Ultan's Hospital, a Protestant background and an early grounding in philanthropic work through their families is evident. The central figure in the hospital from 1919 until she died in 1955 was Dr Kathleen Lynn. Lynn was born in January 1874 in Mullafarry, near Killala, Co. Mayo, the second daughter of Robert Lynn, a Church of Ireland clergyman, and his wife Catherine (née Wynne) of Drumcliffe, Co. Sligo. As the daughter of a clergyman, she was exposed through her mother's good works, as was expected of a clergyman's wife, to the ideals of philanthropy. Almsgiving and visiting the sick were part of Mrs. Lynn's daily life and the young Kathleen 'vividly recalled the poverty she saw as a young girl' (Ruane, 2001). Another woman doctor associated with St Ultan's from its foundation was also the daughter of a Church of Ireland clergyman. Dr Ella Webb (nee Ovenden), born in 1877, was the daughter of Rev. Charles Thomas Ovenden, Dean of St Patrick's Cathedral, Dublin. She attended Alexandra College, later gaining a science degree from the Royal University of Ireland in 1899 before attending the Catholic University School of Medicine in Cecilia Street, Temple Bar which had opened its doors to women three years previously. She graduated in 1904, won a travelling scholarship to Vienna and was awarded a doctorate in medicine in 1906. While not the daughters of clergymen, Drs Elizabeth Tennant (born c. 1867), Katherine Maguire (born 1963) and Dorothy Stopford Price (born 1890) were also Protestants; a further connection between the three of the five female doctors associated with St Ultan's from the beginning was their education in Alexandra College.

Protestant schools for girls were founded from the 1860s with the most important and influential in Dublin being Alexandra College founded in 1866, by Ann Jellicoe, a pioneer in Irish women's education. Jellicoe had higher ambitions for women's education, and she opened University education and public examinations to women' (O'Connor and Parkes, 1984). By 1869 she had persuaded Trinity College Dublin to set up examinations for women so that 'female students could be examined in university subjects and thereby display their academic ability' (Parkes, n.d.). Alexandra had a broad curriculum which included 'English language and literature, mathematics, history, natural science, geography, Latin, mental and moral philosophy, music, drawing, and callisthenics' (McLellan and Hadden). Maguire, Webb and Lynn were all students at Alexandra College and were all influenced by their exposure to its strong academic curriculum, and its ideals of charitable good works and care, as well as its strong association with the Irish suffrage movement. In the late 19th century, the main suffrage organisation was the Irish Women's Suffrage and Local Government Association (IWSLGA), which, in 1898, was the name given to the already-existing Dublin Women's Suffrage Association (founded in 1876). The woman with the closest association with both DWSA and IWSLGA was Anna Haslam. Haslam, from a Quaker background, had long been involved, with her husband Thomas, in campaigns aimed at upgrading girls' secondary education, which they both saw as vital for women's advancement and mission (Cullen, 2009). Haslam visited Alexandra College regularly to give lectures to the students on women's contributions to society and on the fight for the female franchise. It is therefore no surprise that Lynn, Maguire and Webb were all involved in the fight for suffrage rights.

Alexandra College and Its Connections to St Ultan's

The impact of Alexandra's training on all three women cannot be underestimated. While Tennant and Maguire did not become as radical or as militant as Lynn, all three were members of the IWSLGA. By1898, all three were also involved in the Alexandra College Guild, which Maguire had encouraged the School to set up. The Guild was launched in 1898 by the then principal of the College, Henrietta White, to build a bond between past and present students, encourage in them an understanding of 'useful work . . . and to interest them in, and inform them about, women's work' (Valiulis, 1997). Its first meeting was addressed by Dr Katherine Maguire, who gave a paper on the 'Social Conditions of the Dublin Poor', in which she encouraged the members to improve the living experiences of the urban poor by 'buying and maintaining tenement houses in Dublin' (Valiulis, 1997). According to Valiulis, it was a private venture with a sound financial basis which it hoped would 'inspire other private individuals to invest in the city's housing and alleviate the condition of the poor' (Valiulis, 1997). Maguire and Lynn would remain enthusiastic members of the Guild long after they had left Alexandra. That it influenced Lynn's social activism on housing is evident when she later adapted the guild model 'for inner city housing and community projects . . . generated by St Ultan's' (Ruane, 2001). Other connections between the women closely associated with St Ultan's were their involvement in networks of medical women. According to Kelly, there were 42 female medical practitioners in Dublin in 1911, most of whom Lynn knew or worked with at some stage in her career. By 1908, some of these women had come together to establish the Irish Association of Registered Medical Women, with Dr Katherine Maguire as its first president (Kelly, 2012). Lynn was also involved from the beginning and became the secretary of the Association in 1911, a post she would hold until at least 1915. As Kelly suggests the existence of the association shows 'a sense of community or network among these early women doctors in Dublin' (Kelly, 2012).

Political Ideologies, Divisions and St Ultan's Women Doctors

Despite their similar upbringings and education, however, there were deep political differences between the women. While all five doctors, Lynn, Tennant, Webb, Maguire and Stopford Price, were interested and active to varying degrees in suffrage activism, their ideas on Irish nationalism and the fight for Irish freedom diverged greatly. Lynn, Maguire and Tennant were very supportive of the militant suffragettes, and in 1913 campaigned for better treatment for three imprisoned English suffragettes. These women had travelled to Dublin to protest at a meeting attended by the British Prime Minister Herbert Asquith. Members of the militant suffrage group, the British Women's Social and Political Union, Mary Leigh and Gladys Evans, followed him, bringing a small hatchet which they flung at him, narrowly missing his head. Both were arrested and imprisoned in Mountjoy Jail where they promptly went on hunger strike. Concern about the health and well-being of the imprisoned women led to a letter, addressed to the Viceroy of Ireland appearing in the *Evening Herald* on 13 August 1912. The signatories included Drs Kathleen Lynn, Katherine Maguire and Elizabeth Tennant, who stated they wished to 'lay a memorial [appeal] on behalf of Mrs Mary Leigh, Miss Gladys Baker and Miss Lizzie Baker' (McAuliffe and Wheelock, 2024). However, Lynn's politics were becoming much more radical than those of her medical colleagues. When Irish suffragettes were imprisoned in Tullamore Jail in Co Offaly, where they could be, Lynn had replaced Dr Elizabeth Tennant as the doctor to the suffragettes on their release, as 'Tennant's loyalties were found lacking' (Ruane, 2012). Lynn's loyalties were by now most definitely with the militant suffragettes, while Tennant disapproved of their window smashing activities.

Dorothy Stopford (as she was then) also disapproved of the militant activities of the suffragettes and considered their militant tactics 'foolish and undignified' (Mac Lellan, 2014). By 1921, however, Stopford was a committed nationalist and had joined Cumann na mBan, the women's militant republican group which, although proscribed, fought side by side with the male republicans of the Irish Republican Army (IRA) during the War of Independence. During this period, 1919–1921, Stopford Price was a medical officer to a Cork brigade of the IRA while working at the Kilbrittan dispensary in west Cork. Lynn was also involved, by 1913, in radical, militant suffrage activism, in trade union politics and in militant nationalism. She would provide succor for the striking workers during Dublin's Lockout strike in 1913 and participated in the 1916 Rising against British rule in Ireland as a chief medical officer with the socialist inspired workers militia, the Irish Citizen Army. In the post-revolutionary period, she continued to be involved in radical, revolutionary and suffrage politics, campaigning for leading female militant, the imprisoned Countess Markievicz who ran in the 1918 general election. This was the first election in which women, albeit only those over the age of 30, could vote and run. Markeivicz was successfully returned as an abstentionist Sinn Féin candidate. Lynn was also a member of Sinn Féin which was, at the time, the political wing of militant republicanism in Ireland. Lynn continued her medical and social activist work, along with her republican activities as a senior member of Sinn Féin. She was 'an early and energetic proponent of vaccination' when the influenza pandemic, the so-called the Spanish flu, arrived in Dublin in late 1918 (Milne, 2018). Lynn then worked alongside female medical colleagues, some of whom who disapproved of her republican sympathies, but worked with her to combat the flu. These included Drs Ella Webb, Katherine Maguire and Elizabeth Tennant, who would soon collaborate with her on another project. They helped operate a deport for inoculations at 37 Charlemont St., in Dublin's southside, a derelict building which, with the help of some of Lynn's revolutionary women comrades, many of whom had been trained in first aid by Lynn, was cleaned and 'made as presentable as possible' (Lynn, BMH).

Early Days at St Ultan's

No. 37 Charlemont, Dublin, was to the space in which Lynn was to spend the rest of her professional career, as it was here on Ascension Thursday 1919, that St Ultan's Hospital for Sick Infants was opened with '£70 in the bank, and . . . two infants in the hospital' (Lynn, BMH). While Lynn, and her lifelong partner and long-time St Ultan's hospital administrator, Madeleine ffrench-Mullen, are often credited with founding the hospital, it was a number of women, medical and non-medical, who collaborated to create a space with two beds, a goat and £70 in the bank in 1919. The immediate impetus behind the hospital was the striking rise in the incidence of infant syphilis in the city in the wake of World War I, but they were also concerned about the very high infant and maternal mortality rates among the poor in the Dublin tenements. As Ó hÓgartaigh has demonstrated, St Ultan's was unusual in the Irish context.

As detailed above, several hospitals had been founded by women, particularly Catholic religious women, but St Ultan's was the only hospital which was entirely managed by women (Ó hÓgartaigh, 2017). In fact, Ó hÓgartaigh argues that from the beginning Lynn and the Board practised a 'positive discrimination policy' and favoured female staff, due, in part, because many female doctors were deprived of professional opportunities enjoyed by their male counterparts. It was not only female doctors who were associated with St Ultan's, but many of the women also initially associated with the hospital were political allies and, among the nursing staff, were women whom Lynn had trained in first aid as members of the Irish Citizen Army and Cumann na mBan. Among the first medical staff, as the hospital slowly expanded, were her associates from Alexandra College and the Association of Registered Medical Women, Drs Maguire, Tennant and Webb.

The Contributions of Dr Webb, Maguire, Tennant and Stopford Price

Dr Ella Webb had worked with the Women's National Health Association (WNHA) founded by Lady Aberdeen in 1907, primarily to fight against the ravages of tuberculosis (TB) in the country. The Association was concerned with issues which would be central to the work of St Ultan's and its doctors, high infant mortality rates especially among the poorest living in unsanitary conditions in the Dublin tenements and most especially, concern with the health and well-being of mothers and infants. Dr Webb, as reported in WNHA's journal *Slainte* in 1910, was concerned about educating women in healthcare, as it was, she said, 'ignorance and not the want of affection in the mothers that was at the root of most of the evils'. The association initiated a nationwide campaign to spread the 'gospel of cleanliness' bringing the 'language and reality of sanitary reform to many parts of Ireland' (Ó hÓgartaigh, 2017). This ideology of cleanliness, proper sanitation, education of mothers in care of their infants was core to St Ultan's practice from the beginning. Infant mortality rates in Dublin shocked and horrified these women doctors. Webb was already committed to combating ignorance in infant and maternal healthcare, while another of the early members of staff, Dr Maguire, who was Ireland's first female paediatrician, had a private practice but operated a free dispensary at Harold's Cross and worked among the poor in Dublin. Politically, she advocated for suffrage for women; however, as a non-militant she was also involved in WNHA. Professionally, she supported women doctors through her membership of the Association of Registered Medical Women, of which she was the first President. Dr Tennant was also associated with St Ultan's from the beginning. She had received her licentiate from the Royal College of Physicians in 1894 and her large general practice in Dublin specialised in midwifery (Walsh, 2014). After its foundation she because a visiting physician to St Ultan's. When she died in 1938 her obituary in the Irish Times claimed that she 'did a great deal to overcome the prejudices which female practitioners had to meet in the days when their numbers were very few' (*Irish Times*, 19 February 1938).

All four women, Lynn, Maguire, Webb and Tennant found that St Ultan's was a place where they could work as equals and, for Lynn especially, it was a space, as Ruane notes, where she could deliver on her 'feminist, Christian and republican ideals' (Ruane, 2001). Lynn's daily diaries record the comings and goings of doctors and nurses and demonstrate it as a female-run space, with 'M ff M' (Madeleine ffrench-Mullen) in charge of staffing and administration (McAuliffe and Wheelock, 2024). This space allowed them to implement new and sometimes radical ideas in infant and maternal healthcare. Lynn and her team were determined that their care was child-centred; they were inspired by visits to hospitals in the USA and Europe where they met leading paediatricians. They introduced new practices in social and infant medicine, including goats' milk (the one goat they had on opening day grew into a small herd kept on site), breast milk pumps, one of the world's first Montessori wards, and plenty of fresh air and sunshine for the patients. Money was always an issue; however, despite this the Board and the doctors introduced innovative treatments. By 1925, Dr Dorothy Stopford Price, had joined the team at St Ultan's. Unlike the other subjects of this essay, Stopford Price had not attended Alexandra College and was a graduate of Trinity College Dublin which had finally allowed women to take degrees in 1904. She began her career as a dispensary doctor; however, by 1923, she had been offered the position of assistant physician in St Ultan's (Mac Lellan, 2014).

While Lynn and Stopford Price would spend most of their medical career in St Ultan's (Lynn also ran a large private general practitioner practice), Webb became very involved in combatting childhood rickets, which was rampant in the unsanitary and unhygienic Dublin tenements. By the 1920s, it was known that sunshine, along with proper nutrition and care, was vital in combatting rickets and soon after the ultraviolet light was of use in the dark overcrowded tenements. She and several other women were instrumental in the setting-up of Children's Sunshine Home in Stillorgan to provide the care necessary to combat rickets among poor children. Webb continued to work in St Ultan's, and both Lynn and Stopford Price helped in the Sunshine Home. After Lynn, Stopford Price is perhaps the best known of the women doctors associated with St Ultan's. Her biographer writes that her work with Dr Maguire in Maguire's slum dispensary 'was a major stimulus to intellectual endeavor, inculcating an interest in medical research' (Mac Lellan, 2014). Maguire encouraged her to read, find things out and publish, which she took to heart, having her first publication in the *Irish Journal of Medical Sciences* in 1930 on the results of a series of vaccinations to treat diarrhoea (Mac Lellan, 2014). This supportive female space was encouraging to a young doctor, so much so that she continued her studies, working under Dr Wassen, who introduced Bacillus Calmette-Guérin (BCG) vaccine in Sweden and completing a post-graduate course in Bavaria in 1934. She was awarded a Doctor of Medicine by Trinity in 1935 for her thesis on 'The Diagnosis of Primary Tuberculosis of the Lunds in Childhood' (Mac Lellan, 2014). By 1937, her training and experiences in travelling and working with the foremost experts in Europe allowed her to introduce the BCG vaccine, which protects against TB, to St Ultan's in 1937. Pulmonary TB was common among those St Ultan's cared for and mortality rates among under 5 years of age remained stubbornly high into the 1940s. Building on Stopford Price's pioneering work with the BCG vaccine in the 1930s, St Ultan's became a centre for TB treatment with ambitious plans for expansion, and in April 1945, the new TB wing in the hospital was formally opened. In May 1946, Lynn proudly reported that the *Irish Times* featured 'Dr Price's B.C.G. vaccination', it was she wrote 'a great day for Teac Ultain & we are all so proud & pleased' (McAuliffe and Wheelock, 2024).

St Ultan's a Radical, Female Space: Impacts, Challenges and Legacies

As a radical female space, St Ultan's allowed many of its female doctors to work free of the constraints of the male-dominated public and religious hospitals. The hospital was an outlier in a State in which public health and education were very much in the domain of the dominant and conservative Catholic Church. The Church and the State viewed women, primarily, as rooted in the domestic sphere. The ideal Irishwoman was, above all, a wife and mother, the home and the hearth were to be her sphere of influence, and her citizenship became, as Valiulis has noted, 'rooted in the private sphere . . . [and] directly related to motherhood within marriage' (2009). The decade 1922 to 1932 had seen the stabilising of the democratic principles of government in Ireland under a Cumann na nGaedhael-led government, but it had also seen the constant chipping away at the civil rights of women and the promotion of the dominant discourses of women in the home/private sphere, where the right to work outside the home, the right to control fertility and reproduction, the right to self-determined female sexuality and access to political power by women was regulated and restricted.

By 1937 the new Irish constitution formally privileged heterosexual marriage and the martial family as the normal and natural unit of society, and women's place within that vision was marital, reproductive and domestic, reflecting a 'synthesis between Catholic, nationalist and democratic values in a way that provided a stable basis for constitutional continuity' for the coming decades (Girvin, 2002). The State accepted the dominant, leadership role of the Church in many areas of social policy including education and healthcare. St Ultan's as a secular, female run, predominantly Protestant space was regarded with deep suspicion by the Church hierarchy and, indeed, by Catholic educated doctors. This culminated in a battle of wills in the 1930s when the Board of St Ultan's and the nearby Children's Hospital, Harcourt St. proposed an amalgamation to create a new National Children's Hospital. Neither St Ultan's nor Harcourt St was under the Catholic management, and the Church wished all hospitals, especially those dealing with women and children, to be under Catholic control. This had both a moral and sectarian underpinning; that secular sex education, information on contraception and sterilisation which might be offered in an amalgamated hospital were causes for concern, while the anxieties about a perceived majority of Protestant doctors, trained mainly in Trinity College, instead of Catholic doctors, trained in UCD according to a Catholic medical ethos, working in both hospitals, were growing. There were also anxieties about the potential for proselytising among Catholic patients in a Protestant run hospital (McAuliffe and Wheelock, 2024).

The amalgamation was a step too far for the conservative forces of the Church, State and medical profession. Although it was intended to deliver a larger and better-resourced hospital capable of providing a higher standard of care to infants and children, it would also do so without the imprimatur of the Catholic Archbishop of Dublin. As Ruane has argued this fight was the first major battles of the Catholic ethics campaign, important in shaping the Catholic position on public policy, social work, hospital care and medical research, a position centred on morality rather than healthcare (2001). Lynn and her Board sought and gained an audience with the Archbishop, Edward Byrne, to make their case, all to no avail. While he received them, their arguments did not change his mind. The Church won this battle, and the proposed amalgamation came to nothing. This demonstrated the limit on the radicalism which the female-run, secular St Ultan's could deliver. With the growing power of the Catholic Church, especially in the delivery of infant and maternal healthcare, St Ultan's was an outlier, one which needed to be keep marginalised as much as possible. The succeeding Archbishop of Dublin, John Charles McQuaid would instead champion a children's hospital at Crumlin, one which operated under a Catholic ethos. However, this did not stop the ambition of Lynn and her staff from delivering the best, modern and innovative healthcare for infants and mothers. The work of Dr Stopford Price was central in combatting childhood TB, and in the late 1930s St Ultan's opened an eight-bed TB unit. Stopford Price founded an Anti-Tuberculosis League in Ireland in 1942, and again soon found herself opposed by the new Archbishop of Dublin, John Charles McQuaid, who demanded that the Red Cross lead the anti-TB fight. The new Anti-Tuberculosis League, led by the Red Cross, was dominated by Catholic social thinking and Stopford Price stepped down. However, she shifted her focus to promoting the BCG vaccine and she continued to administer the vaccine at St Ultan's. It became in the 1940s a national centre for TB inoculation and in 1949 the Minister for Health, Noel Browne, had approved the location of the National BCG Committee at St Ultan's, with Stopford Price as its first Chair.

Conclusion

Despite opposition and suspicion from conservative Catholic doctors and the Catholic Church, St Ultan's was, and remained for several decades until its closure in the early 1980s, a female space where doctors could care for women and children, provide jobs for female professionals and train the next generation of women doctors. While many such female-run hospitals were similar in their philanthropic ethos, St Ultan's was a more radical space, as many of the women doctors there were also committed socialists, radical feminists and Irish republicans. Tennant, Webb and Maguire were committed to social medicine and healthcare provision among the poor and most vulnerable, as well as committed to female suffrage and the development of medicine as a profession for women. Lynn and Stopford Price, as militant republicans, had been actively involved in the Irish War of Independence, while Lynn and her partner M ff M, the long-time hospital administrator, were committed socialists.

The legacies of religious run and influenced hospitals continue to be an issue in Ireland, particularly when women's and children's healthcare is considered. As argued by Earner Byrne and Urquhart (2019), Irish women had not only to deal with their own healthcare within a system which viewed the female 'reproductive body through a faith-based lens', but they also had to navigate 'moral, legal and social controls' when dealing with pregnancy. These controls included a complete ban on contraceptives, a moralising and carceral attitude to pregnancy outside of marriage and an absolute ban on contraceptives from 1935. Children or unmarried others were often born in Mother and Baby Homes where care was lacking and morality rates shocking high. The legacies of healthcare delivered from a moral rather than a medical perspective continues to impact in the arguments about the co-location of the ageing and over-crowded National Maternity Hospital at Holles St's, to St Vincent's hospital campus, which is still owned by the Religious Sisters of Charity, who historically ran a number of Magdalen Laundries in which women, some of them unmarried mothers, were institutionalised for years for perceived sins of moral transgression. The argument that the Sisters transferred its ownership to the new company, St Vincent's Holdings CLG, has done little to assuage the disquiet of many activists, medics and feminists who recall, all too well, the Catholic control of their reproductive and maternal bodies, and those of their children, in religion-influenced healthcare settings. The example of a secular, female-run hospital such as St Ultan's is one which provides inspiration on models which would work for women and children, especially as despite the political differences between Lynn and some of her medical comrades, they were able to work effectively together in this female space. All had devoted their careers to social medicine and helped the poorest and most vulnerable, something which helped them overcome all political differences. For these women, their commitment to innovative medical practices, and campaigns for improved public health, housing and education, informed their practice in their professional and public lives.

Viewing St Ultan's as a distinctly different hospital, a radical female space, founded, staffed and run by women, determinedly secular in the Catholic Irish Free State – where the Catholic Church and its ethos dominated healthcare – and radical in the development of innovative best practice and standards of infant care and treatment despite regular funding crises allows a new and unique interpretation of its history, influences and legacies, as well as the challenges its staff faced in a traditionalist, conservative faith-based healthcare system. While some of the St Ultan's doctors and their work have been considered individually, analysing their collective work within St Ultan's allows us to rethink of the radical contribution of women doctors to Irish medical, social and feminist histories.

References

Cullen, Mary (2009) 'Anna Haslam's contribution to the cause of women's rights in Ireland', The National Archives, Retrieved November 19, 2024, from https://www.nationalarchives.ie/wp-content/uploads/2019/03/Anna-Haslam-Essay_MaryCullen.pdf

Earner Byrne, Lindsey and Urquhart, Diane (2019) *The Irish Abortion Journey*, London, Palgrave Macmillan.

Elston, Mary Ann (2001) '"Run by women, (mainly) for women": Medical women's hospitals in Britain, 1866–1948', in Laurence Conrad and Anne Hardy (eds) *Women and Modern Medicine*, Clio Medica Series, Rodopi.

Geddes, JF (2010) '"Too high a percentage of failures"? Cover-up at the new hospital for Women', *Journal of the Royal Society of Medicine*, 103(9): 348–351.

Girvin, Brian (2002) *From Union to Union: Nationalism, Democracy and Religion in Ireland – Act of Union to EU*, Dublin, Gill & Macmillan.

Kelly, Laura (2012) *Irish Women in Medicine, c 1880s–1920s; Origins, Educational and Careers*, Manchester University Press.

Kelly, Laura (2017) *Irish Medical Education and Student Culture, c.1850–1950*, Oxford University Press.

Luddy, Maria (1995) *Women and Philanthropy in 19th Century Ireland*, Cambridge University Press.

Luddy, Maria (1996) 'Women and philanthropy in nineteenth-century Ireland', *Voluntas: International Journal of Voluntary and Nonprofit Organizations*: 350–364.

Lynn, Kathleen, Bureau of Military History Witness Statement, Lynn BMH WS 357, Part II, p. 11, Retrieved from https://bmh.militaryarchives.ie/

Mac Lellan, Anne (2014) *Dorothy Stopford Price; Rebel Doctor*, Irish Academic Press.

McAuliffe, Mary (ed) (2013) *Fanny Taylor Irish Homes and Irish Hearts (Classics of Irish History)*, UCD Press.
McAuliffe, Mary and Wheelock, Harriet (2024) *The Diaries of Kathleen Lynn; Revealing History Through Personal Writing*, UCD Press.
Milne, Ida (2018) *Stacking the Coffins: Influenza, War and Revolution in Ireland, 1918–1919*, Manchester University Press.
O'Connor, Anne V and Parkes, Susan M (1984) *Gladly Learn and Gladly Teach: A History of Alexandra College and School, Dublin, 1866–1966*, Dublin, Pigeon House Books.
Ó hÓgartaigh, Margaret (2017) *Kathleen Lynn; Irishwoman, Patriot, Doctor*, Irish Academic Press.
Parkes, Susan M (n.d.) '"Anne Jellicoe" dictionary of Irish biography', Retrieved December 10, 2024, from https://www.dib.ie/biography/jellicoe-anne-a4268
Raftery, Deirdre and Delaney, Catriona (2022) 'Irish nuns and education in the anglophone world, 1800–1900', *Feminist Theology*, 30(3).
Ruane, Medb (2001) 'Kathleen Lynn (1874–1955)', in Mary Cullen and Maria Luddy (eds) *Female Activists: Irish Women and Social Change 1900–1960*, Dublin, Woodfield Press.
Ruane, J (2012) Ireland's ethno-religious conflicts: path dependence and its legacies, In: P. J. Duffy & W. Nolan (Eds) *At the Anvil: Essays in Honour of William J. Smyth*, pp. 631–652 (Dublin: Irish Geography Publications).
Taylor, Fanny (1856) *Eastern Hospitals and English Nurses: The Narrative of Twelve Months Experience in the Hospitals of Koulali and Scutari by a Lady Volunteer*, London.
Valiulis, Maryanne Gialanella (1997) 'Toward 'the moral and material improvement of the working classes': The founding of the Alexandra college guild tenement company, Dublin, 1898', *Journal of Urban History*, 23(3)
Valiulis, Maryann Gialanella (2009) 'Virtuous mothers and dutiful wives; the politics of sexuality in the Irish free state', in Maryann Gialanella Valiulis (ed) *Gender and Power in Irish History*, Dublin, Irish Academic Press.
Walsh, Brendan (2014) *Knowing Their Place: The Intellectual Life of Women in the 19th Century*, The History Press Ltd.

5 Ada Shillman

Midwife to the Jewish Community in Dublin

Mary Curtin, Lorraine Carroll and Caroline Keegan

Early Years

Ada Shillman (pronounced AY-DAH), née Mirrelson (1859–1933), was a trailblazing Jewish midwife and health advocate. Born in Kuršėnai, in the Courland province of Latvia, she was the youngest child of Yehunda Leib and Breina Mirrelson. Her family was notable for their achievements; two of her brothers were prominent rabbis and another brother prospered as a businessman managing forests.

In 1880, Ada married Julius Maurice Shillman (also known by his Hebrew name Yehuda Meishe). Julius hailed from Kreutzburg (modern-day Krustpils), Latvia. His father, Dr Isaac Shillman, was both a Felscher – a medical practitioner or surgeon's assistant – and an apothecary, the equivalent of a modern-day pharmacist. Ada Shillman's mother-in-law was a midwife to the local community, demonstrating the family's commitment to healthcare and the caring professions. Inspired by his parents' professions, Ada's husband Julius began his training to follow in his father's footsteps as a Felscher. This occupation required substantial education and hands-on practice. His career, however, never came to fruition and instead, the young married couple left their native country for Ireland – a journey that reflected the broader migration patterns of many Jewish families during the late 19th century.

Widespread challenges of the Jewish community in Eastern Europe at the time included poverty, restrictive policies and limited opportunities for advancement (Staliunas 2015). Motivated by the difficult economic conditions prevalent in Lithuania and the surrounding regions at the time, Ada and Julius emigrated to Ireland from Latvia in 1882, seeking better opportunities and a new beginning. Many people who made the journey at the time were fleeing not only financial hardship but also the increasing anti-semitism and instability in the Baltic provinces of the Russian Empire, seeking safety and stability in Western Europe and beyond (Staliunas 2015). Ada and Julius embarked on a transformative journey, leaving Riga, Latvia, on a tramp

DOI: 10.4324/9781003546610-5

steamer bound for Ireland. They disembarked at Queenstown (Cobh) and settled in Cork City, which marked the beginning of their integration into Irish Jewish life. After settling in Cork, Julius and Ada Shillman expanded their family, welcoming four children – three daughters and a son. From here, Ada would enter a rapidly changing midwifery landscape.

Maternity Care and Regulation of Birth Attendants

At the time of Ada's arrival to Ireland, the Great Britain Acts of Union (1800) had united both countries to create the United Kingdom of Great Britain and Ireland, and imposed colonial rule that governed all aspects of Irish life, including law and healthcare legislation. One of the oldest and most influential institutions of Irish medicine was the Royal College of Physicians of Ireland (RCPI), established in 1654. In 1667, it received its Royal Charter from King Charles II, which granted it authority over the practice of medicine in Ireland (Fleetwood 1983). The RCPI's responsibilities included supervising and licensing apothecaries, surgeons and midwives, though the regulation of midwifery remained notably informal. Unlike apothecaries and surgeons, midwives were not subject to statutory regulation, a gap that left the occupation largely in the hands of untrained practitioners. As there was no statutory requirement to regulate midwives, the majority of individuals who attended women in childbirth were without formal medical training (Breathnach 2016). These 'lay midwives', often referred to as 'bhean ghluine (knee woman)', or 'bhean cabhair (helping woman)' in Irish, were deeply embedded in their communities. Their titles described what they did rather than an unequivocal label indicating a profession or healthcarer. In English, they were commonly called 'handywomen', and Delay (2023) observes that the terms defied 'clear linguistic categorisation' and were interchangeable with the work of nursing and midwifery. The knowledge and skills of lay midwives were typically passed down through generations. Many inherited and learned their craft from mothers and grandmothers, while others gained experience through observation and informal apprenticeships within their community. Intuition and practical experience were their fundamental methods as they facilitated births and supported mothers and infants in local communities. Their care was deeply rooted in communal trust and tradition, serving as the backbone of childbirth support for much of Ireland's population, especially in rural areas (Delay 2023).

By the late 19th century, Ireland began to witness the emergence of more formalised midwifery training programmes, driven by broader trends in medical professionalisation and public health reform (Breathnach 2005). Lying-in hospitals played a central role in this transformation. These hospitals, primarily located in cities such as Dublin, Limerick and Cork, offered structured midwifery training programmes lasting approximately three months. While these programmes represented a significant step towards professionalising midwifery, their reach was limited. Training opportunities were often restricted to older women of good reputation who sought to enhance their skills, and the care provided by these hospitals predominantly served the poor and destitute (Breathnach 2005). For most Irish women, especially those in rural areas, access to trained midwives or hospital-based care remained out of reach. Even when trained dispensary midwives were assigned to rural districts, they were frequently ignored as many communities were not prepared to flout tradition (Robins 2000), risk their relationship with the local handywoman or were unable to converse with district midwives if they did not speak Irish. Kearns (2004) describes early 20th-century Dublin women as preferring home births to lying-in hospital births as they felt more cared for by women in the home. The divide between urban and rural healthcare systems, as well as formal and informal care, highlighted epidemic poverty and stark inequalities that persisted well into the 20th century.

The shift towards obstetric-led birth and formal midwifery education in Ireland was gradual. Many women, particularly in rural areas, sought to maintain longstanding birthing traditions with known handywomen, reflecting a deep cultural attachment to these practices (Delay 2023). As Ireland remained under British rule, the education and regulation of the midwifery workforce were directly influenced by colonial policies. By 1890, the RCPI had become actively involved in endorsing a system of formal midwifery education and regulation that it could oversee. However, efforts to pass a Midwives Bill in the House of Commons in 1891 were unsuccessful.

As the 20th century approached, the RCPI continued to push for stricter regulation of midwifery, including restrictions limiting midwifery practice to 'natural births' now known as physiological birth, and requiring midwives to defer to 'medical men' in difficult cases (McMahon 2005). From 1890 to 1902, the RCPI continued to petition for the regulation of midwifery under medical control. An example (RCPI 1902) shows an objection by the college to the title of 'midwifery' preferring the title 'midwifery-nurse', which Mc Mahon (2005) speculates represents the reality of what the RCPI envisioned, a practitioner clearly under the auspices of medicine. The move would solidify the distinction between formally trained district midwives, who worked under a doctor's supervision, and lay midwives, who remained unregulated. The RCPI campaigned to ban women without formal qualifications from registering as midwives and fought for the certificates of Irish awarding bodies to be recognised by British institutions. Despite making progress, the Irish perspective was not always given priority or prominence by the UK parliament or its legislation. The passing of the Midwives Act (1902), however, marked a turning point by including Ireland in its scope. The Act recognised Irish hospitals as accredited training institutions and formalised the standards for midwifery education and practice.

The introduction of Britain's Midwives Act in 1918 was an additional turning point in the regulation of midwifery practice, effectively reshaping the landscape of maternal healthcare. This legislation sought to standardise and regulate the practice of midwifery. The Midwives Act made it illegal for unregulated individuals to support births, bringing the role of handywomen to a definitive end. Handywomen, as skilled and experienced lay practitioners, had been relied upon by countless families, especially in rural and working-class communities, where access to formal medical care was limited and more traditional practices favoured. While these women possessed significant practical knowledge, their lack of formal training and certification placed them outside the bounds of the new legal framework. As a marginalised group many handywomen continued to practise outside of the law particularly in rural areas where professionally trained nurses were scarce. Often nurses were also only literate in English, inexperienced in childbirth and therefore the handywoman was sought after by local communities. While there are some sparse accounts of handywomen who worked in collaboration with district nurses and general practitioners, the majority were shunned or prosecuted through licensing hearings for non-registration (Delay 2023). By the late 20th century, medicalisation and regulation had ended the matriarchal position of the handywoman, criminalising and further marginalising the traditional female role (Delay 2023).

The Central Midwives Board in 1918 became the regulatory body for the supervision of midwives. Tasked with overseeing the training of midwives, evaluating performance and enforcing penalties for breaches or offenses, the Board became the cornerstone of the professionalisation of midwifery. The Board not only standardised midwifery education but also introduced accountability mechanisms, ensuring that midwives adhered to ethical and professional standards. Mandatory state registration for midwives followed in 1919, requiring all midwives to be licensed and enrolled on a national roll. This requirement was later reinforced by amendments to the Midwives Act in 1931, which reinforced the prohibition on unlicensed practitioners or lay 'handywomen'. These changes aimed to elevate maternal healthcare standards while eradicating informal and unregulated practices which were perceived as a risk to public health.

Social, Cultural and Religious Influences

It was within this complex political and professional landscape that Ada Shillman began her early midwifery career. Records in the National Archives indicate that Ada decided to follow in the footsteps of her mother-in-law and become a midwife. She enrolled at the Cork Lying-in Hospital and three months later, in the year 1888, she received a certificate recognising her qualification as a midwife. It is unclear whether this was unusual for a migrant woman to take this route at the time, and there are no records available at the time to confirm this. However, the first records held by the Nursing and Midwifery Board of Ireland archives suggest that this was not normal with the overwhelming majority of registrants being Irish and of Roman Catholic or Church of Ireland denomination. Ada's practice straddled the transitional period before and after the implementation of midwifery legislation in Ireland. According to her son's biography held in the National Archives in Dublin, Ada's profession as a midwife played a key role in the Shillman family's relocation to Dublin in 1892. The move was prompted by Ada's journey to Dublin to support a friend in her confinement who had experienced several previous pregnancy losses. The Shillman family established their home at Warren Street, Dublin 8, a move that proved significant in their lives and Ada's career, as it provided greater professional opportunities within the larger Jewish community of Dublin.

Ada Shillman's arrival to Dublin in 1892 coincided with a significant wave of Jewish migration to Ireland. By 1891, the Jewish population of 258 had dramatically increased, from just 258 individuals to 1,779 – a reflection of broader migratory trends (Rivlin 2011, p. 123). Despite this growth, the Jewish community remained a minority in Ireland, where Catholics constituted 90% of the population according to the 1911 census (Central Statistics Office [CSO] report). Ireland itself faced challenges distinct from its neighbouring countries, including poverty and a declining population. These factors, paradoxically, created economic riches for the male Jewish population, who often found employment in trades such as drapery, selling clothing and dry goods (Ó Gráda 2006, p. 48). Furthermore, Jewish working men often accepted payment for goods in weekly instalments, which complimented the poor socioeconomic status of many Dubliners of that time (Rivlin 2011).

Ada Shillman lived and worked in Ireland during a time when the Catholic Church dominated the country's cultural and social landscape. For Ireland's Jewish population, a small but distinct minority, this dominance presented both challenges and opportunities. By the late 19th and early 20th centuries, Ireland's Jewish community had grown in number, largely through waves of migration from Eastern Europe. Though small compared to the broader population, Jews in Ireland enriched the country's cultural diversity. While the Catholic Church exerted significant influence and control over healthcare and social services in Ireland, Ada's practice was firmly rooted in the traditions and customs of her faith. Her ability to adhere to Jewish traditions while navigating a society deeply influenced by Catholicism highlights her resilience and adaptability.

Cultural and religious practices among Dublin's Jewish population shaped the approach to childbirth. Jewish mothers-to-be often avoided maternity hospitals, which were perceived as unfamiliar and unsympathetic to Jewish customs, dietary laws and the broader needs of Jewish observant families. As a result, there was a strong reliance on midwives for home births, preserving both the privacy and religious traditions integral to Jewish life. Among the midwives serving Dublin's Jewish community, Ada Shillman emerged as a prominent and trusted figure (Ó Gráda 2006, p. 170).

Ada Shillman's midwifery career in Dublin also coincided with a time of high maternal and infant mortality for women and children in Ireland. In 1920, records suggest maternal mortality rates were considerably higher in Ireland (6.26/100,000) than comparable countries such as England and Wales (4.33/100,000), Scotland (6.15/100,000) and, further afield, Denmark (4.33/100,000) (Breathnach 2016). In 1916, 372 women were reported to have died because of complications in pregnancy and childbirth. In contrast, almost 100 years later, in 2014, this was reduced substantially with two women dying of complications relating to pregnancy and birth. However, this does not negate the catastrophic consequences of maternal death but instead highlights the risk associated with childbirth at the time of Ada's career and the responsibility midwives like Ada Shillman held. The CSO reports infant mortality in 1916 at its highest in Dublin City, where Ada Shillman worked, at 153.5/100,000 births with the main cause of death under 12 months due to malnutrition and weakness. This was nearly double the national average of the time (81.3) (CSO 2024). These statistics underscore the challenges faced by midwives like Ada and provides a view to understand the impact of poverty and poor health on survival outcomes. Illness had a real impact on a family's ability to survive in Dublin at the time, before the conception of welfare by the state (Rivlin 2011, p. 121). Yet, of note, evidence suggests that Jewish born children had a lower rate of infant mortality which was at the time attributed to cleanliness and general hygiene standards in nutrition and living standards that also reduced the chance of illness and infectious diseases although the exact reason why was not measured at the time (Ó Gráda 2006).

Ada's Professional Journey

Ada Shillman's entry into independent midwifery practice was shaped as much by personal adversity as by societal circumstances. Her husband's declining health curtailed his ability to work, thrusting Ada into the role of primary breadwinner for her family. In an era when women were often confined to domestic roles, Ada's situation left her with little choice but to seek work outside the home. Historically, the Jewish male experience has been documented, sometimes to the detriment of the female Jewish experience. Women were typically considered to be relegated to what would now be considered as stereotypical roles of their time (Wynn 2024, p. 164). Yet there is evidence that Jewish women often worked in a variety of roles that also provided them with an opportunity to maintain their position in the home to minimise poverty at the time. The choice of profession, however, for Ada Shillman was of interest even within Jewish society as although midwifery provided a great service to women, it was also considered 'unclean' and so, considered to be of a 'lower status'. Yet for Ada, the profession offered a pragmatic solution to her family's financial difficulties and a way to contribute meaningfully to the welfare of her community. Her ability to rise above the cultural stigma and establish herself as a respected figure within the Jewish community speaks to her determination and resilience.

What set Ada Shillman apart was not merely her midwifery practice but the collaborative and networking approach she developed in what was a highly gendered field (Wynn 2024, p. 182). As a midwife, Ada forged connections with families, community leaders and other women, creating a support network. In doing so, she positioned herself as both a caregiver and a community leader. It was this beginning that placed Ada Shillman as a revolutionary for women's health.

Ada's midwifery practice reflected a holistic approach that would resonate with modern healthcare ideals. She provided comprehensive care that included antenatal, birth and community care in the form of follow up home visiting after birth for 12 days. This provision of care, provided by one caregiver could be considered revolutionary in the modern day, which is often seen as the gold standard of care that healthcare professionals aspire to (Sandall et al. 2024). The Births, Deaths (Ireland) Act 1864 mandated the civil registration of births, marriages and deaths in Ireland for the first time. Ada Shillman's practice adapted to include this legislative requirement; however, the registration district for registering births, marriages and deaths was situated a tram ride away, challenging Ada's resources to pay the tram fare to register each child after birth, so she would wait in order to register a number of births at the same time. Ada was diligent with meticulous record-keeping which is evident in her 'birth book', now preserved in the Jewish Museum in Dublin. This book provides valuable insights into her work, documenting births across socioeconomic and religious boundaries.

Ada's professional commitments coincided with her growing family. In Dublin, four more children, a son and three daughters were born into the Shillman family. The family of eight was not unusual for that time; however, this was unusual in the context of Ada Shillman's role outside of the home, which is more like modern-day healthcare professionals than her own contemporaries who stayed at home at the time. The expansion of Ada's family coincided with Ada's increasing contributions to maternal and community healthcare. This provides further evidence of Ada Shillman's unusual place in society at the time as a woman, and as a midwife, solidifying her legacy as a pioneering figure within Dublin's Jewish community.

Positioning and Collaboration within Maternity Healthcare

The increasing Jewish population of the time required considerable thought as to how to support and integrate their community into society. This was achieved by the wealthy established Irish-Jewish population who provided welfare and support directly to those in need (Rivlin 2011). It was this approach that conceived the establishment of the Board of Guardians in 1882 which was formed to support the poor Jewish immigrants and originally financed through permanent subscriptions from the wealthier Jewish population. This organised approach may be considered more unusual by today's standards but can appear as an outward appearance of the Jewish philosophical way of life. It was also ahead of its time, and prior to the national welfare state provision. Within Judaism, the presence of charity was considered a duty. This may have contributed to Ada Shillman's approach to her own practice as a midwife. Ada Shillman often received reimbursement for her skills by means other than monetary payment. Ada often provided food, milk or swaddling clothes to households that were most in need. Ada Shillman also tailored her costs to the women and families that she cared for in what today we would refer to as 'means-testing', measuring sources of income to understand an individual's need. This can be seen in her 'birth book' which is housed in the Jewish Museum. This book provides evidence that Ada Shillman attended women across the socio-economic spectrum and shows some blank spaces where some women were provided care for free. Although care was often provided to women of the Jewish faith, this was also not absolute, and women of other faiths were provided care if they sought it. Ada's broader understanding of challenges faced by expectant mothers led her to advocate for organised charitable support. In 1898, this advocacy resulted in the establishment of the Dublin Jewish Ladies Charitable Society of which Ada Shillman was a founding member. Anecdotally, its formation originates from the story of a Jewish woman who found herself stranded in Dublin. Her husband had continued an onward journey to the USA. This was not unusual for those who could not afford the direct journey to the USA at the time and often stopped, or worked while raising funds to complete the final leg of their journey; however, it highlighted the need for a supportive network around migrant Jewish women in Dublin at the time (Rivlin 2011). This initiative highlights Ada's role not only as a midwife but also as a community leader. It was these acts of charity that made Ada became very well known within her community and was often referred to as the 'mother of the community'.

Ada Shillman's career as a midwife in early 20th-century Dublin defied not only stereotypes of her profession but also the broader societal expectations placed on migrant women of her time. Her contributions extended far beyond the Jewish community, cementing her reputation as a pioneering figure in maternal healthcare. Her midwifery prowess was recognised by both the Jewish community and the medical community. Her collaborations, most notably with Dr Bethel Solomons, a prominent Jewish obstetrician, highlight a story of mutual respect, innovation and commitment to advancing healthcare in a challenging era.

Dr Bethal Solomons, born into a distinguished family in Dublin, studied medicine at Trinity College Dublin in 1902. By 1926, he was Master of the Rotunda maternity hospital, one of the oldest maternity hospitals in Europe. Dr Solomons was known for his progressive views, supporting women's suffrage and advocating for the inclusion of women in the Royal College of Physicians of Ireland (Wynn 2024, p. 182). This progressive outlook likely provided common ground with Ada Shillman, whose unconventional role as a midwife and migrant woman had already distinguished her in the Jewish and medical communities.

The collaboration between Ada Shillman and Dr Solomons was both professional and groundbreaking. Together they attended numerous birthing cases, with Dr Solomon later recalling in his memoir, *One Doctor in His Time*:

> she built up an enormous practice and attended most of the Jewish women in the city. We did many cases together and I cherish her memory as a magnificent woman.

To achieve such an acknowledgement indicates a confidence in Ada's ability to provide safe care at a time of high maternal and infant mortality. Further, to be acknowledged by the medical profession of the time demonstrates the level of respect accorded to her which validates Ada's skills, professionalism, and the community's confidence in her expertise as a midwife.

Beyond their clinical work, Ada Shillman and Bethal Solomon co-founded a free medical dispensary in Stamer Street (1913) to support the Jewish population in Dublin. Even though Dr Solomons was a male with a strong standing in society, he was a joint manager of the dispensary with Ada Shillman, providing evidence of their successful and equitable collaboration and mutual respect. According to the writings by Ada's son, Bernard Shillman, which are held in the National Archives, the dispensary opened twice a week and continued well into Ada's later years. In Natalie Wynn's book, *Community, Identity, Conflict – The Jewish Experience in Ireland 1881–1914*, it is suggested that 318 women were treated in the first year which was approximately 20% of the Dublin Jewish population at the time. Further, although there are no records to support it, it is thought that many women brought their children for treatment, expanding the dispensary's impact. This effort reflected a holistic approach to healthcare that integrated maternity, paediatric and general medical services – an innovative model for its time. A model sought after today!

Ada Shillman held a key position within the Jewish community and for many non-Jewish families too. This standing and her involvement with charitable Jewish associations of the time placed her in a unique position to canvas and progress opportunities to provide affordable treatments to ordinary mothers and families for all. One such collaboration supported another female leader and activist of the time – Dr Kathleen Lynn. Dr Lynn acknowledged a 'Jewish nurse', who is considered widely to be Ada Shillman who fundraised within the Jewish community for St Ultan's Children's Hospital. In a newspaper cutting dated 25 July 1933, Dr Kathleen Lynn reported a substantial funding contribution, so much so that it suggested it was enough to equip the first floor of the hospital building. This provides evidence of a charity that was far beyond the realm of the Jewish community and benefitted all children who required healthcare at the time.

Ada Shillman continued her contributions to maternal healthcare and her community well into her later years. The precise timeline of her active midwifery practice however remains unclear. Her birth register, an invaluable record of her midwifery practice, contains entries up to 1908, indicating that she remained engaged in supporting women during childbirth until at least that year. The introduction of the Midwives Act in1902, which aimed to regulate and restrict the activities of handywomen and untrained birth attendants, did not impact Ada's practice. Having received formal midwifery training at the Cork Lying-in Hospital, Ada was equipped to meet the professional standards required under the Act. The official state registration of midwives did not commence until 1919, and archival data from the Nursing and Midwifery Board of Ireland did not list Ada Shillman in its 1919 register. This suggests that she had ceased practising her midwifery practice by that time, likely due to advancing age. Nevertheless, Ada earned a place of deep respect and affection within Dublin's Jewish community. Despite her advancing age and declining health, she remained devoted to her support of health provision for the community until illness forced her to stop.

Embodied Leader, Professional and Revolutionary

Ada Shillman was a migrant, a mother and a midwife. None of these provided her with high standing in the community at the time. However, her approach to healthcare, such as means-testing her clients, and the direct supportive measures she provided individually, to the Jewish community and to the society resulted in a philosophy and practice of care that could be judged as ahead of their time by standards of today. Her recognition of the work that could be done through networking and collaboration, with colleagues, obstetricians and the wider medical community in setting up the first hospital for infants in Ireland was highly successful. Such approaches and management in healthcare are highly sought after today.

Ada's entry into midwifery, born of necessity, ultimately became a revolutionary act. By challenging societal norms and navigating the dual challenges of poverty and cultural expectations, she carved out a path not only for herself but for other women in her community. Her work bridged the gap between necessity and innovation, proving that, even within restrictive societal frameworks, women could assert agency and effect change. In the face of personal hardship and systemic limitations, Ada Shillman's career embodied the transformative potential of women's roles in healthcare. Her story is a testament to the resilience of women who, through their work, redefine their circumstances and create lasting impacts on their communities.

One hundred years after Ada and her contemporary's system of caregiving, evidence-based maternity research advocates woman-centred models of care (Sandall et al. 2024; WHO 2024) based in communities for healthy childbearing women. The benefits of building relationships with caregivers including a known and trusted midwife is supported by research today and heralded as best practice for healthy women. International policy (WHO 2024; NICE 2021) along with the first Irish Maternity strategy (2016–2026) recommends establishing maternity care models and midwifery services in communities. They advocate choices for women which include community homebirth maternity services similar to midwifery practice facilitated by Ada. These skills and services were lost to communities with the medicalisation of childbirth and the move into institutions for birth heralding the demise of the community midwife, community values and feminised healthcare culture.

Ada Shillman passed away on 11 October 1933, coinciding with the Jewish festival of Hoshana Rabba, a day of significance in Jewish tradition. Ada was laid to rest in the Jewish Cemetery at Dolphin's Barn in Dublin, a testament to her lifelong connection to the Jewish community she served so faithfully. Her gravestone bears a heartfelt epitaph that encapsulates her legacy:

> Lady of great charm and of outstanding character, her hands accomplished a lot and she was perfect in her deeds, to the poor and the destitute she helped with her body and her soul, her goodness and her kindness – source of her compassion.

Ada's death was mourned deeply by her children, grandchildren and the wider community, reflecting her pivotal role as a caregiver, advocate and motherly figure. Her kindness, service and advocacy for the vulnerable left an enduring mark on Dublin's Jewish history, ensuring her memory lived on as a pillar of compassion and community leadership.

References

Breathnach C. 2005. *The Congested Districts Board of Ireland, 1891–1923.* Dublin: Four Courts Press.

Breathnach C. 2016. Handywomen and birthing in rural Ireland, 1851–1955. *Gender & History*, 28(1):34–56.

Central Statistics Office. 2024. *Life in 1916 Ireland: Stories from Statistics.* Central Statistics Office. https://www.cso.ie/en/releasesandpublications/ep/p1916/1916irl/introduction/.

Delay C. 2023. 'In all circumstances': Home births and collaborative health care in Ireland, 1900–1950. *Bulletin of the History of Medicine*, 97(3):394–422. https://doi.org/10.1353/bhm.2023.a915268. PMID: 38588193

Department of Health. 2016–2026. *Creating a Better Future Together, Maternity Strategy.* Dublin, Ireland: Department of Health.

Fleetwood JF. 1983. *The History of Medicine in Ireland.* 2nd Ed. Skellig Press.

Kearns K. 2004. *Dublin's Lost Heroines: Mammies and Grannies in a Vanished City.* Dublin: Gill and Macmillian.

McMahon A. 2005. *Care to Remember: Nursing and Midwifery in Ireland.* Mercier Press.

National Institute for Health and Care Excellence. 2021. *Postnatal Care (NG194).* www.nice.org.UK/guidance/ng194

Ó Gráda C. 2006. *Jewish Ireland in the Age of Joyce: A Socioeconomic History.* Princeton: Princeton University Press.

Rivlin R. 2011. *Jewish Ireland: A Social History.* Dublin: History Press Ireland.

Robins J. 2000. *Nursing and Midwifery in Ireland in the Twentieth Century.* Dublin: An Bord Altranais.

Sandall JFTC, Devane D, Soltani H, Gillespie P, Gates S, Jones LV, Shennan AH, and Rayment-Jones H. 2024. Midwife continuity of care models versus other models of care for childbearing women. *Cochrane Database of Systematic Reviews*, 4.

Staliunas D. 2015. Lithuania during the 'storms in the South' (early 1880s). In *Enemies for a Day: Antisemitism and Anti-Jewish Violence in Lithuania Under the Tsars* (pp. 85–128). Central European University Press. https://doi.org/10.7829/j.ctt14qrxxb.8

World Health Organisation. 2024. *Transitioning to Midwifery Models of Care.* Launch of the World Health Organization's Global Position Paper, Geneva.

Wynn N. 2024. *Community, Identity, Conflict: The Jewish Experience in Ireland, 1881–1914.* New York, NY and Oxford: Peter Lang.

6 Elizabeth Abimbola Awoliyi

The Architect of Maternal Public Health in Nigeria

Aisling Walsh

Introduction

> Hers has been a great pioneering work. In medicine, the flag she unfurled when she came back from the UK a doctor, in 1938 has never wavered. There is no doubt that her personal success has been a victory for Nigerian womanhood.
>
> (Daily Times Nigeria, 1 August 1959)

This newspaper article, entitled *Hundreds of Mothers in Lagos Owe Much to Her*, outlined Dr Elizabeth Abimbola Awoliyi's medical and public health-career to date in 1959, which reads more like a public healthcareer of the 21st century rather than the mid-20th century. Dr Awoliyi was Nigeria's first female medical doctor, who broke barriers in not only a male-dominated but also a Western-dominated field. So, what was it about this clinician that was so unique to her time and context, and what lessons can we learn from here for healthcare management today?

To begin, we must imagine life for expectant mothers in Nigeria in the first half of the 20th century. Healthcare access for women was limited. High levels of infant mortality were identified in the Annual Medical Reports for Nigeria, with a rate of 127 deaths per thousand live births recorded for Lagos in 1939, and a maternal mortality rate of 8.9 per thousand in 1934 (Van Tol, 2007). Dr Awoliyi specialised in women's health, principally in maternal and child healthcare. She was particularly focused on reducing infant mortality and improving prenatal care. Her strengths lay not only in the focus on the direct reduction in maternal and child mortality rates but also on her broader public health reach, including leadership in and management of public health initiatives, at a time when public health was in its infancy in West Africa.

The most frequently employed definition of public health is given as follows: 'The science and art of preventing disease, prolonging life and

DOI: 10.4324/9781003546610-6

promoting, protecting and improving health through the organised efforts of society' (Acheson, 1988, p. 1). Society includes organisations, communities and individuals.

Three broad domains of public health are considered:

1. *Health protection:* including the control of infectious diseases, managing health emergency responses and environmental health hazards.
2. *Healthcare services delivery:* including engagement in service delivery, promoting clinically effective practice and governance, planning and prioritising services, and engaging in research, audit and evaluation.
3. *Healthcare improvement:* or health promotion, what we can do to improve health at individual and population level. This includes improving health behaviours over the life course as well as the social determinants of health and reducing inequalities.

A key target of Sustainable Development Goal (SDG) 3 is to ensure universal access to sexual and reproductive healthcare services, including for family planning, information and education by 2030. Dr Awoliyi had begun to envisage this nearly a century before the SDGs were developed. Her contribution to public healthcare and management focused primarily on health services delivery and healthcare improvement through health promotion, therefore this chapter will concentrate on these two domains. A domain of 'public health agent' is added, to analyse the extent of her individual influence both within direct healthcare delivery and healthcare management, despite the barriers she faced. Table 6.1 outlines the focus of the chapter, structured through the two public health domains and the domain of public health agent, through which her achievements will be analysed. The chapter will celebrate Dr Abimbola Awoliyi as one of the architects of maternal public health in Nigeria.

Table 6.1. Assessing the contribution of Dr Awoliyi to maternal and child health in Nigeria

Public health achievement	*Application to Dr Awoliyi's work*
Public health agent	• Nigeria's first female medical doctor • Influence of Irish and British medical education on Awoliyi's public health approach
Health services delivery	• Impact of colonial and post-colonial maternal and child public health in Nigeria
Healthcare improvement and promotion	• Family planning • Social determinants of health

Public Health Agent: Nigeria's First Female Medical Doctor

> When Dr Abimbola Awoliyi came home in 1938, she made history. She was the first West African Woman ever to qualify as a doctor, and because even male doctors were then still very few, very much of her success was kept behind lock and key – although in fact her personal achievement was a victory for Nigerian motherhood.
>
> (Daily Times Nigeria, 1 August 1959)

Elizabeth Abimbola Awoliyi (neé Akerele) was born in Lagos in 1910, to Rufina and David Avoristo Akerele. Elizabeth's upbringing and career success was rooted in a progressive outlook on education. Her father was an educator and was committed to giving his daughter the best possible opportunities despite the societal norms of the time. This was at a time when Nigeria offered limited educational prospects for women, and expectations for girls were primarily focused on domesticity. Yet Elizabeth's family encouraged her dream of pursuing a career that was unconventional for women. Elizabeth completed her primary schooling at St Mary's Convent School in Lagos and secondary education at Queen's College Yaba. She excelled academically and earned a scholarship to study medicine in Ireland.

She became the first woman from Nigeria to obtain a degree in medicine. The journey was not without its challenges. She had to overcome the racial and gender biases prevalent in the 1930s (described in sections 'Status of Women in Nigeria in the First Half of the 20th Century' and 'Influence of Irish and British Medical Education on Awoliyi's Public Health Approach'), but her determination was resolute. Elizabeth graduated as a medical doctor in 1938, during which time Nigeria remained under British colonial rule. Being the first female doctor in Nigeria, Awoliyi demonstrated perseverance and resilience, overcoming societal expectations of women in the early 20th century. What drove her to persevere despite so many structural obstacles?

Status of Women in Nigeria in the First Half of the 20th Century

In order to appreciate the significance of the achievements of Dr Awoliyi, we must describe the status of women at the time in Nigeria. Agunbiade (2022) discusses how historiographical accounts are mostly written from male perspectives, with women hardly mentioned:

> the height of anti-colonial agitation and nationalism in Nigeria in the 1930s and 1940s, are widely-documented as a male-driven process. In many books on Nigeria's colonial past, the male political class and business elites are placed at the core of the narratives. At best, women are treated superficially as micro-narratives.
>
> (Agunbiade, 2022)

Agunbiade's research has shown however that during this time, women across the country played critical roles as activists and advocates for political rights, women's enfranchisement and social justice, roles that have not been acknowledged by historians. This is certainly the case of Awoliyi herself also. When researching for this chapter, there was little to be found, instead necessitating the puzzle of her career to be pieced together, through accounts of the institutions in which she worked, and references to terms such as 'Lady Medical Officer' being used, rather than naming Awoliyi in her own right.[1] To add to the lack of evidence of women's roles in public life at the time, Agunbiade wrote how she keyed in 'women in West Africa' at the National Archives, with very little return. 'Even in writing of history books, the roles that women played are not included or at best are diminished and marginalised' (Agunbiade, 2022).

At the beginning of the 20th century, there emerged a group of Western-educated women in Nigeria (Panata, 2020), of which Awoliyi was to become. Gradually from the 1920s, this new class of women started to infiltrate positions in the economic social and political spheres, from which they had previously been barred. Panata discusses this as unsettling existing gender roles:

> Global discussions over the 'New Woman,' Christian and colonial discourses around femininities and masculinities and the so-called 'traditional Nigerian women's roles' mingled and overlapped.
>
> (Panata, 2020, p. 142)

Despite the reporting (Denzer, 1989) that from the mid-1940s, there was an increasing demand for careers for women; these were as teachers, nurses and secretaries. Doctors were not mentioned. Van Tol (2007) reports that a considerable role was also played by Western-educated African medical staff in delivering maternal and child health services. By 1934, there were 484 African nurses of various levels of training in Nigeria, which had raised to 1000 in 1947 (Van Tol, 2007). There was no such increase in the number of female doctors during this time.

> The wife was encouraged to get an education but she was not supposed to reach the same academic level as her husband as he should remain her master. She should be hardworking and independent, although some men worried about her neglecting her household duties if she worked outside the home.
>
> (Panata, 2020, p. 160)

Awoliyi married fellow doctor and surgeon, Dr SO Awoliyi, in 1942. They travelled to the United Kingdom in 1949 to embark on a period of further study. In 1955, she obtained a Diploma in Child's Health and was awarded a Member of the Royal College of Physicians. She was also appointed as a senior specialist gynaecologist and obstetrician by the Federal Ministry of Health in 1962. In 1957, she became the first African woman to be inducted into the Royal College of Obstetricians and Gynaecologists in London. She had to balance her family life (she had two children) with a demanding career, facing social and professional challenges as a woman in the medical field.

Universal adult suffrage was introduced to Lagos in 1948. By 1950, one editorial in the Nigerian Tribune wrote: 'Women may seize power.' This was a testimony to the strength of women's activism in society at the time (Agunbiade, 2022). This was at a time when Awoliyi's medical career was thriving, so perhaps may have made her path a little bit more feasible.

Influence of Irish and British Medical Education on Awoliyi's Public Health Approach

It wasn't just women that were unusual in medicine at the time. The vast majority of African doctors were essentially excluded from the West African Medical Service (WAMS) and there was only a small number of African male doctors in Nigeria in the first half of the 20th century. 'Recruitment of doctors into WAMS was characterised by racial discrimination as only doctors with European parentage were enlisted into the medical services' (Adetiba and Msindo, 2022, p. 594). The first Nigerian doctor to practice within the country was Nathaniel King who qualified in 1874. It was not until 1930 that the Yaba Medical Training College in Lagos began training assistant medical officers, and not until 1952 that the first teaching hospital in Nigeria, the University College Hospital Ibadan, was established, allowing for domestic training of medical and nursing personnel (Abubakar et al., 2022). This meant that Awoliyi was left with no choice but to travel abroad to pursue her medical education. Interestingly, a search for information on Dr King yielded an approximately similar number of results than the search for Awoliyi.

Elizabeth Awoliyi travelled to the UK and Ireland to pursue her medical education. Unlike that in Britain, Irish medical education in the early 1920s appeared to have a surprisingly inclusive attitude to women, with women and men treated equally in terms of hospital experience, lectures, which they attended together, and prizes and scholarships, which were open to women on the same terms as men. However, there were separate dissecting rooms to avoid one gender distracting the other (Kelly, 2010). In 1911 in Dublin, there were only 42 female medical practitioners. Just 21 women students matriculated in medicine for the 1921–1922 session (Kelly, 2010). This meant that Awoliyi was not only in the minority in terms of her gender but also in terms of her ethnicity, at a time when intersectionality was not even considered.

Women's contribution to medicine was mainly in women's health and childcare and psychiatry, where they were perhaps perceived as less of a threat to their male colleagues. This may have been the reason that Awoliyi decided to specialise in Obstetrics and Gynaecology. She became Nigeria's first female Specialist in Gynaecology.

She left Nigeria in 1929, and in 1930, she entered the Rotunda Hospital and Trinity College for the licentiate in Midwifery and the Diploma in Obstetrics and Gynaecology. Awoliyi was added to the Royal College of Surgeons in Ireland Roll of Licentiates in July 1936, and was the first West Africa woman to appear on it (Figure 6.1). There is no doubt that her education in Ireland exposed her to a more global perspective on medicine and public health, which she applied to the Nigerian health system on her return.

Health Services Delivery

Healthcare access for Nigerian women was limited in the mid-20th century, and maternal mortality rates were high (Van Tol, 2007). Dr Awoliyi took a special interest in women's health, particularly in maternal and childcare.

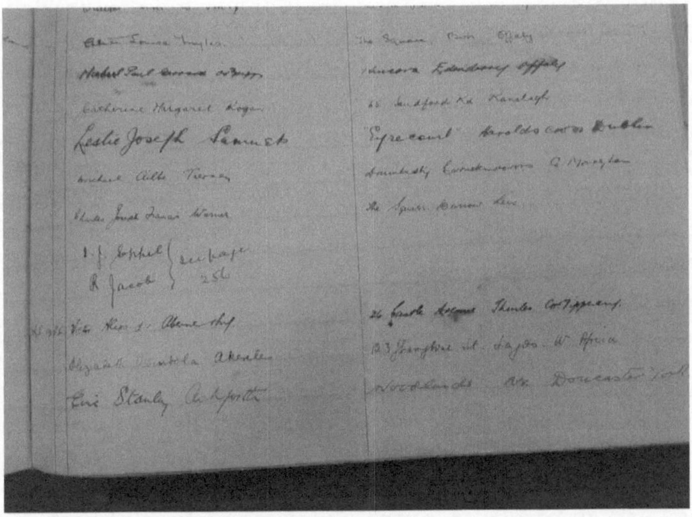

Figure 6.1 Elizabeth Awoliyi's signature on the RCSI Roll of Licentiates.

She became a vocal advocate for better maternal health facilities and worked tirelessly to improve health services and supports for women in Nigeria, working from being a junior medical officer to a position of leadership.

Impact of Colonial and Post-Colonial Maternal and Child Public Health in Nigeria

In Nigeria, public health development can be traced to three periods: pre-colonial, colonial and post-colonial eras (Atting, 2019). Services for maternal and infant welfare introduced in British Nigeria between 1925 and 1945, were part of a widespread effort aimed at the reduction of infant and maternal mortality rates across the British Empire (Van Tol, 2007). Maternal and health services in Nigeria were based on policies transferred to the colony from Britain (Jones, 2004), (Atting, 2019). The first calls for infant and maternal services were reported in the Annual Medical Reports for Nigeria from the early 1920s, as a result of the high rates of infant mortality (Van Tol, 2007). Renovation of Lagos's Massey Street Dispensary commenced in 1925, with a focus on maternity and women's and children's diseases (Van Tol, 2007).

Upon returning to Nigeria in 1938, Awoliyi was immediately faced with the reality of practising medicine in a country still under colonial rule, and with an underdeveloped healthcare system, especially in maternal and child health services. She faced difficulties navigating Nigeria's colonial context and its impact on the health system, while at the same time she was experienced in colonial type healthcare as a result of her studies in Ireland and the UK. Nwashindu et al. (2023, p. 1), argued that 'public health in colonial Africa was not public in application but selective, discriminatory, and racial'.

She was appointed first as a junior medical officer at the Massey Street Hospital in Lagos in 1938. It had grown into a major centre for maternal and child health, playing a significant role in combating maternal and infant mortality and childhood diseases. During this period, Lagos was experiencing rapid urbanisation, and the need for healthcare services, especially for women and children, was essential. Her work there was influential in improving maternal and child mortality rates. She was promoted to Chief Consultant Gynaecologist and then Medical Director/Chief Medical Officer in 1960, a position she held until her retirement in 1969. She was the first woman to hold this position.

The Annual Medical Reports recorded dramatic reductions in infant mortality rates, from 238.3 per thousand in 1925 to 128 per thousand by 1945, and 'were attributed to the success of these antenatal and child welfare clinics and, in particular, to the unwavering efforts of both nurses and local women trained as health visitors in bringing health and hygiene advice to African mothers' (Van Tol, 2007). Within Lagos, the improvement in outcomes during this time can also be attributed to the leadership of Awoliyi and her team. The profile of Dr Awoliyi featured in the Daily Times Nigeria in 1959 praised her achievements in improving standards of healthcare for expectant mothers: 'Today, hundreds of mothers in Lagos and the improved birth rate which places Lagos ahead of the rest of the country owe much to Dr Abimbola Awoliyi.'

Awoliyi was working against the backdrop of a focus on curative rather than preventive medicine in the 1930s, with a lack of focus on public health. This emphasis on curative medicine was criticised by some contemporaries, and later by historians, as a major shortcoming of the British provision of medical services in colonial Africa (Silla and Addae, 1996). Another important factor Awoliyi was working against was the prevalence of practising of traditional medicine and the reluctance to attend for health services.

> In the days when ignorance and superstition were rife, and native doctors were held in awe by the majority of the people, it was difficult to persuade expectant mothers to take advantage of modern medical services; and these mothers were taken to hospital only as a last resort, to obtain death certificates. All sorts of persuasive means has to be used to educate the general public. Her personality and intensive propaganda in all it's forms played an important part in a time when it was possible to post to Massey Street Dispensary a Nigerian Lady Medical Officer who naturally understood the background and customs of the people.
>
> (Daily Times Nigeria, 1 August 1959)

This demonstrates Awoliyi's ability to bridge the gap between the colonial medical administration and the traditional health system. Jakovljevic et al. (2021) reported that the Global North and its medical institutions did not recognise the importance of indigenous health programmes of the Global South (p. 30). Awoliyi herself is not mentioned in name in the colonial accounts of the time, nor are any Nigerian medical personnel. There is no direct evidence to show how she worked with traditional medicine in Nigeria, but there is no doubt that she had local populations on her side, as is evidenced by the references to her popularity above.

The Nigerian medical services were reorganised in 1945 as part of the British ten-year development plan for the colony. African medical personnel were trained and there was an expansion of maternal and child services. In the lead up to decolonisation, the colonial government took on more of a supervisory role while local health services were coordinated and carried out by the local native administration (Van Tol, 2007). This would indeed have given Awoliyi a greater opportunity to create her own system within Massey

Street Hospital to focus on her public health vision. Jones (2004) describes many actors both within and outside the colonies as being responsible for shaping British colonial medicine. Awoliyi was given certain agency to shape policies within Massey St and not simply a pawn of the Empire.

She was also appointed as a Senior Specialist Gynaecologist and Obstetrician by the Federal Ministry of Health, Nigeria, in 1962, two years after independence. There is no evidence of a shift in Awoliyi's approach following independence, but rather that it was a continuation of the mix of the colonial and native administration regime. This would have been in line with her Western education.

Not only can Awoliyi be credited with contributing directly to the decline in maternal and child mortality rates, through her role as Medical Director, she also used her platform to mentor younger doctors, advocating for better working conditions for female health professionals. Under her leadership, the hospital became a centre of excellence in the treatment of women's health issues and maternal care, leading to significant improvements in patient outcomes.

Healthcare Improvement and Health Promotion

Dr Awoliyi was not only a practising doctor; she was also a pioneer in public health education, believing that community health was as important as individual care. She regularly held public forums and lectures to educate Nigerian women on reproductive health, childcare and nutrition. In addition to routine care, Massey Street Hospital also became involved in public health initiatives such as family planning, nutrition education, and public health campaigns to raise awareness about child health and hygiene. This was against the backdrop of a push against preventive services, a focus on curative medicine, and staff cuts in Nigeria at the time (Atting, 2019; Abubakar et al., 2022).

Family Planning

Although the first family planning clinic was opened in Lagos in 1958, there was no formal family planning programme until 1964. During the period 1958–1964, approximately 600 contraceptive patients were registered. Reasons for these low attendance figures include lack of resources and government support, and the widespread use of traditional contraceptive techniques, including the use of charms (Morgan, 1972). Large families were culturally encouraged in Nigeria, and the colonial government did not focus on formal family planning as part of reproductive health. The use of modern contraception rose steeply post-independence, during the 1960s and early 1970s (Caldwell and Ware, 1977), which coincided with Awoliyis' efforts in the area.

Awoliyi became the second president of the National Council of Women Societies (NCWS) from 1964 to 1971. It was a leading organisation advocating for women's rights and empowerment. She was a consultant to the organisation's Family Planning Clinic, which later became the Planned Parenthood Federation of Nigeria. Many women lacked access to information and services related to reproductive health. Recognising these challenges, Awoliyi, through the NCWS, began advocating for family planning, as part of its broader mission to improve the status of women in Nigeria. Awoliyi utilised the NCWS, recognising early on the crucial role that family planning could play in improving women's health and advancing gender equality (Caldwell and Ware, 1977).

In the late 1960s and early 1970s, family planning became a critical issue globally, with international organisations such as the **United Nations Population Fund** and **World Health Organization** promoting birth control and child spacing to improve health outcomes. The NCWS, through Awoliyi's leadership, aligned with these global efforts, and began to integrate family planning advocacy into its programmes.

Social Determinants of Health

Elizabeth Abimbola Awoliyi's influence extended beyond health. She was also a leader in women's rights and an active member of several organisations advocating for the empowerment of women. She lobbied for policies that increased access to education for girls, leading to higher enrolment rates and greater education and employment opportunities. She was also an active member of several other organisations including the Child Care Voluntary Association where she was President of the Business and Professional Women's Association. Through her leadership and medical expertise, she played a crucial role in shaping the humanitarian efforts of the Nigerian Red Cross, particularly in health and community outreach. Awoliyi was also an active member of the Motherless Babies Home Governing Council of Nigeria. These homes catered primarily to children whose mothers had died during childbirth or due to disease. Awoliyi was awarded a Member of the Order of the British Empire in 1958 for services to child welfare.

Conclusion

Elizabeth Abimbola Awoliyi died in 1971 at the age of 61. Her legacy will now be discussed within the broader context of modern-day Nigeria in terms of (1) women in medicine in Nigeria, (2) maternal and child health and (3) lessons for contemporary health management.

Women in Medicine in Nigeria

> The average Nigerian woman, albeit educated, is expected to prepare for family and place the needs of the family ahead of hers. This extra pressure to be the main carer in the family, to cater to her husband and children impacts her opportunity to pursue her career and hone her skills. Although, some women manage to balance this cultural pressure with their educational and career goals it is an obstacle for many.
>
> (Idowu, 2021)[2]

Unfortunately, this quote about the struggles of being a female doctor in Nigeria in 2021 reads remarkably similar to the quote by Agunbiade in the section 'Status of Women in Nigeria in the First Half of the 20th Century', even though almost a century has passed. Another Nigerian female doctor describes how they were expected to work twice as hard as men to prove their capabilities; however, the influx of women into medicine the last number of years shows that things are beginning to change.[3] In 2022, males comprised 65% of the doctors in Nigeria, with female doctors at 35% (SNB, 2023). Even though Awoliyi's career was filled with significant milestones, it was not without its difficulties. She often faced discrimination because of both her gender and race, especially in the early years of her career. As a black female doctor practising in a male-dominated profession, she had to work twice as hard to earn the respect of her colleagues and patients.

Many Nigerian doctors travel further afield to practice. The World Health Organization has included Nigeria on its red list to discourage other countries from actively seeking health professionals to relocate to higher income countries. Between 2015 and 2021, it is estimated that nearly 5,000 Nigerian doctors relocated to the UK.[4] Reasons for this include poor pay and conditions and a lack of healthcare technologies. Awoliyi was an example of a doctor who wished to return to her country to improve the plight of women and children with the benefits of a global perspective on medicine. This did not preclude her from appreciating and respecting traditional medicine and cultural norms within Nigeria at the time. It is perhaps the sensitivity to this usual colonial tension between the Western and traditional medicine and customs that contributed to her success. No doubt she has inspired generations of Nigerian women, not only to embark on a career in medicine but also to aspire to leadership roles.

Maternal and Child Health

Van Tol (2007) claims that successes in reproductive health have been a consequence of colonial efforts. While this may be partly true, it ignores the efforts of local doctors such as Awoliyi and is a further example of history not recording the work of Awoliyi and other Nigerian female

Table 6.2 Lessons learned from Awoliyi's work and implications for contemporary healthcare management

Domain	*Lesson*	*Implications for contemporary health management*
1. Public health agent	***Gender equity in healthcare:*** Awoliyi demonstrated how empowering women in medicine can improve maternal and child healthcare.	Promote gender equity in medical education to ensure diverse perspectives in health management and service delivery.
	Healthcare leadership: Awoliyi overcame societal obstacles to become a leader in medicine and public health. She also advocated for better working conditions for female health professionals.	Train healthcare leaders to navigate health management challenges such as resource constraints and gender and cultural biases, encompassing intersectionality.
2. Health service delivery	***Prioritise maternal and child health services***: Awoliyi championed maternal and child health at a time when such services were lacking in Nigeria, with an appreciation for the intersection between traditional and modern medicine.	Invest in maternal and child health initiatives, particularly in underserved communities, by expanding prenatal care, safe delivery services and postnatal support.
3. Healthcare improvement and promotion	***Advocacy for public health services with a focus on the social determinants of health:*** Awoliyi was a vocal advocate for preventive healthcare, especially for women and children, with a focus on the social determinants of health.	Strengthen community-based health education programmes that target in particular those who are vulnerable.
	Collaboration between health stakeholders: Awoliyi worked with diverse stakeholders at international, sub-national and community level to improve healthcare delivery in Nigeria.	Foster collaboration between government state sector, non-profits and international organisations to improve healthcare infrastructure, funding and accessibility.

and male health professionals. However, despite early successes during the mid-late 20th century, Nigeria ranks the fourth highest maternal mortality ratio worldwide (Hopkins, 2023). In 2020, the maternal mortality rate was 1,047 deaths per 100,000 live births. The neonatal mortality rate was 35 deaths per 1000 live births in 2021. The 2023 UN report on Trends in Maternal Mortality from 2000 to 2020 revealed that nearly 28.5% of global maternal deaths happen in Nigeria. The reasons for this are too numerous to be discussed in this chapter, however, a lack of investment in public health, and a dysfunctional health system are significant factors, in addition to a less than adequate management within the system. Maternal and child mortality rates declined during Awoliyi's career, which can be attributed to her individual public health agency, influence and leadership, and against a backdrop of a focus more broadly on maternal and child health.

Lessons for Contemporary Health Management

Dr Awoliyi's work offers several lessons that remain relevant for contemporary health management, which are presented in Table 6.2 under each of the three domains: public health agent, health service delivery and healthcare improvement and promotion.

The organisations that Dr Awoliyi helped to lead and manage continue to advocate for women's rights and health. She opened doors for generations of African women in medicine and played a critical role in shaping the future of healthcare management in Nigeria. Even after her passing in 1971, her legacy continued through various programmes and initiatives. The Massey Street Hospital, where she served as Chief Medical Officer, remains a centre of excellence in maternal healthcare. This chapter has celebrated Dr Awoliyi as one of the architects of maternal public health in Nigeria. Almost a century after she graduated as a medical doctor, her work provides us with useful lessons for effective healthcare management, organisation and service delivery today.

Notes

1 Van Tol (2007) references Massey Street Hospital being supervised by 'the first Lady Medical Officer (LMO) appointed to practice in Nigeria' (p. 112) rather than referring to Awoliyi by name.
2 https://dopeblack.org/the-struggles-of-being-a-female-doctor-in-nigeria/
3 https://humanglemedia.com/the-nigerian-doctor-8-being-a-health-worker-affects-my-mental-health/
4 https://www.theguardian.com/global-development/2023/may/22/nigerias-doctors-furious-over-plans-for-five-years-of-mandatory-service

References

Abubakar, I., Dalglish, S. L., Angell, B., Sanuade, O., Abimbola, S., Adamu, A. L., Adetifa, I. M. O., Colbourn, T., Ogunlesi, A. O., Onwujekwe, O., Owoaje, E. T., Okeke, I. N., Adeyemo, A., Aliyu, G., Aliyu, M. H., Aliyu, S. H., Ameh, E. A., Archibong, B., Ezeh, A., Gadanya, M. A., Ihekweazu, C., Ihekweazu, V., Iliyasu, Z., Kwaku Chiroma, A., Mabayoje, D. A., Nasir Sambo, M., Obaro, S., Yinka-Ogunleye, A., Okonofua, F., Oni, T., Onyimadu, O., Pate, M. A., Salako, B.

L., Shuaib, F., Tsiga-Ahmed, F. and Zanna, F. H. 2022. The lancet Nigeria commission: Investing in health and the future of the nation. *Lancet*, 399, 1155–1200.

Acheson, D. 1988. *Independent inquiry into inequalities in health.* The Stationary Office.

Adetiba, A. and Msindo, E. 2022. Chiefs and rural health services in South-Western Nigeria, c. 1920 – c. 1950s. *Social History of Medicine*, 35, 589–611.

Agunbiade, T. 2022. *A stash of gems on women from the Nigerian national archives – Tayo Agunbiade.* Women's History Network.

Atting, I. 2019. *Chapter thirteen public health system in Nigeria.* https://www.researchgate.net/publication/331650664_CHAPTER_THIRTEEN_PUBLIC_HEALTH_SYSTEM_IN_NIGERIA

Caldwell, J. C. and Ware, H. R. E. 1977. The evolution of family planning in an African city: Ibadan, Nigeria. *Population Studies*, 31(3), 487–507.

Denzer, L. R. 1989. *Women in government service in colonial Nigeria, 1862–1945.* African Studies Center, Boston University.

Hopkins, J. 2023. *Nigeria: Maternal & newborn health country profile.* Institute of Human Virology Nigeria, Ukaid.

Idowu, M. 2021. The struggles of being a female doctor in Nigeria. *Dopeblack.* https://dopeblack.org

Jakovljevic, M., Liu, Y., Cerda, A., Simonyan, M., Correia, T., Mariita, R. M., Kumara, A. S., Garcia, L., Krstic, K., Osabohien, R., Toan, T. K., Adhikari, C., Chuc, N. T. K., Khatri, R. B., Chattu, V. K., Wang, L., Wijeratne, T., Kouassi, E., Khan, H. N. and Varjacic, M. 2021. The global south political economy of health financing and spending landscape – history and presence. *Journal of Medical Economics*, 24, 25–33.

Jones, M. 2004. *Health policy in Britain's model colony: Ceylon (1900–1948).* New Delhi: Orient Longman.

Kelly, L. 2010. 'Fascinating scalpel-wielders and fair dissectors': Women's experience of Irish medical education, c. 1880s–1920s. *Med History*, 54, 495–516.

Morgan, R. W. 1972. Family planning acceptors in Lagos, Nigeria. *Studies in Family Planning*, 3, 221–226.

Nwashindu, V., Onu, A. and Okonkwo, U. 2023. 'How public is public health?': A historical appraisal of public health services in colonial Enugu-Nigeria, 1917–1960. *Cogent Arts & Humanities*, 10, 2231710.

Panata, S. 2020. 'Dear readers . . .': Women's rights and duties through letters to the editor in the Nigerian press (1940s–1950s). *Sources*, 1.

Profile of Elizabeth Abimbola Awoliyi (Daily Times Nigeria). 1 August 1959. *Nigerian Daily Times.*

Silla, E. and Addae, S. 1996. *The evolution of modern medicine in a developing country: Ghana 1880–1960.* Durham Academic Press.

SNB. 2023. *2023 social statistics report.* SNB.

Van Tol, D. 2007. Mothers, babies, and the colonial state: The introduction of maternal and infant welfare services in Nigeria, 1925–1945. *Spontaneous Generations*, 1, 110.

7 Edwina Jeruto Kwallah

Organising Against Gender-Based Violence

Purity Mwendwa

Introduction

Globally, women have been in the frontline delivering formal and informal healthcare and social support (Boniol et al., 2019), but their roles and contribution to the sector have received little attention (World Health Organization, 2019). In addition, women remain largely underrepresented in health management and global health leadership roles (Smith & Sinkford, 2022). This chapter examines the work of Edwina Jeruto Kwallah in Kajiado county in Kenya. Edwina has been at the forefront of organising against gender-based violence (GBV) in Kajiado West sub-county through her work with Cara Projects (Cara). The chapter begins by defining and outlining the forms and drivers of GBV and then delves into the various types and drivers of GBV. This is followed by an examination of gender equality and women's empowerment in Kenya. The chapter then looks at how Edwina's work with communities has helped promote the protection of women and girls in her community. The chapter concludes with a reflection on how this work has helped shape narratives and practice as it relates to GBV and women's leadership more generally.

Defining Gender-Based Violence

The United Nations defines GBV as 'any act of gender-based violence that results in, or is likely to result in, physical, sexual or psychological harm or suffering to women . . . whether occurring in public or private life. GBV could include violence against men, provided the violence stems from a man's gender identity or presentation' (United Nations Population Fund, n.d.). And while GBV can affect both genders, including sexual minorities, women and girls are more likely to be victims (United Nations Population Fund, 2022). The UN Sustainable Development Goal (SDG) 5 Target 3 is to eliminate all harmful practices, such as child, early and forced marriage and female genital mutilation (United Nations, n.d.).

DOI: 10.4324/9781003546610-7

Child marriage is defined as 'the marriage of a girl or boy before the age of 18 years' and affects more girls than boys (UNICEF, 2019). While there has been a decline in child marriages globally, some regions of sub-Saharan Africa (SSA) continue to record high incidences; with one in three young women marrying before attaining age 18 (United Nations Children's Fund, 2023). Some of the factors associated with child marriage include residing in rural/remote areas, having no formal/low education levels, low social economic status/poverty (Subramanee et al., 2022) and a high prevalence of female genital mutilation (FGM) (Ahinkorah et al., 2023).

FGM 'comprises all procedures that involve partial or total removal of the external female genitalia, or other injury to the female genital organs for non-medical reasons' (WHO, 2024). FGM violates the human rights of women and girls and is a manifestation of gender inequality and is used to control women's sexuality (United Nations Children's Fund, 2021). At least 200 million girls and women have undergone FGM in 31 countries with representative data on prevalence (United Nations Children's Fund, 2020). And while girls who experience child marriage and FGM tend to have some common characteristics, the drives of both practices differ distinctly. Child marriage is closely linked to poverty (lack of economic opportunities) where families choose to marry off their child to secure finances (through dowry/bride price) or in the hope that marriage would provide a secure future for the girl-child (United Nations Children's Fund, 2021). FGM is closely tied to cultural and traditional beliefs and norms (Berg & Denison, 2013) and depending on where (community) it is carried out, it serves as a symbol of ethnic identity and belonging (Sheikh et al., 2023). When girls undergo FGM they are forced to abandon their dreams and aspirations as most eventually get married off early. It has taken over five decades to fight practices such as FGM, because they are deeply embedded in culture and traditions. In countries such as Kenya, historically this has meant enacting government policies and laws aimed at curbing the practice (28 Too Many, 2018), employing community-based approaches to change attitudes about FGM through health education and sensitisation campaigns (Matanda et al., 2023) and delivering 'alternative' rites programmes (ARPs) that seek to retain a community's cultural traditions without having to perform FGM (Esho et al., 2023).

Kenya has put in place a number of legal and policy guidelines that aim to protect children from GBV. These include the Children's Act, 2001, Section (14), the Sexual Offences Act, 2006, the Prohibition of Female Genital Mutilation Act, 2011 and the Marriage Act, 2014. In line with Target 5.3 of the SDGs, the country also commits to eliminate child, early and forced marriage by 2030 (African Union, 2023). Yet, Kenya is one of the countries in SSA where child marriage and FGM continue to be practised with an estimated prevalence of 23% for child marriage (KDHS, 2014) and

15% FGM (KDHS, 2022). These practices are particularly prevalent among pastoralist and nomadic communities including the Samburu, Maasai, Pokot, Rendille and Somali ethnic groups in Kenya (UNICEF, 2018). Patriarchal norms, poverty and traditional pastoral lifestyles encourage the continuation of these harmful traditional practices (Lowe et al., 2022). In addition to having in place legislative frameworks and policies that protect women and girls from GBV, Kenya has committed to advancing gender equality and the empowerment of women and girls (USAID, 2022) which aligns with Goal 5 of the SDG agenda. One key target to this goal is to 'Ensure women's full and effective participation and equal opportunities for leadership at all levels of decision-making in political, economic and public life' (United Nations Sustainable Development Goals, n.d.).

It took almost 50 years post Kenya's independence for the role of women in leadership to be fully recognised. This was incrementally achieved through women's own activism over decades (e.g. through the Beijing conference) which sought to promote women's rights and gender equality (United Nations, 1996). Historically, and in most societies, women's positions and standing in society have been underpinned by patriarchal systems which give men an upper hand and authority, right from the family level to the political, legal and economic spheres. This experience is/was not unique to Kenya. Modern-day developed societies, e.g. countries like Ireland, tell a similar story (O'Connor, 1998). In Kenya, patriarchy dates back to the pre-colonial times, where leadership and political decisions were the preserve of men, although there is some evidence from communities in Kenya which present counter arguments (where women had more decision-making power) (Wai, 1994). Colonialism entrenched patriarchy, curtailing women's roles in public life and leadership and restricted them to domestic life and in some cases stripped women of the rights to own land and property (Hepburn, 2023). Independence from colonial rule brought with it some changes, expanding some rights, education and employment opportunities (Hepburn, 2023); however, few women held positions of leadership or influence in public life despite the end of colonial rule.

Kenya ushered in a new constitution in 2010 that provided a major shift in the legal system putting in place measures to remedy decades of women's exclusion in political life. The constitution states in part that 'Women and men have the right to equal treatment, including the right to equal opportunities in political, economic, cultural and social spheres' (Government of Kenya, 2010). Among the major changes brought about by the new constitution is to increase women's leadership in politics. Accordingly, 'not more than two-thirds of the members of elective public bodies shall be of the same gender' (Government of Kenya, 2010). Despite these deliberate efforts and legislative measures to ensure women are included in political life, there is still a long way to go as women continue to be inequitably represented in the areas of education (highest level), leaderships roles and employment opportunities (USAID, 2022). The next section considers the context in which Edwina's work is located a followed by a more detailed account of her work and its impact.

Organising Change: Edwina's Work

Edwina's work is situated in Kajiado County, one of Kenya's 47 counties located in the South of the country. It has a population of 1,117,840, with a female population of 50.1% (The Kenya Population and Housing Census of 2019). Kajiado county is multi-ethnic, with the Maasai community dominating rural areas. The county is semi-arid and nomadic pastoralism is the main practice in rural areas. Kajiado has five sub-counties, with Kajiado West being the largest in km^2 (7,862) with a population of 202,573 as of the year 2022. The population of women of reproductive age (15–49) was 27.1% in 2019 and the percentage of women aged 15–49 with no formal education was 11%. In Kenya, FGM prevalence is 15% compared to 63% in Kajiado. Approximately 36% of women aged 15–49 have experienced physical violence since age 15 (Kenya Demographic and Health Survey (KDHS)). The county has in place strategies that sensitise communities about FGM, child marriage and early pregnancies (UNFPA Kenya, 2021). According to the 2019 KDHS report, over 2000 teenage girls were reported pregnant in Kajiado West sub-county alone, all of whom had undergone FGM.

There have been various approaches and strategies to addressing GBV. Examples have included programmes that seek to empower girls by providing them with life skills, vocational trainings, mentorship, educational opportunities through scholarships, legal representation and psychosocial support as well as providing girls with menstrual products (Girlsnotbrides, n.d.). At the community level, efforts to raise public awareness about the harmful effects of GBV through community dialogues have gained in importance. There are a few organisations that serve as rescue and recovery centres for those affected by GBV. Cara is one such organisation that was set up by a group of Irish volunteers in 2008. This non-governmental organisation (NGO) was founded in 2008 with a focus on child protection and GBV working primarily with women and girls. Edwina Jeruto Kwallah was pivotal to its establishment and work.

At the age of 29, Edwina – then a young mother of two boys aged 3 and 6 – was introduced to an Irishman Paddy O'Connor by the children officer in charge of the Ngong municipality in Kajiado county. Edwina had volunteered at the children department after completing her attachment in the same office. Paddy had a negative experience with the founder of a charitable children's institution who, it was alleged, had been misappropriating funds collected from family and friends. Paddy was on the brink of giving up on supporting vulnerable children in Kenya until the children office intervened by introducing Edwina to him. However, their initial interactions were fraught as Edwina was perceived as a spy and a threat, leading her to leave the shelter.

Paddy then approached Edwina to collaborate on establishing a shelter together under an organisation they would later establish and register. Around this time, an Irishwomen named Roisin Kelly joined the duo. The trio co-founded and registered Cara Projects, with Paddy taking on the role of president, Roisin as the secretary, and Edwina as the treasurer of the Kenyan registered NGO. Paddy and Roisin focussed on resource mobilisation primarily in Ireland, while Edwina managed the administrative aspects of Cara Projects in Kenya. Initially established as a Girls Rescue Centre, Cara Projects has since evolved into an organisation with integrated programmes including advocacy, women empowerment, home-based support and a sustainable building programme.

Cara aims to fulfil three main objectives: work with the Children's Office to rescue neglected/abused young girls through the Cara Girls Rescue Centre (CGRC), empower girls and women through the Cara Projects Empowerment Centre and promote gender equality and ensure sustainable development for mothers and children through advocacy. Cara recognised the need to provide a sanctuary for girls at risk of GBV. The organisation provides a safe haven at the CGRC for up to forty girls from ages 2 to 16 years.

Edwina (42 years of age) was born of parents from the Maasai and Kalenjin communities of Kenya. Edwina is the last born in a family of two boys and two girls. She is married, and together with her husband, they have two teenage boys. Edwina grew up in the foothills of Ngong in Kajiado county where she was a shepherd girl to her father's sheep, when not in school or helping with house chores. She attended formal education and was placed in boarding school at the age of 11. This taught her independence. While in high school, she formed a club where they would collect unused toiletries and send them to children's homes. While at the University, she used most of her lunch breaks to visit the terminally ill children at the Kenyatta National Hospital in Nairobi. Edwina has always had a passion for children and for serving the less fortunate in society. She has been a volunteer for various children's services and participated in policy formulation at various levels. Although many females in her family, including her mum, underwent FGM, Edwina says 'I am fortunate to have escaped the ordeal. I'm grateful to my family and especially my father for this.'

Edwina has been leading the Cara team that comprises five departments: shelter, advocacy, women empowerment, community-based support and a sustainable housing programme. Through Cara, Edwina offers a voice and helping hand to scared children, children betrayed by their own families and communities, those abused and mistreated. Since 2008, Cara has been able to provide a safe haven for over 600 children some of whom have acquired formal education, accessed counselling, medical attention, legal aid and re-integration back into society. Cara employs a holistic model of care with affected girls which includes psychosocial and trauma-informed practice. To build the capacity of teenage mothers, Cara has in place the 'Girl Boss' programme, which provides young mothers with entrepreneurial and leaderships skills to help build their confidence and secure financial independence (UNANIMA International, 2024). Cara also works with governments both county and national, other charitable children's institutions, networks dealing with child protection and sector working groups that touch on gender equality and child protection. In recognition of Edwina's leadership, she received an award from the Red Cross for Community Service of the Year 2022. In 2024, she was recognised for her work as a child protection champion by Kajiado West sub-county in Kenya.

Edwina has participated in shaping a number of policies which include policies on care reforms, eradication of FGM in Kajiado county, halting harmful practices, gender mainstreaming, promoting policy on menstrual health management for girls in schools, ending child marriage and achieving 100% transition from primary to secondary school.

The policy that holds significant importance for Edwina is the one addressing the eradication of FGM, specifically tailored for Kajiado county. The prohibition of FGM was established in 2011 as a strategic measure to eliminate this practice in Kenya. In order to ensure the effective implementation of this legislation, the county government of Kajiado formulated an anti-FGM policy as a legal framework for eradicating this harmful tradition. FGM is deeply entrenched in the cultural fabric, and while certain cultural practices are commendable and worth preserving, FGM is regressive and must be abolished in Kajiado county. For decades, this practice has inflicted physical, social and emotional harm upon women and girls in Kajiado, stripping them of their dignity and denying them life opportunities. This practice constitutes a violation of human rights and has had profound adverse effects on the county's social, economic and political development. Therefore, the Kajiado policy for eradicating FGM defines the practice as a form of GBV that severely undermines the well-being of females.

Edwina's work to empower and provide a safe haven for girls in her community has not been without challenges. It is common for children who testify against their family to be denounced, which can make re-integration challenging and at times impossible. Funding has also been an issue. The need in this community far outweighs the funding available to ensure the delivery of effective and sustainable interventions. There have been instances where Edwina's work could not garner adequate support from some local authorities, which complicated the efforts to support girls in need. There are also cases where girls themselves fail to co-operate, believing that the situation they find themselves in is normal and acceptable, which is attributable to peer pressure and the strong cultural and traditional environment they have grown up in.

The progress towards tackling FGM has been slow exemplified by the fact that FGM was outlawed 14 years ago, yet it continues to impact Kenyan children. Although statistics indicate a decrease in the prevalence of FGM, the ongoing advocacy and battle against it persist. Women residing in remote and rural areas bear the brunt of this practice, as FGM serves as a precursor to various forms of GBV inflicted upon women.

Recent work conducted on FGM in Kajiado notes the need for organisations working to end traditional practices such as FGM to challenge cultural practices so as to end the continued harm to girls (Mwendwa et al., 2022). This, however, is not always easy to achieve. Working closely with communities and including men in these conversations, in culturally acceptable ways, is seen as one of the ways to help change mind sets about negative cultural practices (Mwendwa et al., 2022). While educating communities about these harmful practices is crucial, it is also important to involve communities in co-designing strategies to fight negative cultural practices. This will ensure that such strategies have local relevance and hence are most likely to have the desired impact.

Conclusion: Quiet Healthcare Leadership

Harmful cultural practices and violence against children continue to be a practice among some communities in Kenya. This has negative implications for the health and well-being of children and hinders their potential to realise their dreams, including taking on leadership positions which are mostly dominated by men. There is growing evidence on what works to combat GBV (Evidence Reviews, 2019). Some suggested strategies include community activism, gender transformative interventions and economic empowerment for women and girls including interventions that seek to challenge social norms at the community level. The importance of male involvement in challenging these practices is gaining importance globally (Varol et al., 2015). Edwina and Cara have been at the forefront of examining ways of promoting male engagement in combating GBV by collaborating with researchers in Kenya and overseas. Increasingly important is providing spaces that can provide safety, shelter and dignity for survivors. Cara not only provides shelter and safety but has also been instrumental in providing girls and women with life and vocational skills to enhance their income generation potential, independence and, ultimately, their leadership potential.

Women, just like men, want to take on leadership positions, and there are ample examples of women who have gone on to break and challenge the negative traditional norms of 'the woman belongs in the kitchen' and taken on top leadership roles amid systemic barriers and gender discrimination (Smith & Sinkford, 2022). The first African woman to win the Nobel Peace Prize was the late Prof. Wangari Mathaai, a Kenyan, who, among other things, fought for women's empowerment and social justice amid opposition from the government at the time. Prof Mathaai was able to inspire other women and challenge stereotypes around women's capability to take on political leadership. However, importantly, her work embodies the use of bottom-up approaches, particularly grassroots movements led by women, to bring about change.

In addition to women wanting to sit at decision-making tables alongside men, it is imperative that women take up (top) leadership positions in society. Not only does this contribute to gender diversity in leadership, it is the right thing and should be the obvious thing to do. A recent report that showcases the work that political foundations in Europe have conducted, in a bid to promote gender equality and women's participation in politics globally, notes that 'Women bring unique experiences, insights and priorities to the table, enrich policy discussions, and promote a more comprehensive understanding of societal needs' (Ceciarini, 2023, p. 3). Excluding women from forums where decisions about them are made is certainly not in keeping with the 2030 Agenda of the UNSDG principle of 'Leave No One Behind' which UN Member States including Kenya have committed to achieve by 2030.

Edwina is part of a line of unrecognised and often unseen women who care for local communities and work to change practices from the bottom-up. Her experiences growing up, and the support from her family, especially her father, helped inspire her work of protecting and empowering young girls and women in the community where she grew up. Edwina's work is situated in a community where patriarchal norms persists and grant men dominance in almost all aspects. Her work is that of someone 'leading change in ways that depart from patriarchal norms, in a society that is strongly entrenched in cultural beliefs' (Nkambule & Perumal, 2024, p. 2). She exemplifies the continuing need to organise and collaborate in the protection and promotion of girls and women, although it can be challenging for a female to take a stance against practices that have been normalised in one's own community. I argue that women and girls see Edwina not only as someone helping to promote their empowerment and independence but also equally as a role model.

As compared to other women who have shaped healthcare and wider cultural debates, it appears that there is much less to say about Edwina Jeruto Kwallah. She has not written treaties in the style of Florence Nightingale or been a subject of record (until now). She is perhaps more like the wise women discussed in Chapter 1 whose contribution is one of quiet service to their communities. Her impact is from the bottom-up, organising services and changing lives collaboratively on the ground. As such, Edwina represents millennia of often-unrecognised women who make a difference daily through direct provision, while also being the frontline change agents that work to enact the cultural and societal changes that others expound. As such, it is crucial that we recognise this type of quiet healthcare leadership directed at socio-cultural revolution.

References

28 Too Many. (2018). *Kenya: The law and FGM.* https://www.fgmcri.org/media/uploads/Law%20Reports/kenya_law_report_v1_(may_2018).pdf

African Union. (2023). *Kenya country profile on child marriages.* https://www.aucecma.org/kenya-country-profile-on-child-marriages/

Ahinkorah, B. O., Hagan Jr, J. E., Seidu, A. A., Bolarinwa, O. A., Budu, E., Adu, C., Okyere, J., Archer, A. G., & Schack, T. (2023). Association between female genital mutilation and girl-child marriage in sub-Saharan Africa. *Journal of Biosocial Science, 55*(1). https://doi.org/10.1017/S0021932021000687

Berg, R. C., & Denison, E. (2013). A tradition in transition: Factors perpetuating and hindering the continuance of female genital mutilation/cutting (FGM/C) summarized in a systematic review. *Health Care for Women International, 34*(10), 837–859. https://doi.org/10.1080/07399332.2012.721417

Boniol, M., McIsaac, M., Xu, L., Wuliji, T., Diallo, K., & Campbell, J. (2019). *Gender equity in the health workforce: Analysis of 104 countries.* World Health Organization, IRIS. https://iris.who.int/handle/10665/311314

Ceciarini, S. (2023). *The work of political foundations in the area of gender equality and women's political participation: A compilation of best practices by ENoP members.* European Network of Political Foundations – ENoP. https://www.enop.eu/wp-content/uploads/2023/08/ENoP_Best-Practices-Compilation_Gender-Equality-and-Womens-Political-Participation.pdf

Esho, T. C., Scholten, J., Conradi, H., Kawai, D., Mbogo, B., Lugayo, D., Opanga, Y., Muhula, S., & Matanda, D. J. (2023). Amref alternative rites of passage (ARP) model for female genital mutilation/cutting, teenage pregnancies, and child, early and forced marriages in Kenya: A stepped-wedge cluster randomised controlled trial protocol. *Journal of Global Health Reports, 7*, e2023031. https://doi.org/10.29392/001c.77597

Evidence Reviews. (2019). *What works – evidence reviews.* https://www.whatworks.co.za/resources/evidence-reviews

Girlsnotbrides. (n.d.). *Successfully addressing FGM/C and child marriage; the case of msichana empowerment Kuria, Kenya.* https://www.girlsnotbrides.org/documents/1458/Successfully_addressing_FGM-C_and_child_marriage_-_MEK.pdf

Government of Kenya. (2010). *The constitution of Kenya.* https://interior.go.ke/sites/default/files/2024-08/1.%20Constitution%20of%20Kenya%202010_3.pdf

Hepburn, S. (2023). *Women in Kenya.* https://doi.org/10.1093/acrefore/9780190277734.013.1607

Lowe, H., Kenny, L., Hassan, R., Bacchus, L. J., Njoroge, P., Dagadu, N. A., Hossain, M., & Cislaghi, B. (2022). 'If she gets married when she is young, she will give birth to many kids': A qualitative study of child marriage practices amongst nomadic pastoralist communities in Kenya. *Culture, Health & Sexuality*, *24*(7), 886–901. https://doi.org/10.1080/13691058.2021.1893821

Matanda, D. J., Van Eekert, N., Croce-Galis, M., Gay, J., Middelburg, M. J., & Hardee, K. (2023). What interventions are effective to prevent or respond to female genital mutilation? A review of existing evidence from 2008–2020. *PLOS Global Public Health*, *3*(5), e0001855. https://doi.org/10.1371/journal.pgph.0001855

Mwendwa, P., Kaimuri, M., Kalondu, E., Karani, C., Behnam, R., Al-Rousan, T., Kroll, T., De Brún, A., & McAuliffe, E. (2022). Female genital mutilation and male involvement: Insights of men and women in two counties in Kenya. *African Journal of Reproductive Health*, *26*(11), 106–118. https://doi.org/10.29063/ajrh2022/v26i11.10

Nkambule, H., & Perumal, J. (2024). An interaction of patriarchy and female leadership: A synthesis of literature on women leadership in Eswatini. *Review of Education*, *12*(1), e3450. https://doi.org/10.1002/rev3.3450

O'Connor, P. (1998). *Emerging voices: Women in contemporary Irish society (1998/reprinted 1999) by Pat O'Connor*. Dublin: IPA (Paperback).

Sheikh, M. M., Cheptum, J. J., & Mageto, I. G. (2023). Factors linked to female genital mutilation practice among women living in Alungu village of Mandera County, Kenya. *The East African Health Research Journal*, *7*(1), 109–115. https://doi.org/10.24248/eahrj.v7i1.716

Smith, S. G., & Sinkford, J. C. (2022). Gender equality in the 21st century: Overcoming barriers to women's leadership in global health. *Journal of Dental Education*, *86*(9), 1144–1173. https://doi.org/10.1002/jdd.13059

Subramanee, S. D., Agho, K., Lakshmi, J., Huda, M. N., Joshi, R., & Akombi-Inyang, B. (2022). Child marriage in South Asia: A systematic review. *International Journal of Environmental Research and Public Health*, *19*(22), Article 22. https://doi.org/10.3390/ijerph192215138

UNANIMA International. (2024). UNANIMA international news from the UN and around the world. *July 2024 Newsletter*, 28. https://brigidine.org.au/wp-content/uploads/2024/07/UNANIMA-International-News-from-the-UN-July24.pdf

UNFPA Kenya. (2021). *Kajiado County models a collaborative approach to ending FGM*. https://kenya.unfpa.org/en/news/kajiado-county-models-collaborative-approach-ending-fgm

UNICEF. (2018). *Situation analysis of children and women in Kenya 2017*. UNICEF.

UNICEF. (2019). *Child marriage*. https://data.unicef.org/topic/child-protection/child-marriage/

United Nations. (1996). *Report of the fourth world conference on women* (ISBN 92-1-130181-5). United Nations. https://documents.un.org/doc/undoc/gen/n96/273/01/pdf/n9627301.pdf

United Nations. (n.d.). *Achieve gender equality and empower all women and girls*. Department of Economic and Social Affairs Sustainable Development. https://sdgs.un.org/goals/goal5#targets_and_indicators

United Nations Children's Fund. (2020). *Female genital mutilation: A new generation calls for ending an old practice*. UNICEF. https://data.unicef.org/resources/female-genital-mutilation-a-new-generation-calls-for-ending-an-old-practice/

United Nations Children's Fund. (2021). *Understanding the relationship between child marriage and female genital mutilation: A statistical overview of their co-occurrence and risk factors*. UNICEF.

United Nations Children's Fund. (2023). *Is an end to child marriage within reach? Latest trends and future prospects. 2023 update*. UNICEF. https://data.unicef.org/resources/is-an-end-to-child-marriage-within-reach/

United Nations Population Fund. (2022). *My body, my life, my world operational guidance. Module 2: Gender-based violence*. https://www.unfpa.org/sites/default/files/resource-pdf/UNFPA-MBMLMW_MOD2-EN.pdf

United Nations Population Fund. (n.d.). *What is gender-based violence (GBV)?* https://www.usaforunfpa.org/what-is-gender-based-violence-gbv/#:~:text=The%20United%20Nations'%20definition%20of,in%20public%20or%20private%20life

United Nations Sustainable Development Goals. (n.d.). *Goal 5: Achieve gender equality and empower all women and girls*. Sustainable Development Goals. Retrieved October 1, 2025, from https://www.un.org/sustainabledevelopment/gender-equality/

USAID. (2022). *Kenya gender equality and female empowerment fact sheet*. https://www.usaid.gov/sites/default/files/2022–05/Gender_Fact_Sheet_for_Kenya.pdf

Varol, N., Turkmani, S., Black, K., Hall, J., & Dawson, A. (2015). The role of men in abandonment of female genital mutilation: A systematic review. *BMC Public Health*, *15*(1), 1034. https://doi.org/10.1186/s12889-015-2373-2

Wai, N. (1994). *Wangu Wa Makeri: A pioneering Kenyan feminist*. Kaswanga Press.

World Health Organization. (2019). *Delivered by women, led by men: A gender and equity analysis of the global health and social workforce* (Human Resources for Health Observer Series No. 24). World Health Organization.

World Health Organization. (2024). *Female genital mutilation: Key facts*. https://www.who.int/news-room/fact-sheets/detail/female-genital-mutilation

8 Examining the Contributions of Catherine Brogan to Healthcare Management

Lessons Learned from Implementing New Approaches to Mental Health Recovery – A Personal Journey

Michael John Norton and Catherine Brogan

Introduction

Recovery in mental health is considered a contested concept due to the various ways it can be interpreted (Norton and Cullen, 2024). Within mental health service provision, there are three types of recovery evident, with some attaining more traction and power than others. The first kind, clinical recovery, emerged from professional-led research and refers to an outcome or state that is observable, measurable and does not vary between individuals (Slade and Longden, 2015). In other words, it focuses on symptom remission and a return to normal functioning (Austin et al., 2021). The second, social recovery, is a form of recovery first noted by Ramon in 2018 and suggests that for recovery to occur, society must have the necessary resources in place to allow individuals to become full and meaningful members of society again (Swords and Norton, 2020). It differs to clinical recovery as it places responsibility on one's society for recovery to occur. Finally, personal recovery, a multifaceted and individually defined concept, is best described through the seminal work of William A. Anthony in 1993 (O'Keeffe et al., 2021). Here, personal recovery is defined as:

> a deeply personal, unique process of changing one's attitudes, values, feelings, goals, skills, and/or roles. It is a way of living a satisfying, hopeful and contributing life even within the limitations caused by illness. Recovery involves the development of new meaning and purpose in one's life as one grows beyond the catastrophic effects of mental illness.
>
> (Anthony, 1993, p. 21)

DOI: 10.4324/9781003546610-8

In this sense, it differs from clinical and social recovery as it observes recovery as a lifelong journey focussed on the maintenance of a quality of life and finding meaning within distress (Norton and Cuskelly, 2021). This chapter focuses on personal recovery and its development and advocacy by Catherine Brogan.

Personal recovery is viewed as both a philosophical concept and a wider service user movement (Norton, 2024). Within an Irish context, the concept is supported by policy to be a cornerstone in mental health service provision, with personal recovery being one of the underpinning principles of Ireland's new policy document 'Sharing the Vision' (Department of Health, 2020; Swords and Norton, 2023). The Health Service Executive (HSE)[1] has an office within its national structures that has responsibility for the implementation of recovery into mental health systems (HSE, 2023). This office – the Office of Mental Health Engagement and Recovery – has co-produced 'A National Framework for Recovery in Mental Health' where four central pillars to creating and sustaining recovery orientation are stipulated along with guidance to support implementation (HSE, 2024).

In support of this work, in 2011, Leamy and colleagues conducted a systematic review and narrative synthesis of the literature into personal recovery. From their review of 97 papers, CHIME was constructed. CHIME is an acronym that stands for five concepts essential for personal recovery: connectedness, hope, identity, meaning and purpose and empowerment (Leamy et al., 2011). CHIME also has an impact of changing organisational culture so that services can become more compassionate and person focussed (HSE, 2024).

Within Irish mental health services, the transformation from clinical to personal recovery is still an ongoing journey. A journey which, like that of personal recovery itself, is lifelong with many peaks and troughs along the way. However, Irish services are considered leaders in this space as much of the global north still operates strictly under a biomedical approach with asylums evident in many areas. To reach where we are today, there are several players who are instrumental in creating the capacity required for this to occur. In this chapter, the aim is to explore the life work and impact of one such player: Catherine Brogan to this field. In doing so, we aim to highlight Catherine as a female leader in mental healthcare and from which highlight her immense contribution to healthcare management through autoethnography.

Autoethnographic Account

Autoethnography is a reflective, narrative approach that supports researchers to deepen their understanding of a phenomena by incorporating their own personal values, experiences and opinions to the conversation (Norton and McLaughlin, 2022; Zierotin et al., 2025). It does this by connecting the self to outside elements such as culture and the surrounding society (Chang, 2016).

In this chapter, the authors utilise an autoethnographic methodology to explore the life work of Catherine Brogan. The narrative will then be analysed by the first author (Michael John Norton) so that her contribution to healthcare management as a woman can be critically explored. We start with Catherine's narrative.

To find out where my motivation for nursing came from, we must travel back to when I was a 12-year-old girl in a boarding school in Cashel, Co. Tipperary. During this time, in early September, I can remember how a nun working within the boarding school asked me to go and comfort another student who was upset because of her poor results in the Inter Cert.[2] Doing what all school children did at a time when the catholic church ran the school system, I obeyed and approached this girl and, doing what came naturally to me, I comforted her by listening and talking to her about these results. Through this action, she managed to see the situation in a different light and left the encounter feeling more hopeful for a better outcome in future exams.

This early encounter led me, at the age of 17, to start holiday work in what was then called the 'county home'[3] in my hometown of Thurles as a nurse attendant.[4] I remember working in a ward which 20 older ladies called home. The main reason for their admission into this facility was old age. They were not acutely ill but were individuals who were there due to accidents that happened when they were younger, or because they had a child out of wedlock or because of an underlying physical and/or intellectual disability. Most spent their lives in their nightdresses wrapped with a dressing gown and were never encouraged to wear or do anything else. I began sitting with these individuals and hearing their life stories. This simple act of listening and curiosity allowed relationships to develop between these ladies and I, from which I began noticing little changes. For instance, they began eating dinner at the table rather than at the bedside. It was at this point I decided to become a nurse.

In 1980, I began my nursing career working at St. Raphaels in Celbridge, Co Kildare, where my interest in working with those with intellectual disabilities and challenging behaviour increased. Although I was unaware of co-production at this juncture, looking back now, I can see how my work back then reflected its underpinning philosophy. One example came from my investigation to understanding why some individuals in my care woke in an agitated and uneasy state during the night. Through observing the meal schedules, along with speaking to service users on the ground, I decided to organise for soup and bread to be provided prior to bedtime. Within a week, the service users' sleep patterns positively changed and their agitation and unease reduced dramatically.

Later, I moved to Stewart's hospital, where I began working with individuals who had enduring mental health challenges and an intellectual disability. It was during this period that I became interested in mental health nursing specifically. During my subsequent training as a mental health nurse, I spent time at St. Brendan's and St. Loman's services where my training in social models of care was put to good use. Again, my curiosity allowed me to engage with services users to understand their lives, who they were, where they came from and what supports they had that were outside of the mental health services. This allowed me to begin to see the person behind the diagnosis, moving my thinking away from the medical model towards influencing change through co-production.

As my career progressed, I wanted to get a broader experience of mental health services beyond the acute units and as such, I transitioned to community mental health in 1994. This started an amazing journey of learning and understanding the lives, hopes and dreams of people experiencing mental health challenges and what my role was in supporting these individuals achieve what they wanted in life. This journey began in a sector headquarters which also served as a day hospital and day centre and as such was always busy. Here, I engaged with people with various mental health challenges including psychosis. In those days, the practice was not to acknowledge the presence of voices people experience. However, I wanted to understand this experience more, so I often engaged in conversation with these individuals to hear their experiences. To my surprise, those I spoke to felt relieved to talk about their voices without fear of judgement or denial. This also allowed individuals to begin to make sense of the experiences and how such experiences impacted their recovery journey.

Working here also allowed me to try out new ways of doing things and I was very lucky to always have the team's support and the support of those attending services. The changes I helped implement were simple but extremely impactful. One was regarding how outings and holiday were planned. Before, service users would just go along with whatever staff had organised with no real input. I wanted to change this by bringing a group together and asking them where they wanted to go and do? This group exercise became an annual event with the service users putting away money every week towards it. In addition, to raise funds for the trip and to support communities to understand the mental health services better, we held open days which raised funds for the holidays by selling the produce created by service users. Without knowing it, I led a process, now known as co-production and applied CHIME to those I supported so that they increased their connections, created a sense of hope, had meaning and purpose in life and in remembering who they are in order to take control over their lives.

On another occasion, I was working on finding community supports for those I was working with. One such support I found was GROW[5] – a community peer support group for those experiencing mental health challenges.

I began liaising with GROW to get those I was working with to attend. However, going to a community group outside the day hospital did not work for these individuals. Instead, I organised for GROW to come to the day hospital and establish a group there. Naturally, in the spirit of co-production, when service users attended, so did I. However, after two or three meetings, I noticed that my presence was having a negative impact and as such, I stood back, and from there, the group took off. However, my involvement to this point in GROW made me wonder about the potential support those with lived experience can give to others in mental health discourse.

In a bid to reduce stigma and promote mental health and the power of lived experience, I stepped away from my nursing role to become a Development Officer with Mental Health Ireland[6] – Ireland's longest running mental health charity. Here, I had the flexibility and autonomy to affect change like never before by networking and forming linkages with communities, organisations and individuals. This also involved bringing organisations and people with lived experience together, which led to the creation of many community events, projects and initiatives. In January 2002, I began working as a Resource Officer for Suicide Prevention and Mental Health Promotion with the HSE where again, I like to think I made a lasting, positive impact. One example of impact I remember was in adding mental health to health promotion material at a population level. This led to another layer of knowledge being accumulated on how to work with communities and those with lived experience. It also made me realise that without organisational commitment it is difficult to make consistent and sustainable change to mental health service provision. This did not deter me, as in 2004, I became Director of Mental Health and Addiction Services in the then Southwestern Mental Health Services. Here I learned the business side of healthcare, including understanding where money came from, how it is spent, what services need developing and how to create business proposals and indeed network with other colleagues in the field.

Around this time, national services were on the cusp of change thanks to the then mental health policy document 'A Vision for Change'[7] and now in my new role as a National Specialist in Mental Health Services had the privilege of being a member of the Implementation group for this policy document within the HSE. For the first time, the voice of people with lived experience and their family member/supporter was mentioned in Chapter 3 of the policy. This was the opportunity I was waiting for and working with several mental health organisations, people with lived experience and family members/supporters, the National Service User Executive was born. This independent group brought the voice of lived experience to the table at local and national level. A major shift happened in 2006 when I led a group of interested mental health champions from different backgrounds who wanted to integrate lived experience into local mental health services. This group travelled to Brighton to meet with likeminded people who were already ahead in this journey. The learning accumulated there resulted in the development of the Dublin City University's (DCU) Co-operative Leadership Programme, which involved service users, their family members and service providers attending DCU as a team from a community mental health service in order to work together to understand each other's perspective and then effect change at a local service level. This lined up nicely with Ireland becoming a member of the International Initiative for Mental Health Leadership (IIMHL)[8] (now the Global Leadership Exchange) – a consortium that brings together mental health leaders to help spread innovation and best practice regarding mental health and addiction services. Again, from an organisational commitment perspective becoming a member of IIMHL had to have government sponsorship behind it. What caught my interest in this group was the recognition of both experiences and expertise as characteristics that make you a leader, not a qualification. In 2010, I was proud to project manage the IIMHL Exchange and Conference in Ireland, where 520 delegates globally attended. My first step in this process was to establish a co-production group to co-produce the agenda for the week event. And in keeping to co-production, service users and family members were involved in the process.

In 2012, Dr Julie Repper came to Ireland to discuss ImROC,[9] their ten organisational challenges and recovery education more broadly. What resulted was the transformation of the National Service User Executive into Advancing Recovery in Ireland (ARI).[10] This new pilot initiative was co-led between a senior staff member [me] and a person with lived experience (Michael Ryan). Our first task was to identify services that were interested but also ready to get involved. Seven sites joined and site visits and learning sets to promote recovery commenced. At this stage nothing was happening in ARI without all relevant voices at the table. One co-produced activity was a recovery-training programme specifically to support staff to become recovery orientated. This training, 'Recovery Principles and Practice Workshop', launched in 2017 in Kilkenny where 300 delegates gathered for a National Learning Set. Shortly after this, the first National Framework for Recovery in Mental Health was co-produced and launch by the Minister for Mental Health alongside the National Lead for Mental Health Operations. This framework identified four pillars necessary for services to achieve to become recovery orientated. In June 2018, I left this post to once again join Mental Health Ireland as their National Training and Development Manager where I liaised closely with the HSE to implement the framework, particularly on the recovery education stream. This happened just as ARI fused with the Office of Mental Health Engagement to become the Office of Mental Health Engagement and Recovery (MHER).

In 2020, I became Deputy CEO of Mental Health Ireland. In this role, I strengthened Mental Health Ireland's relationship with MHER, working closely with them to expand the lived experience workforce, particularly within recovery education and family peer support. I also supported the development of the first user-led Community Café. In addition to this, I also became president of Mental Health Europe in May 2021 where I continued to promote recovery and co-production to countries who were earlier in their recovery orientation journey. In December 2023, I retired from Mental Health Ireland to set up my own consultancy business. This allowed me to apply for the position of Chair of the National Implementation and Monitoring Committee – the overarching body responsible for the implementation and monitoring of 'Sharing the Vision'. Today, I am involved in both roles while also working as a Senior Policy Officer for Co-creation with Mental Health Europe. In this role, I continue to utilise my life experiences to reshape mental health services in Ireland, Europe and beyond.

Catherine Brogan's Impact to Healthcare Management as a Female Leader

From the above life experiences of Catherine Brogan, we can how she has impacted healthcare management in her field as a prominent female leader. This, of course, was first shaped by her early life experiences when she comforted another student in her school, through to a curiosity driven willingness to listen and ultimately involve those she saw as people (not just patients) in their own development and care. In so doing, she demonstrated a willingness to step outside the status quo, to risk and to innovate. She was willing to move beyond the constraints of the biomedical model and convention, as demonstrated when dealing with those with psychosis where she actively enquired about their voices to understand them and the person who hosted them. This had the positive side effect of supporting these individuals to express their experiences without fear of stigma to the benefit of their mental well-being. This reflected Catherine's person-centred approach to her practice, which ultimately positively impacted individuals' sense of identity and their overall recovery journey practices that, at the time, would not have been conventional in the care and treatment of those with mental health challenges.

Catherine's desire to involve people in decisions about their lives and their care was novel given the way mental health services operated in Ireland at that time. Indeed, her formative work demonstrated the early use of both co-production and utilising lived experience to support others in recovery: approaches that are now only becoming commonplace in mental health service provision in Ireland, but were unheard of when Catherine first implemented these ideas. Later in Catherine's career she brought these skills into a forum where others could become aware of these approaches and learn to implement them. This started with her involvement in the implementation of 'A Vision for Change' where she was central in implementing Chapter 3 of the policy.

Catherine was and still is a powerhouse when it comes to co-production and the use of lived experience. She was central in bringing the recovery movement to an international audience, with Ireland's involvement with the IIMHL, and when employed with Mental Health Europe (as President and then more recently as a Senior Policy Advisor on Co-Creation). Within Irish services, Catherine's notability as a leader in the field of healthcare management truly came to light when she was chosen to co-lead ARI with Michael Ryan. Her work here involved supporting Irish services in becoming more recovery orientated by harnessing the skills Catherine perfected over a lifetime of experiences – including that of co-production and recovery education. Catherine had and still has a curiosity to explore how lived experience as knowledge can be used to support others in recovery. Through the set-up of recovery colleges within Irish services, Catherine was able to fuse the act of co-production with the equal and mutual involvement of lived experience to showcase how services can do more than treat a mental health challenge but also educate and learn from those that use services for the betterment of the service as a whole. Indeed, her work to date has made her not just a leader in recovery, but in co-production and in the use of lived expertise for the betterment of services.

From Catherine's narrative, a lesson for healthcare management moving forward is the power of co-production to achieving healthcare management goals. Co-production is defined by Norton (2022) as:

> the creation and continuous development of a dialogical space where all stakeholders, including service users, family members, carers, supporters and service providers enter a collaborative partnership with the aim of not only improving their own care but also that of service provision
>
> (p. 27)

The use of co-production at an individual level can lead to a number of benefits including: personal confidence and growth (Salisbury, 2020), the ability to attain an identity that is more meaningful than that of the passive service user and recognition that a person's lived experience as knowledge can be used to provide meaning and purpose in one's life. At an organisational level, working in co-production is also of benefit to the healthcare organisation. Within an Irish context, working in co-production is a mechanism by which the regulatory and policy goals placed on the organisation are realised (Batalden et al., 2016). In addition, working in co-production means that there is a stronger likelihood of adherence to treatment modalities thus enhancing safety within therapeutic environments (Bamber, n.d.; Norton and Swords, 2021). This is noted in Catherine's narrative on numerous occasions including when enquiring about the psychiatric symptoms experienced by individuals with psychosis. By understanding these experiences, Catherine enhanced meaning-making for these individuals, and with this insight came mechanisms to understanding distress rather than mitigating risks associated with such distress, e.g. physical restraint.

Despite these various advantages of co-production at both an individual and organisational level, co-production also has challenges including the organisational culture of the mental health services (Dalgarno and Oates, 2018; Boyle, 2019; Norton, 2022). Mental health services are based on an evidence-based model that is centred around getting tasks done on time and only basing interventions on high-quality evidence. Co-production is inherently messy. It involves numerous stakeholders, knowledge-sets and a copious amount of time for it to be utilised properly. In today's mental health services, utilising co-production authentically can be difficult, with many opting to utilise lower levels of participation instead. However, as is evident by Catherine's narrative, when someone takes the time to listen empathically to your story and really values your input, then true transformation can occur leading to a lasting impact not just on the individual, but also the services at large (Norton and Swords, 2021). Within Irish mental health services, co-production is a recognised mechanism used to change the organisation to one that emphasises personal recovery (HSE, 2024).

Catherine's gender has also had a massive role in the way she continues to lead organisations towards recovery-orientation. Due to Catherine's gender, she entered the nursing profession where she instigated the changes noted above to the betterment of both the organisation and the services she worked for. Being a woman allowed her to take a more compassionate approach to interacting with individuals in her care. In this way, her gender caused Catherine to view issues differently and from which, she identified, when no one else did, that working together was the best way to instigate and sustain organisational change within mental health services. In addition, her caring and empathetic ear, granted to her from training and her way of being, allowed her to identify the hidden knowledge individuals possess from having a lived experience of mental health difficulties. An example of this is through her conversations with individuals with psychosis where, instead of viewing psychosis as a debilitating life-long disease with a poor prognosis, Catherine, through her life experiences, saw it as a source of knowledge that if carefully utilised, can increase the sense of safety within a number of different acute and community environments.

Because of her gender, at the tender age of 12, it was assumed that she had a caring component to her identity and, as such, was instructed by a nun to support an older student in distress. If Catherine were a male, this would have been far less likely to happen. In addition, the career choices that Catherine took were shaped by her gender, particularly her nursing career and her health promotion experiences with numerous non-governmental organisations. Despite well-acknowledged barriers that women and female nurses face, Catherine climbed the ladder to what is now a prominent advocacy and leadership position within the spaces of co-production, recovery, lived experience and organisational cultural change. Her experiences as a women have shaped her style of work in order to become a more compassionate, thoughtful and empathetic leader in the arena of mental health – something that is often lacking in modern organisational and leadership contexts.

Notes

1 The name of the Irish statutory health service that supports individuals regarding their physical, mental and intellectual health needs.
2 An examination that takes place between primary school and leaving cert that helps identify areas of improvement for the leaving cert. It is now called the Junior Cert.
3 Essentially a nursing home.
4 Now known as a healthcare assistant.
5 Grow, https://grow.ie/
6 Mental Health Ireland, https://www.mentalhealthireland.ie/
7 A Vision for Change, https://www.hse.ie/eng/services/publications/mental-health/mental-health-a-vision-for-change.pdf
8 International Initiative for Mental Health Leadership, https://www.iimhl.com/homepage
9 Implementing Recovery Through Organisational Change, https://www.imroc.org/
10 Advancing Recovery in Ireland, https://www.hse.ie/eng/services/list/4/mental-health-services/advancingrecoveryireland/

References

Anthony, W.A. (1993) Recovery from mental illness: The guiding vision of the mental health service system in the 1990s. *Psychosocial Rehabilitation Journal 16*(4), 11–23. doi: https://doi.org/10.1037/h0095655.

Austin, S.F., Hjorthoj, C., Baagland, H., Simonsen, E. & Dam, J. (2021) Investigating personal and clinical recovery processes in people with first episode psychosis. *Early Intervention in Psychiatry 16*(10), 1102–1111. doi: https://doi.org/10.1111/eip.13258.

Bamber, H. (n.d.) *'Managers and Clinical Leads' Perspectives of a Co-Production Model for Community Mental Health Service Improvement in the NHS: A Case Study* (Published Professional Doctorate Dissertation), University of Salford.

Batalden, M., Batalden, P., Margolis, P., Seid, M., Armstrong, G., Opipari-Arrigan, L. & Hartung, H. (2016) Co-production of healthcare services. *BMJ Quality and Safety 25*, 509–517.

Boyle, R. (2019) *The Magic of Co-Production in the Making of a Norwegian Recovery College: A Qualitative Case Study* (Masters Dissertation), NLA University College, Bergen, Norway.

Chang, H. (2016) *Autoethnography as Method*. Routledge, Oxon, United Kingdom.

Dalgarno, M. & Oates, J. (2018) The meaning of co-production for clinicians: An exploratory case study of practitioner trainers in one recovery college. *Journal of Psychiatric and Mental Health Nursing 25*(5–6), 349–357. doi: https://doi.org/10.1111/jpm.12469.

Department of Health. (2020) *Sharing the Vision: A Mental Health Policy for Everyone*. https://www.lenus.ie/bitstream/handle/10147/633416/76770_b142b216-f2ca-48e6-a551-79c208f1a247%281%29.pdf?sequence=1&isAllowed=y.

Health Service Executive. (2023) *Mental Health Engagement and Recovery Office Strategic Plan 2023–2026: Engaged in Recovery*. https://www.hse.ie/eng/services/list/4/mental-health-services/mental-health-engagement-and-recovery/mher-strategic-plan-engaged-in-recovery.pdf.

Health Service Executive. (2024) *A National Framework for Recovery in Mental Health 2024–2028*. https://www.hse.ie/eng/services/list/4/mental-health-services/mental-health-engagement-and-recovery/resources-information-and-publications/a-national-framework-for-recovery-in-mental-health.pdf.

Leamy, M., Bird, V., Le Boutillier, C., Williams, J. & Slade, M. (2011) Conceptual framework for personal recovery in mental health: Systematic review and narrative synthesis. *The British Journal of Psychiatry 199*(6), 445–452. doi: https://doi.org/10.1192/bjp.bp.110.083733.

Norton, M.J. (2022) *Co-Production in Mental Health: Implementing Policy into Practice*. Routledge, Abingdon, United Kingdom.

Norton, M.J. (2024) Recovery education through the pandemic: The use of artificial intelligence to create an adaptive learning environment. In: M. Ibrahim, M. Aydogmus & Y. Tukel (Eds.) *AI in Education: New Trends and Promising Directions in Modern Education*. (pp. 195–214). Palet Yayinlari.

Norton, M.J. & Cullen, O.J. (2024) Recovery in mental health, addiction and dual diagnosis. In: M.J. Norton & O.J. Cullen (Eds.) *Different Diagnoses, Similar Experiences: Narratives of Mental Health, Addiction Recovery and Dual Diagnosis* (pp. 35–41). Emerald Publishing Limited.

Norton, M.J. & Cuskelly, K. (2021) Family recovery interventions with families of mental health service users: A systematic review of the literature. *International Journal of Environmental Research and Public Health 18*, 7858. doi: https://doi.org/10.3390/ijerph18157858.

Norton, M.J. & McLaughlin, M. (2022) Fusion of clinical and lived experiences of psychosis: Lessons learned and implications for future clinical teaching. *Psychiatry International 3*, 286–296. https://doi.org/10.3390/psychiatryint3040023.

Norton, M.J. & Swords, C. (2021) Creating equality for those in crisis: Transforming acute inpatient mental health services through co-production. *Academic Quarter 23*, 64–79. doi: https://doi.org/10.5278/academicquarter.vi23.7029.

O'Keeffe, D., Sheridan, A., Kelly, A., Doyle, R., Madigan, K., Lawlor, E. & Clarke, M. (2021) A qualitative study exploring personal recovery meaning and the potential influence of clinical recovery status on this meaning 20 years after a first-episode psychosis. *Social Psychiatry and Psychiatric Epidemiology 57*, 473–483. doi: https://doi.org/10.1007/s00127-021-02121-w.

Ramon, S. (2018) The place of social recovery in mental health and related services. *International Journal of Environmental Research and Public Health 15*(6), 1052. doi: https://doi.org/10.3390/ijerph15061052.
Salisbury, C. (2020) *Using Co-Production in Interventions to Reduce Health Inequality: A Qualitative Study of Process and Impact* (Published PhD Dissertation), University of East London, United Kingdom.
Slade, M. & Longden, E. (2015) Empirical evidence about recovery and mental health. *BMC Psychiatry 15*, 285. doi: https://doi.org/10.1186/s12888-015-0678-4.
Swords, C. & Norton, M.J. (2020) Is sharing really caring? A vision or an aspiration? Ireland's new mental health policy 2020. *Irish Journal of Psychological Medicine*. doi: https://doi.org/10.1017/ipm.2020.118.
Swords, C. & Norton, M.J. (2023) Individual recovery or collective recovery? Do we really consider both in current Irish mental health policy and provision? *Irish Journal of Psychological Medicine*. doi: https://doi.org/10.1017/ipm.2023.25.
Zierotin, A., Norton, M.J., O'Donoghue, B., O'Connor, K. & Clarke, M. (2025) Physical health in psychosis: A perspective on the recovery paradigm. *Irish Journal of Psychological Medicine*. doi: https://doi.org/10.1017/ipm.2025.1.

9 Ann Beckett

A Pioneering Irish Occupational Therapist

Judith Pettigrew, Mairead Cahill and Jennifer O'Mahoney

Introduction

> Occupational therapists like to pride themselves on their self reliance, lateral thinking, intuition, ability to work in extreme circumstances and a facility to relate to all sorts of people in all sorts of places.
>
> If ever there was a therapist who embodied all these abilities it must be Ann Beckett.
>
> (Patterson, 1992)

So began a biographical piece in the *Irish Journal of Occupational Therapy* based on an interview with Ann Beckett (1927–2002), the first diploma-qualified occupational therapist to practice in Ireland.[1] Through her clinical work, her role as a manager, an educator and as one of the founders of the Association of Occupational Therapists of Ireland, Beckett played a key role in establishing the profession of occupational therapy in Ireland (Figure 9.1).

This chapter analyses her career focusing, in particular, on her role as a manager and educator. It builds on O'Mahoney's (2015) work highlighting the influence of Dr Elizabeth Casson on Beckett, who founded the first school of Occupational Therapy in the UK – Dorset House – which Beckett attended. Casson was strongly influenced by social reformer Octavia Hill, who worked as a housing manager and organiser of recreational activities focusing on the arts before studying medicine. Although the influence of social reformers and the Arts and Crafts movement on the profession of occupational therapy, and particularly its American founders (Wilcock, 2002), has been widely recognised, this chapter highlights for the first time the direct influence of the social reform movement on Irish occupational therapy through the influence of Casson on Beckett.[2]

The chapter begins with a biographical section introducing Beckett's family background and childhood. This is followed by a section on her introduction to occupational therapy and subsequent training at Dorset House. In 1948, Beckett returned to Ireland to develop occupational therapy and

DOI: 10.4324/9781003546610-9

Figure 9.1. Ann Beckett
Copyright: Ann Beckett Committee

worked in several Dublin hospitals and clinics as a therapist and a manager. The chapter concludes by addressing her role as an educator and founding member of the Association of Occupational Therapists of Ireland. Ann Beckett is revered in Irish occupational therapy and the profession's most prestigious award is named after her. However, her work in the broader field of rehabilitation in Ireland, especially in the field of adaptive equipment and assistive technology, has been overlooked, and some of the reasons for this are considered.

Biography

The Becketts (originally named Becquet) were of Huguenot descent, suggesting that they moved from France to Ireland for economic and religious freedom in the 18th century (Lee, 2009). As they became respected members of the Protestant business community, they moved from the linen industry into the construction and building trades (Bair, 1990). Ann Beckett's grandfather, William Frank Beckett, and his brother became master builders constructing several civic buildings in Dublin including the National Library of Ireland and the National Museum (Knowlson, 2004). By the mid-19th century, the family had their own crest with *Prodesse Civibus* ('Serve the Citizens') as its motto (Knowlson, 2004). Ann Beckett's uncle, James, followed the family business and built the cottages on Gerald Street in Dublin which, it is thought, he named after his brother, her father, Gerald Beckett (Bunbury, 2009). Her father read medicine at Trinity College Dublin and after practising abroad returned to Ireland. He was known for his wide variety of interests and was capped for Ireland in rugby and water polo. He also enjoyed music and played the piano with his nephew, the writer, Samuel Beckett (Bair, 1990). Her mother, Margaret (Peggy) Robinson Collen, was born in Portadown, Co. Armagh, and was a member of a noted family of builders from Northern Ireland.

Childhood

Ann Beckett and her twin brother John were born on 5 February 1927 in Sandyford, Co Dublin. In 1930, her father was appointed Medical Officer of Health for County Wicklow and in 1933 the family moved to Greystones, County Wicklow (O'Mahoney, 2015). Her childhood home was in the progressive Burnaby Estate, the first of its kind in Ireland, built in the style of the Arts and Craft Movement (Howard, 1965). Beckett attended Alexandra College private school, the first educational establishment for women in Ireland that aspired to university education for its pupils (O'Connor and Parkes, 1983). Though she enjoyed school, she was happier exploring the Wicklow countryside than engaging in academic work (Patterson, 1992). She often accompanied her father on his countywide calls which may have helped shape her positive relationships with medical professionals later in her career. When she was 10 years of age, Beckett got a painful infection in her leg which required surgical intervention. Her lower leg was amputated when she was 14, which she saw as an overwhelmingly positive experience. A participant in O'Mahoney's study for her master's thesis on Beckett recalls that 'she would always maintain that she was so pleased that her parents made the decision, and that really her life took off after that' (O'Mahoney, 2015). Beckett's experience of physical challenge and her capacity to transcend the resulting physical limitations had an impact on her as an occupational therapist. She explained 'It gave me the ability to have an understanding of people with a disfiguration, it has never held me back' (Patterson, 1992).

Introduction to Occupational Therapy

Though the profession of occupational therapy – founded in the United States (US) in 1917 and started in the UK in the 1920s – was in its early days, entering the caring professions was strongly promoted within the Protestant liberal tradition and led by medical men like Beckett's father (Fealy, 2004). Beckett's career choice was also influenced by World War II as she and a friend saw a magazine article showing photographs of ex-servicemen being treated by an occupational therapist and thought 'this is for us!' (Patterson, 1992).

Beckett started training at Dorset House School of Occupational Therapy in Bromsgrove, Worcestershire in 1945. Dorset House was established by Elizabeth Casson, a psychiatrist, who had encountered occupational therapy on a visit to the US. There was a strong communal ethos at Dorset House and individuals were encouraged to feel useful and worthwhile. According to Wilcock (2002) the communal nature:

> seemed to draw upon and epitomize the communal Utopias that were conceptualized in nineteenth century philosophy and social activism . . . It seemed to have much in common with the ideology and action associated with the Settlement movement, in both England and the USA, which found a central place for people of different persuasions, social standing and capacities to share resources and grow, helping each other in many ways
>
> (Wilcock, 2002, p. 124)

Casson emphasised that there were no professional or social distinctions between members of staff and there was a strong participatory ethos in the School. In her highly participatory, inclusive and egalitarian approach these influences are clearly reflected in Ann Beckett's later work as a therapist, manager and educator.

The Dorset House course was three years long, a third of which was spent acquiring and practising clinical skills (Wallis, 1987). The programme was both academic and practical. The first year was spent intensively learning craft activities which at the time was the main occupational therapy treatment medium. In 1946, Beckett's second year of training, Dorset House moved into premises on the grounds of the Churchill Hospital, Oxford – a former Emergency Medical Service hospital and later an Italian Prisoners of War Camp (Jones, 2013).

The course allowed students to choose to practice in either psychiatric occupational therapy or occupational therapy applied to physical conditions after their second year (unlike contemporary programmes, which require practice in both areas). Beckett had negative experiences in psychiatric hospitals. She found some of the practices of the time disturbing including electroconvulsive therapy[3] and insulin treatments[4] which she assisted at. Pre-frontal leucotomies were also performed. She stated that 'The psychiatric frightened the life out of me' (Patterson, 1992). This was in contrast to her experiences in physical rehabilitation, which she enjoyed and which she chose to specialise in for her final year.

Return to Ireland

Beckett always planned to return to Ireland and pioneer occupational therapy. She came from a background which encouraged this – both of her brothers pioneered their professions. Her twin John S. Beckett became a composer and musician who was innovative in the realm of early music in Ireland (Gannon, 2016) and her older brother Peter G.S. Beckett became a pioneer figure in Irish psychiatry who was appointed the first Professor of Psychiatry in Trinity College, Dublin and later became the Dean of the School of Medicine in Trinity (Webb, 2012). Her first cousin Samuel Beckett was an extremely successful avant-garde novelist, playwright, theatre director and poet (Knowlson, 2004).

On her return to Ireland in 1948 Beckett had an interview with the Minister for Health Noel Browne to discuss opportunities for occupational therapy in the health service. While Browne was aware of the occupational therapists' role, he could not see any openings for her as there were already occupational therapists employed in the health service who were either nurses (who had trained on short courses or on the job) or former tuberculosis (TB) patients (Patterson, 1992). TB is an airborne infectious disease caused by Mycobacterium tuberculosis and the ninth leading cause of death globally (Sweeney et al., 2019). It primarily affects the lungs, especially in children or immunocompromised individuals, but remains dormant in most infected people (Hershkovitz et al., 2008). In Ireland, TB mortality was high in the late 1800s and early 1900s, peaking in 1904, unlike in Scotland and England, where rates were declining (Jones, 2001). It remained a leading cause of death until the 1940s but aligned with European rates by the 1950s (Jones, 2001; Sweeney et al., 2019).

Occupational Therapy Practice and Management

Although deeply disappointed in not getting a post in the health service, Beckett soon got a position with the Irish branch of the British Red Cross, making her the first diploma educated occupational therapist to work in Ireland (Pettigrew et al., 2017). Here she set up a workshop for returning ex-servicemen many of whom had contacted TB while serving on the Atlantic Convoys (Patterson, 1992). She was particularly successful at integrating the ostracised TB patients into the workshop and facilitated many ex-servicemen to return home. Beckett felt that this job – in which she stayed for six years – taught her more than anything she had learned in college and in particular how to get on with people and manage a large caseload. At the height of the polio epidemic Beckett was appointed to set up an occupational therapy department within a rehabilitation unit at Cherry Orchard Hospital in Dublin. Here she worked on the wards without inoculation and encountered her first piece of environmental control equipment when working with patients in iron lungs (Patterson, 1992). This started her passion for using electronic equipment to facilitate patients to manage their everyday lives and environment.

In 1956, Beckett moved to the Central Remedial Clinic (CRC). She was given a very small department in the basement and worked hard to get accepted by the physiotherapists who 'started by feeling OT [occupational therapy] had nothing to do with what they were trying to achieve and ended by seeing it had everything to do with it' (Patterson, 1992). Beckett deemphasised the role of crafts which was already waning in the profession. While many occupational therapists still used crafts as treatment during the 1940s and 1950s the field faced growing demands from medicine to adopt a more objective approach and establish an empirical foundation for its interventions (Duncan, 2020). Beckett focused on clients – instead on facilitating – to manage their activities of daily living and with her emphasis on the importance of electronic equipment she brought in electric typewriters and an electric wheelchair. She considered herself fortunate to have worked with the medical director Dr Kieran Barry, who hugely supported occupational therapy.

Ann Beckett introduced many changes during her time at the CRC including starting a sheltered workshop with light and heavy occupational therapy workshops, a three-week vocational assessment and a vocational rehabilitation unit. When the CRC moved to its new purpose-built premises in Clontarf, she established a new occupational therapy department with a kitchen and activities of daily living area and a seating clinic, using the heavy workshop to design, alter and adapt wheelchairs. She also played a mentorship role in setting up an aids and appliances facility with the National Rehabilitation Board and encouraged the development of a paediatric service.

Colleagues, students and clients remember Beckett as a warm and humorous person, who truly enjoyed interacting with a diverse range of people. An interviewee in O'Mahoney's study stated, 'I would say her main passion of course is people, she just loved people'. As a manager, Beckett followed the approach that Casson, had set in seeing the Clinic as a place where everyone felt 'valued and valuable' (Wilcock, 1999). Under her management staff, students and clients used first names, shared break times and socialised together. The client–therapist relationship was also facilitated by her amputation and she would talk openly about her prosthetic leg as her 'woodner'. Beckett's approach embodied client-centredness, shared decision-making, collaboration and empowerment. By sharing her own experiences to build trust and engaging with clients as equals, Beckett, like other occupational therapists of the time, reflected what we now recognise as a collective-based model of health and social care. Beckett stated that she 'didn't really think about the personality' of those she worked with (Patterson, 1992). Instead, she saw herself as focusing on practical solutions to physical problems. This, however, seems at odds with the view of those who worked with her. One of O'Mahoney's interviewees recalled that she was 'very aware of social dynamics in her dealing with people actually, very clued into that more emotional side'. Another, a former patient, describes meeting her in the CRC 'I wouldn't have had really good confidence . . . she did it in a nice way and a kind way, you know, and encouraged you'.

The extended Beckett family were known to have diverse and well-rounded interests. A friend of Samuel Beckett's, the writer A.J. Leventhal, stated that 'all the Beckett's can either sing or swim' (Knowlson, 2004). Ann Beckett had a wide variety of interests including swimming, music, gardening, woodwork and bird watching. She made every effort to find similarly enriching activities for her clients. She developed workshops around meaningful activities including printing, compositing, mechanics, woodwork, finishing and painting, typing and crafts. A former colleague interviewed by O'Mahoney remembers Beckett's intervention with a client who loved woodwork – she had him make his own bath-board, a 'work of art, or a work of woodwork' – making his engagement 'meaningful and acceptable to him' (O'Mahoney, 2015).

Beckett saw the occupational therapist and client relationship as a dual relationship, with each learning from the other, which enabled 'both to achieve together what neither could achieve alone' (Glyn Owens, 1955, p. 95). Later in her life she worried that the client–therapist relationship did not play as central a role as previously. Talking in 1992, she said, 'They [occupational therapists] are not having that lovely spark of relationship with one client to develop some particular part of their lives' (Patterson, 1992). The client–therapist relationship being diminished may result from changes in the Irish health service in the previous decade, which had become increasingly target-driven and resource-constrained (Wiley, 2005).

Beckett's own experience with illness and amputation shaped the way she viewed her clients' abilities: she saw her amputation as having a positive effect on her life and her career (O'Mahoney, 2015). She saw the problems of disability as challenges which could be overcome. For example, while working in the CRC she encountered a man who had lost fingers and had difficulties with his speech. He had been a carpenter. A participant in O'Mahoney's study recalled that Beckett spotting his talent 'negotiated that he would be part of that department [occupational therapy] and he was . . . for many, many years' (O'Mahoney, 2015). He devised a measuring chair for children and made and finished equipment to a high standard. A former client explained how Beckett's belief in her ability impacted her life and led her to employment in the CRC administration. It later led to her subsequent involvement in advocating for the rights of people with disabilities (O'Mahoney, 2015).

Central to occupational therapy is an 'optimistic faith in the potential of every individual to grow, change, and move toward purposefulness' (Yerxa, 1979). Professor Chris Mayers, a colleague of Ann Beckett's at St Joseph's

College of Occupational Therapy described Beckett as someone who epitomised optimistic faith:

> Ann sat down with her clients, who became her friends, and problem-solved with them; regardless of how severe the dysfunction was, she majored on the abilities of these people and motivated them
>
> (Mayers, 2000)

Beckett's belief extended to students who had placements with and were taught by her. She was hugely encouraging of younger staff and students, bringing new knowledge to the occupational therapy department. Former students remember her faith in their ability and in the profession as a significant learning experience which solidified their belief in occupational therapy. Referring to the CRC a former student recalled:

> We loved going there am . . . because Ms. Beckett was the leading lady and she was always on the floor and full of enthusiasm and she made you feel very involved. . . . if a wheelchair was given to her . . . she had an artificial limb you know and she'd give it a kick with her wooden limb and set it back into place you know. Nothing was a problem to her . . . she had an amazing personality which counts for a lot you know . . . I loved working with her you know. She quickly made-up her mind too about you, what made you tick and she sort of filled you in . . . She got you going. You were very fulfilled and you felt important and your morale was high . . . I had to repeat a physical exam for my finals and it was back to her, I was lucky I came back to her and she brushed me up completely, what I needed
>
> (Pat Murray, 2014 personal correspondence with Brid Dunne and co-author Judith Pettigrew)

Ann Beckett has been described as having a 'love affair' with gadgets, which she felt she inherited from her grandfather (Patterson, 1992). This was supplemented by the in-depth craft training she got in Dorset House, which she said was 'as good as a carpenter' (Patterson, 1992). Beckett brought these skills to occupational therapy by making and designing her own assistive devices. One of O'Mahoney's (2015) participants described her as 'almost like an inventor as well, she would invent things that were custom made – she used springs to help a client use the typewriter, hooks to help a man who'd lost his fingers' (O'Mahoney, 2015). The devices she made were of high quality – one participant remembered calling to the Polio Fellowship, after Beckett had retired, where 'there were little touches of Ann around the place – there was a grab-rail she'd made from the branch of a tree . . . beautifully finished and varnished and I just thought what a lovely touch, very homely'. Beckett's adoption of early assistive technology included powered wheelchairs which resulted in setting up a wheelchair and seating service and computers. She was also instrumental in a mentorship role in the development of a service displaying early technology pieces such as a through-floor lift, beds and special commodes, she also gave demonstrations on national television highlighting the role that adaptive equipment can play in enhancing people's lives.

After 16 years, Beckett found her time more and more taken up by administration which gave her less time to work with clients, staff and students, and decided to leave. On the day she left in 1974, she was presented with a car, in appreciation of the outstanding contribution she made to the CRC.

Educator

Beckett subsequently went on to work at St Joseph's College of Occupational Therapy, Dun Laoghaire. The curriculum at that time required the students to learn a large number of activities and Beckett's brief was to teach some of these practical classes including printing, activities of daily living, woodwork, gardening and music (Patterson, 1992). She initially found teaching terrifying but enjoyed it when she settled in. As an educator she was endlessly enthusiastic, knowledgeable and innovative. She had excellent relations with students and was approachable, engaging and encouraging. She taught the first author who remembers her talking through ideas for innovations, not all of which were successful including the design for an adapted semi-standing toilet which Beckett disappointedly admitted would not work due to the anatomy of the bowel.

Founding and Leading the Association of Occupational Therapists of Ireland

Gaining 'professional and scientific authority' (Peters, 2011, p. 199) and marketing the profession was a priority for occupational therapy from 1950 to 1980. While the development of occupational therapy in Ireland was shaped by specific political, institutional and social contexts the process of professionalisation and the strategies used to achieve it were like those used in the USA, Canada and the UK (Quiroga, 1995; Wilcock, 2002; Friedland, 2011). One of the most important strategies was one that Beckett was at the heart of – the founding of a professional association. In 1965, Beckett and four others founded the Irish Association of Occupational Therapists. Drawing on her managerial and organisational skills, she co-wrote the constitution along with fellow founder Sister Eugene Butler. When the Association attempted to join the World Federation of Occupational Therapists (WFOT) in 1967, they asked their solicitor to form a limited liability company. He 'returned to Council with the unexpected news that there was

ALREADY a company registered as the "Irish Association of OTs". This caused consternation among the qualified OTs' (AOTI, 2015). The association had been founded by nurses and craftworkers who worked in occupational therapy predominantly in psychiatric hospitals. Beckett was at the forefront of the negotiations with the rival association and recalled that 'For several years there was a lot of hassle which caused unpleasantness' (Beckett paraphrased in Patterson, 1992). Eventually Beckett and her colleagues abandoned the name and registered as the Association of Occupational Therapists of Ireland (AOTI) (Cahill and Pettigrew, 2020). AOTI was admitted to WFOT in 1970.

Understanding the importance of a professional association to the future development of occupational therapy in Ireland, Beckett promoted the Association to students and colleagues. A former student recalled that she was 'very central to encouraging that development with us' (O'Mahoney, 2015). Drawing on her early computer skills she also set up the first database of AOTI members.

After her retirement in 1991 Beckett continued working for charities and institutions including the Open Door Day Centre in Bray, Co. Wicklow, the Cerebral Palsy Clinic in Sandymount, Dublin and the Sue Ryder Foundation, Dalkey, Dublin. Following her death in 2002, the Ann Beckett Award was set up by a group of her colleagues with the purpose of celebrating her life and work and showcasing occupational therapists practical occupation based interventions. It is not an academic award; however, true to the core themes of Beckett's work as an occupational therapist, the Committee 'look for practical projects which showcase active engagement in meaningful activity, and demonstrate creative ideas which involve clients and inspire colleagues'. Epitomising Beckett's love of nature, the award is a sculpture of 11 birds in flight.

However, Beckett's national-level role in developing and championing adaptive equipment and assistive technology has not been well recognised (although a medical equipment provider does sponsor the award named after her). Beckett was at the tail end of an era when occupational therapists handmade adaptive equipment for their clients. By the 1970s and increasingly afterwards, this equipment was commercially made and marketed by a growing number of medical equipment providers. The making of adaptive equipment is seen by contemporary occupational therapists as a somewhat surprising and perhaps quaint relic of a bygone era. Ann Beckett's expertise in this area, however, was exceptional and combined with her innovativeness she played a significant and championing role in the early development of adaptive equipment and assistive technology in Ireland. Due to timing and the rapid commercialisation of the sector, Ann Beckett's individual client-centred approach and her membership in a small, low-profile predominantly female profession, her national achievements are not as recognised as they deserve.

Conclusion

Ann Beckett's pioneering work strongly influenced the development of occupational therapy in the Republic of Ireland. As the first diploma-qualified occupational therapist in the country, she was pivotal in establishing and promoting the profession through her clinical practice and roles as a manager, educator and founder of the Association of Occupational Therapists of Ireland. Her professional relationships and management style were influenced by Elizabeth Casson, who, in turn, was influenced by the social reform movement and by her work with Octavia Hill. There was a strong communal and participatory ethos in Casson's Dorset House, and this is reflected in Ann Beckett's approach to her work as a manager, clinician and educator.

Wilcock writing in 2002 suggested that Casson's approach (and therefore Beckett's):

> points the way for occupational therapists to embrace, once more, a participatory model of learning and to work towards overcoming the constraints and difficulties of the consultative model of practice which is in vogue. This latter model is imposed largely by managerial, economic, rationalist philosophies of life, and the current approach of medical science.

In her critique of the 1990s' practice and the client–therapist relationship Beckett expressed concerns similar to Wilcock's. In the intervening years, occupational therapists have looked to the founding era for inspiration; although the consultative model remains the development of the social science–orientated theoretical discipline of occupational science, a range of person-centred models of practice herald a more participatory approach. These approaches are in keeping with Beckett's emphasising the importance of innovation, inclusivity and collaboration in occupational therapy practice and management.

Notes

1 Occupational therapy intervention uses everyday life activities (occupations) to promote health, well-being and people's ability to participate in the important activities of their lives. This includes any meaningful activity that a person wants to accomplish, including taking care of themselves and their family, working, volunteering and going to school, among many others (adapted from American Occupational Therapy Association, https://www.aota.org/about/what-is-ot).

2 The foundation of occupational therapy was informed by diverse movements which included Moral Treatment, Mental Hygiene, the Arts and Crafts movement, the Settlement House movement, and the need to rehabilitate injured World War I soldiers (Wilcock, 2002). Occupational therapy was officially named in 1917 in Clifton Springs, New York, USA, when the National Society for the Promotion of Occupational Therapy (NSPOT) (subsequently the American Occupational Therapy Association in 1923) was formed (Quiroga, 1995).

3 While the precise mechanism of action is not fully understood, electroconvulsive therapy functions by using electrical stimulation to trigger seizure activity in the brain's frontal lobes (Ruffalo, 2018). In the 1940s, when Beckett would have encountered electroconvulsive therapy, it was typically administered without anaesthesia or muscle relaxants, leading to full-body convulsions. There was a risk of physical injury from the jerking during the seizure (Kelly, 2023).
4 Pioneered by Austrian psychiatrist Manfred Sakel in 1933, insulin coma therapy involved giving insulin to people with schizophrenia. It was widely adopted in Europe and North America and promoted by government public health authorities. It was used until the early 1960s (Freudenthal and Moncrieff, 2022).

References

Association of Occupational Therapists of Ireland. (2015) *The AOTI archives*. Association of Occupational Therapists of Ireland, July.

Bair, D. (1990) *Samuel Beckett: A biography*. Simon and Schuster.

Bunbury, T. (2009) *Dublin Docklands – an urban voyage*. Dublin Docklands Development Authority.

Cahill, R., & Pettigrew, J. (2020) 'Development of occupational therapy in Grangegorman hospital, Dublin: 1934–1954'. *Irish Journal of Occupational Therapy*, 48(1), pp. 69–87.

Duncan, E. (2020). *Foundations for practice in occupational therapy*. 6th ed. Elsevier.

Fealy, G. M. (2004) '"The good nurse": Visions and values in images of the nurse'. *Journal of Advanced Nursing*, 46(6), pp. 649–656.

Freudenthal, R., & Moncrieff, J. (2022) '"A landmark in psychiatric progress"? The role of evidence in the rise and fall of insulin coma therapy'. *History of Psychiatry*, 33(1), pp. 65–78.

Friedland, J. (2011) *Restoring the spirit: The beginnings of occupational therapy in Canada, 1890–1930*. McGill-Queen's Press-MQUP.

Gannon, C. (2016) *John S. Beckett, the man and the music*. Lilliput Press.

Glyn Owens, C. (1955) 'Recollections 1925–33'. *Occupational Therapy*, 18, pp. 95–97.

Hershkovitz, I., Donoghue, H. D., Minnikin, D. E., Besra, G. S., Lee, O. Y., Gernaey, A. M., Galili, E., Eshed, V., Greenblatt, C. L., Lemma, E., Bar-Gal, G. K., & Spigelman, M. (2008) 'Detection and molecular characterization of 9000-year-old mycobacterium tuberculosis from a Neolithic settlement in the Eastern Mediterranean'. *PLoS One*, 3(10), p. e3426.

Howard, E. (1965) *Garden cities of to-morrow*. MIT Press.

Jones, G. (2001) *'Captain of all these men of death': The history of tuberculosis in nineteenth and twentieth century Ireland* (No. 62). Rodopi.

Jones, W. L. (2013) *Ministering to minds diseased: A history of psychiatric treatment*. Elsevier.

Kelly, B. D. (2023) *Asylum: Inside Grangegorman*. Royal Irish Academy.

Knowlson, J. (2004) *Damned to fame: The life of Samuel Beckett*. Grove Press.

Lee, G. L. (2009) *The Huguenot settlements in Ireland*. Heritage Books.

Mayers, C. A. (2000) 'The Casson memorial lecture 2000: Reflect on the past to shape the future'. *The British Journal of Occupational Therapy*, 63(8), pp. 358–366.

O'Connor, A. V., & Parkes, S. M. (1983) *Gladly learn and gladly teach: A history of Alexandra college and school, Dublin, 1866–1966*. Dublin: Blackwater Press.

O'Mahoney, J. (2015) *'Ann Beckett': A passion for people. An analysis of the contribution of an occupational therapy pioneer* [Masters thesis, University of Limerick].

Patterson, M. (1992) 'Ann Beckett interview'. *Irish Journal of Occupational Therapy*, 22(1), pp. 31–33.
Peters, C. O. (2011) 'Powerful occupational therapists: A community of professionals, 1950–1980'. *Occupational Therapy in Mental Health*, 27(3–4), pp. 199–410.
Pettigrew, J., Robinson, K., Dunne, D., & O' Mahoney, J. (2017) 'Major trends in the use of occupation as therapy in Ireland 1863–1963'. *Irish Journal of Occupational Therapy*, 45(1), pp. 4–14.
Quiroga, V. A. M. (1995) *Occupational therapy: The first 30 years 1900 to 1930*. Bethesda, MD: American Occupational Therapy Association.
Ruffalo, M. L. (2018) 'A brief history of electroconvulsive therapy: The story of a misunderstood but effective treatment'. *Psychology Today*, 3 November.
Sweeney, E., Dahly, D., Seddiq, N., Corcoran, G., Horgan, M., & Sadlier, C. (2019) 'Impact of BCG vaccination on incidence of tuberculosis disease in southern Ireland'. *BMC Infectious Diseases*, 19, pp. 1–5.
Wallis, M. A. (1987) '"Profession" and "professionalism" and the emerging profession of occupational therapy: Part 2'. *The British Journal of Occupational Therapy*, 50(9), pp. 300–302.
Webb, M. (2012) 'Trinity's psychiatrists: From serenity of the soul to neuroscience'. *Irish Journal of Psychological Medicine*, 29(2), p. 136.
Wilcock, A. A. (1999) 'Creating self and shaping the world'. *Australian Occupational Therapy Journal*, 46(3), pp. 77–88.
Wilcock, A. A. (2002) *Occupation for health: A journey from prescription to self health, a history of occupational therapy in the United Kingdom during the twentieth century and a source book of archival material*. British Association and College of Occupational Therapists.
Wiley, M. M. (2005) 'The Irish health system: Developments in strategy, structure, funding and delivery since 1980'. *Health Economics*, 14(S1), pp. S169–S186.
Yerxa, E. (1979) 'The philosophical base of occupational therapy'. *Occupational Therapy: 2001 AD*, pp. 26–30.

10 Morrnah Nalamaku Simeona's Updated Ho'oponopono

Bridging Indigenous Wisdom and Contemporary Health

Eleni Tzouramani

Introduction

Human societies across history and cultures have developed diverse theories and worldviews to explain the interconnectedness of life (Gergen, 2015). These approaches have been developed to help us address key existential questions and influence our shared understanding of the world (Cammell, 2015). In addressing existential questions and shaping our worldviews, we, the whole of humanity, have developed diverse theories and practices on the relational nature of life. Wisdom traditions such as Taoism's interconnectedness of all things and Buddhism's emphasis on the interconnectedness of all phenomena in an illusory world, along with philosophical ideas like Goethe's 'multiplicity in unity' Bortoft (1996) and Gergen's (2009) conceptualisation of the 'relational being' in psychology, collectively contribute to a nuanced understanding of existence. Including Indigenous perspectives that are less widely recognised outside their communities further enriches this spectrum of co-existing realities, offering new possibilities for their advancement.

Few women are acknowledged or mentioned in the history of health (Green, 2008; Martins, 2020) and even fewer in the domains of non-mainstream medicine and alternative healing. I am referring to this chapter's protagonist as Morrnah, using her first name, for several reasons. The first is because this is how she is mostly known rather than with her surname or 'Kahuna' title. The second is to allow for equality and closeness which resonate with her ideas. Finally, this is to honour her dissent from traditional systems of power or hierarchical dynamics.

To provide a clearer understanding of the ways in which these ontologies can be both experienced and practised in the workplace, this chapter is based on qualitative content analysis of material from various workshops which included discussions and applications of Self I-Dentity through Ho'oponopono (SITH®). It also draws on the eight 'Blue Ice Books' (Rafaelovich et al.,

DOI: 10.4324/9781003546610-10

2013a, 2013b, 2013c, 2013d, 2013e, 2013f, 2013g, 2013h), a collection of compiled transcripts and reflections from a radio programme that explored the philosophical basis and practical use of SITH®. The reflections in this chapter are drawn from my personal engagement with the practices and I have also had the privilege to interview Kamailelauli'I Rafaelovich (KR), the president of The Foundation of I, Inc. Freedom of the Cosmos and IZI LLC among other roles. Kamailelauli'I (KR) met Morrnah in 1969 and was present during the years that Morrnah received inspirations from Divinity through meditation which led to the development of the SITH® process (IZI LLC, n.d.). KR collaborated with Morrnah to meditate, refine and publish the SITH® process.

This chapter begins with an exploration of Morrnah's life story, her background as a Hawaiian Kahuna Lapa'au and the influences that shaped her development of the traditional communal practice of Ho'oponopono into a self-directed, inclusive and universally accessible method focused on 'cleaning' subconscious memories as a healing modality. Morrnah's work is then placed within broader debates in healthcare that critique conventional approaches for compartmentalising the body and reducing health to quantifiable metrics. Morrnah's ontology of unity integrates the physical, emotional, relational and spiritual dimensions in healthcare by reframing health as a holistic, interconnected experience. This perspective resonates with patient-centred and interdisciplinary approaches by valuing relational ethics, subjective experience and spiritual well-being. The chapter then explores how Morrnah's approach recognises the role of subconscious memories, relational imbalances and cultural perspectives in health as opposed to treating illness as an isolated physiological dysfunction. By addressing the role of subconscious memories, relational imbalances and sociocultural narratives Morrnah's approach validates Indigenous and other marginalised healing traditions that have been historically dismissed by dominant health discourse. This discussion also looks at the ways in which this approach disrupts hierarchical structures within healthcare by shifting the focus from external authority to shared responsibility and co-creation. This approach also challenges the paternalistic structures in conventional medicine where expertise is revered and patients are passive recipients of health interventions. Morrnah's work focusing on co-creation and shared responsibility helps empower individuals as active agents in their healing process. This is similar to feminist critiques of healthcare, the autonomy and diffused power. Empirical evidence in different therapeutic contexts support the effectiveness of Morrnah's updated Ho'oponopono as a patient-driven intervention. The chapter also explores how Morrnah's work helps move healthcare from monocultural to pluralistic approaches. Historically, Indigenous practices have been marginalised, leading to the exclusion of their diverse knowledge and reinforcing structural inequities within medicine. Morrnah's work, based on an ontology of unity, reframes health beyond physiological measures and through the interconnectedness of individuals, communities and the natural environment. Her efforts to introduce this work to hospitals and universities helped promote more inclusive, culturally responsive approaches. Finally, the chapter reflects on Morrnah's stance towards visibility where despite the worldwide reach of her work, she prioritised the work over self-promotion in consistence with feminist ethics of care that question traditional success narratives. Her legacy reimagines healthcare as a participatory, inclusive and co-creative practice, grounded in an ontology of unity.

Morrnah's Biography

Morrnah Nalamaku Simeona was born in Honolulu on 19 May 1913. From the outset of her life, she was deeply enmeshed in a rich cultural lineage; her mother Lilia was one of the last remaining kahunas of the Hawaiian dynasty and so Morrnah was raised within a worldview where everything is alive and learnt the sacred kahuna practices from a young age. Her upbringing was marked by a tension: on one hand she belonged to a highly regarded family of healers and spiritual leaders, her mother being one of the few remaining Kahuna Lapa'au Kahea and a lady-in-waiting to Queen Lili Uoqailani, the last monarch and only female ruler of the Kindgom of Hawaai (Khalsa, n.d.). On the other hand, Morrnah experienced the disdain of neighbours who would remark, 'There go those Kahunas' (Bowman, 1982). The word 'Kahuna' comes from the combination of the words 'Ka' (light) and 'Huna' (sacred secret, divine wisdom) signifying the kahunas vital role in Hawaiian life as custodians of reconciliation, healing, mediation between the natural and spiritual realms and maintaining balance in the community. Morrnah was recognised at the age of 3 as carrying this living tradition (Khalsa, n.d.). She was trained in La'au Lapa'au (herbal remedies), LomiLomi (Hawaiian healing massage), La'au Kahea (healing chants) and Ho'oponopono (family and community reconciliation). Ho'oponopono means 'to make right', and traditionally it involved a healing session with the entire family facilitated by a moderator, where each family member would ask for forgiveness.

Morrnah is said to have been influenced by attending catholic school, studying Indian philosophy and Taoism as well as reading Edgar Cayce's work (IZI, n.d.). Throughout her life Morrnah worked in various roles, including as a teacher for disabled children, a nurse in the blood bank, a driver and instructor for the American Red Cross and as the owner and operator of health spas, all while keeping her role as a kahuna relatively low key. Her contributions to her community were many and important.

In 1976, at the age of 63, Morrnah began developing an updated version of Ho'oponopono, which primarily involved a 12-step process. According to Kamailelauli'I Rafaelovich (KR), considerable effort and meditation were dedicated to every word and sentence of the prayers. Morrnah did not share this updated practice until 1980. This updated practice is simple and accessible, allowing individuals to use it independently without the need of a moderator or the presence of others. Morrnah said 'it is a matter of going beyond traditional means of accessing knowledge about ourselves' and she developed this version as 'a problem solving method that anyone, young or old, male or female, regardless of religion or race, can practice on their own in the present moment without special help from anyone' (IZI LLC, n.d.).

Despite facing criticism from purists for incorporating Western and other influences, Morrhan's ideas gained widespread recognition. She started giving lectures and her teachings were translated into multiple languages. She run workshops and symposia worldwide and taught the SITH® course at institutions such as the University of Hawaii and Johns Hopkins University. Morrnah also founded Pacifica Seminars (Micklei, 2021) and the Foundation of I (IZI LLC, n.d.). In 1983, at the age of 70, Morrnah was officially recognised a Kahuna Lapa'au and the Hon-pa Hongwanji Mission of Hawaii, with both the Houses of the Legislature honouring her with the title 'Living Treasure of Hawaii' (Infante, 1992; Khalsa, n.d.; Micklei Media, 2021). In the same year, she was invited to speak at a world peace meeting hosted by the United Nations in New York.

Morrnah passed away in Germany on 11 February 1992 at the age of 79. In 1990, Morrnah founded Pacifica Seminars in Germany with two friends with whom she went to live in 1991. During her final year, no classes were held but instead, the three friends travelled over 37,000 miles through the countryside surrounding Munich, where Morrnah was fulfilling her new mission of 'environmental protection on a spiritual scale', purifying the landscapes, rivers, streams and lakes (Micklei Media, 2021, n.d.).

Her passing was marked with a tribute titled 'Ke Ola' or 'Going Home', organised by the Foundation of I in Hawaii followed by a private scattering of ashes, honouring her wishes. Morrnah's obituary was published in the Honolulu Advertiser, where she was remembered as an honoured Hawaiian healer, a living treasure and a pioneer of Ho'oponopono. The article detailed her international teachings, her work across continents and her contributions to healing practices. Her peaceful nature, humility and devotion to helping humanity were emphasised as key aspects of her life and legacy. Morrnah's legacy continues to inspire individuals worldwide, reflecting her dedication to spiritual healing for both people and the planet.

Morrnah's Transformation of Ho'oponopono

The traditional Ho'oponopono process, an ancient Polynesian healing and forgiveness process, includes first acknowledging that everyone is responsible for everyone else's actions, expressing remorse and offering forgiveness to restore harmony and balance. Consequently, Ho'oponopono translates to disentangling or putting things right when resolving interpersonal conflict. Wall and Callister (1995) explain that Hawaiians started using the word 'entanglement' – originally taken from the context of fishing, such as a tangled fishing line or a sea turtle caught in the net – as a metaphor for interpersonal conflict. The 12 steps that Wall and Callister (1995) list for employing Ho'oponopono as a conflict resolution method, include questioning of participants, honest confession to the gods and to each of the disputants, talking about actions for resolution or 'disentanglement' and mutual forgiveness. As a problem solving and reconciliation practice, Ho'oponopono extends to procedural justice and management practice for conflict resolution, teamwork and responsible leadership.

Morrnah's updated version still includes 12 steps, but they are different from the traditional version and no longer require the involvement of the wider family or community. As KR explained in her interview, this update did not start as a deliberate effort to change Ho'oponopono (K. Rafaelovich, personal communication, 8 August 2024). Instead, this new version emerged through meditation. KR described this as a long process of deep work and extensive periods of meditation dedicated to each sentence. She emphasised the importance of maintaining the integrity of these sentences and said that 'every word was a serious commitment because this Self I-Dentity Ho'oponopono process has to be spiritually correct for all identities through all space and time to use' (K. Rafaelovich, personal communication, 8 August 2024). This chapter does not aim to detail the specific processes or various versions of Ho'oponopono; however, it focuses on how Morrnah's ideas and contributions offer an ontology where the entire world fully co-participates and where past present and future are connected. Contributing to this ontology is a perception of time that acknowledges past – including ancestors, present and future. It also includes a perception of wholeness where even a speck of dust participates in life enactment in the moment and a perception of co-creation that acknowledges that our individual and collective responsibility is one and the same.

Morrnah's updated version includes a set of practices and 'cleaning tools'. The long version includes breathwork and prayers for forgiveness and requests for memories to be released, while the shorter version tools have been developed to help one achieve the full process instantaneously. The practice is focused on erasing memories in the subconscious that manifest in our reality as problems until they are released. They can be memories from our own lives, the lives of our ancestors, collective memories embedded in culture or even memories of places and spaces we have visited. Our purpose in life is to clean these memories and keep cleaning. Since this is based in an ontology of unity, as we clean, collective memories are released. This ontology also sees as everything being alive meaning even inorganic things, such as a chair, can hold memories which we can clean using the tools.

At an interview for the Honolulu Advertiser, Morrnah said 'naturally I've become a radical because I am changing a concept' (Bowman, 1982). Morrnah's update challenges separation ontologies where separate, self-contained individuals engaged in an objective process of seeking and offering forgiveness from each other. It even goes beyond ideas of relationality and interconnectedness where interdependent actors would negotiate meanings and forgiveness and where each individual's identity remains separate and influenced or challenged by the interaction. Instead, Morrnah's process does not require any external interaction while at the same time it is not based on a long internal process. It is a process that recognises that the individual and the collective are one.

From Fragmented Bodies to the Whole Person

Explaining concepts of unity is inherently challenging within the acceptable scientific discourse. Max Weber argued that dividing science from religion has led to making them both inadequate and ultimately leading to the disenchantment of the modern world (Weber, 2009). In a well-cited systematic review, de Brito Sena et al. (2021) evaluate evidence for spirituality's significant impact on physical, mental, emotional and social health, suggesting that spirituality deserves more attention in research, clinical practice and the training of health professionals. They make a case for clearer definitions of spirituality to better understand 'which dimensions of spirituality influence more positively health-related endpoints' (p. 2) and provide a framework for this. Their efforts are bound by the limitations of 'acceptable' epistemologies and remind me of what KR told me during the interview: 'I understand your questions, but it's a rational discussion of what's an irrational experience' (K. Rafaelovich, personal communication, 8 August 2024). As long as we rely only on tools developed for positivist scientific analysis, it will be difficult to research what KR mentions here as an 'irrational experience'. Regardless of Descartes' perhaps misunderstood efforts to explain the connection between mind and body (Duncan, 2000), positivist scientism created a split between mind and body leading to both medicine's and social sciences' limitations (Mehta, 2011). Specifically in medicine, clinical practice treated the body in a compartmentalised and objectified way, disregarding the patient's lived experience (Foucault, 2003).

Despite a recent 're-discovery' of preventative methods, herbal medicine and energy healing through a resurgence of 'well-being', mainstream medicine rejects traditional healing methods instead of assimilating them. Traditional healers have been ridiculed and even persecuted for their methods (Micozzi, 2002). Engaging with this updated version of Ho'oponopono would require a shift in the ways in which we understand reality. While advocates of interconnectedness and holism have made considerable efforts to develop more comprehensive epistemologies, what mostly distinguishes this process from other ontologies of interconnectedness is the concept of the void – the going back to the knot, the liminal space where every possibility exists as potential.

Morrnah's updated Ho'oponopono shifts the focus of health from fragmented parts to the whole person, challenging the objectification of the body by presenting a holistic perspective on health that respects the patient as a multidimensional being. Conventional biomedicine often views the body as a fragmented object for clinical intervention, prioritising quantifiable physiological metrics over patients' lived experience (Bologh, 1981; Lawton, 2003; Marcum, 2005). This reductionist approach has been critiqued by sociologists of health and illness and medical anthropologists for fragmenting the individual and minimising the social, emotional and spiritual dimensions of health (Bologh, 1981; Lawton, 2003; Marcum, 2005; Waitzkin, 1989). Kretzer et al. (2007) have shown in an empirical study that Morrnah's updated Ho'oponopono can lower blood pressure and also enhance spirituality, bridging the gap between physical and psychospiritual dimensions of health. Feminist scholars, including Haraway (1988) and Browne and Fiske (2001) further argue that this objectification is not value-neutral but rooted in patriarchal and colonial structures that have historically dehumanised marginalised bodies, treating them as objects of knowledge or intervention instead of active, meaning making agents.

Morrnah's ontology also directly challenges the siloed approach in most healthcare organisations where departments and practitioners often work in isolation. This ontology encourages an integrated perspective where every aspect of health is interconnected, dissolving institutional barriers and developing systemic collaboration. Integrating Morrnah's Ho'oponopono could enable healthcare professionals to better address the psychosocial and spiritual needs of patients within a more inclusive and compassionate organisational culture.

From the Physical to the Emotional, Relational and Symbolic Dimensions of Health

Conventional biomedicine often overlooks the importance of emotional factors in understanding and addressing health (Foucault, 2003; Duncan, 2000; Marcum, 2005). Morrnah's practice does not address illness as an isolated malfunction within the body but as an imbalance within relational emotional and spiritual networks. Her perspective of Ho'oponopono as 'a problem solving process to release memories that are experienced as problems' (IZI LLC, n.d.) works by addressing relational disharmonies and restoring peace. Instead of focusing solely on physical symptoms, this practice encourages forgiveness, introspection and personal accountability. Khalsa (n.d.) cites Morrnah saying, 'we are the sum total of our experiences, which is to say that we are burdened by our pasts. When we experience stress or fear in our lives, if we would look carefully, we would find that the cause is actually a memory. It is the emotions which are tied to these memories which affect us now. The subconscious associates an action or person in the present with something that happened in the past. When this occurs, emotions are activated and stress is produced.' This worldview suggests that health is not isolated within biological parameters but emerging from the relational, emotional and spiritual links between individuals, their communities, ancestors and environments.

Beyond the emotional, Morrnah's approach includes the symbolic, recognising the importance of cultural and spiritual meanings shaping health. Vitale (2014, p. 26) writes that 'Morrnah believed that the imagined world was as solid as the real world. She often said you don't need water as a cleansing tool, for example, that you could in fact imagine water'. This perspective expands health into a realm of cultural interpretation, personal meaning and spiritual alignment where health is a cultural construct shaped by diverse narratives and contexts (Kelly, 2024). This symbolic inclusion is significant for Indigenous and marginalised populations, whose health experiences are tied to cultural and historical narratives often overlooked by conventional healthcare systems (Phillips-Beck et al., 2020). Systemic discrimination and scientism have devalued traditional practices, creating mistrust towards biomedical models that disregard the symbolic and spiritual dimensions of health that are central to many Indigenous worldviews (Browne & Fiske, 2001; Phillips-Beck et al., 2020). Morrnah's updated Ho'oponopono bridges this gap by elevating traditional practices while adapting them for broader accessibility. By addressing the psychospiritual and symbolic dimensions, it validates cultural narratives and fosters trust among communities often excluded from mainstream healthcare. This approach makes traditional knowledge relevant to contemporary needs, promoting engagement. The inclusivity of Morrnah's model creates a framework where healing is relational, empowering and aligned with the lived realities of diverse populations.

From Expert-Based Models to Co-creation

Morrnah's updated Ho'oponopono challenges the paternalistic structures of conventional healthcare where authority is mostly concentrated in clinicians who act as gatekeepers of medical knowledge. These systems often reduce patients to passive recipients, limiting their agency and reinforcing hierarchical dynamics (Marcum, 2005; Phillips-Beck et al., 2020; Waitzkin,

1989). Conventional biomedical models privilege quantifiable metrics over lived experience, overlooking the subjective, cultural and relational aspects of health (Foucault, 2003; Rocca & Anjum, 2020; Marcum, 2005). This dynamic perpetuates epistemic injustices by devaluing alternative ways of knowing, especially those from Indigenous or marginalised traditions (Haraway, 1988; Phillips-Beck et al., 2020). Feminist critique looks at the ways in which these structures reflect broader hierarchical patriarchal systems. The authority of medical professionals is often legitimised through a form of scientism that excludes non-dominant voices and maintains power asymmetries between healthcare providers and patients (Phillips-Beck et al., 2020; Waitzkin, 1989). These critiques are particularly important for marginalised populations whose health experiences are often shaped by systemic discrimination and a historical erasure of their cultural practices (Browne & Fiske, 2001). By exalting expert authority and reducing patients' roles to compliance with prescribed treatment, conventional healthcare systems fail to account for the complex, multidimensional nature of healing.

Morrnah's work offers a practical, accessible modality for integrating relational ethics into healthcare organisations. Based in unity and accountability, this modality aligns with feminist ideas of inclusivity and empowerment, challenging hierarchical systems and supporting shared responsibility. Her emphasis on co-creation offers a framework for transforming patient-provider relationships, moving from paternalistic models to collaborative care (Gilligan, 1982; Haraway, 1988). Morrnah's vision disrupts these hierarchical dynamics by dismantling the expert–patient hierarchy. She recognised that in Ho'oponopono, there is no need for a kahuna to act as a mediator or even for the physical gathering of the whole family. Her updated approach reframes healing as a process that does not rely on external authority but empowers patients as active participants with significant cultural, emotional and spiritual insights. The emphasis on 'cleaning' memories as a practice of accountability has been embraced by wellness practitioners worldwide, inspiring adaptations in psychotherapy, coaching and organisational management (Vitale, 2014). The removal of the 'expert' as the ultimate authority shifts the focus from hierarchy to collaboration, aligning with broader critiques of expertise as a mechanism of exclusion (Ho, 2009; Hogle, 2002). The study by Kretzer et al. (2007) practically demonstrates this shift by showing positive outcomes in lowering hypertension and improving psychosocial well-being through teaching individuals to 'clean' their own memories and take responsibility for their healing. In mental health therapy, Ho'oponopono has also been adapted as a structured method to address tensions and emotional distress with a focus on 'cleaning' subconscious memories (Thakurdas, 2008). This modality has also been used as a method to reduce clinician burnout, especially in psychotherapy and counselling, encouraging therapists to take accountability for their own subconscious perceptions (Vitale, 2014). In decentralising authority, Morrnah's practice restores agency to patients and offers a more egalitarian and inclusive framework of healthcare.

This approach goes beyond discussions over paternalism and offers an alternative ontology of healing, based on interrelation and unity. Healing, in Morrnah's work is not a linear process dictated by an external authority but an act of transformation within an interrelated whole. It reflects principles of feminist ethics which emphasise the relational dimensions of care and the need to balance individual autonomy with interdependence (Gilligan, 1982; Gómez-Vírseda et al., 2020). Feminist ethics challenge traditional hierarchical model of healthcare by redefining autonomy as relational instead of self-contained, positioning it within an interconnected understanding of well-being. Similarly, in Morrnah's practice, healing is a co-creative process with shared agency placing health and illness within a comprehensive, interconnected unity instead of within the individual.

From Monocultural to Pluralistic Healthcare

Indigenous and non-Western healing traditions have frequently been marginalised as 'alternative' or 'complementary', reflecting perspectives that dismiss local knowledge as inferior or superstitious (Cameron, 2010; Micozzi, 2002). These perspectives are based on positivist logic and often mono-dimensional understandings of illness and healing, favouring quantifiable metrics while undermining cultural particularities and interconnected understandings. This context creates a structural inequity where Indigenous knowledge systems are excluded or seen as incompatible with clinical practice (Browne & Fiske, 2001; Cameron, 2010; Micozzi, 2002).

Historically, the dominance of Western biomedicine has reinforced a singular, universalised understanding of health and illness, dismissing knowledge systems rooted in ancestral, spiritual and community-based wisdom traditions. This marginalisation is criticised as reflecting the colonial power structures that devalue and suppress Indigenous practices as unscientific or superstitious (Hellowell & Schwerdtle, 2022; Micozzi, 2002; Phillips-Beck et al., 2020) limiting their integration into clinical settings (Browne & Fiske, 2001; Micozzi, 2002). This has practical consequences, reducing patients' opportunities to engage with healing modalities that align with their cultural identities and perpetuating cultural dissonance and inequities in healthcare systems (Browne & Fiske, 2001; Phillips-Beck et al., 2020). As Browne and Fiske (2001) argue, these exclusions reinforce disparities in care by prioritising biomedical universality over culturally responsive practices.

Morrnah's efforts to integrate Ho'oponopono into hospitals and universities worldwide, including documented engagements in the United States,

Europe and Asia, helped redefine the boundaries of healthcare. By elevating Indigenous Hawaiian healing traditions from the margins to equal standing with Western biomedical models, her work challenged the hierarchical dominance of biomedicine. The importance of integrating Indigenous knowledge systems into healthcare is emphasised by scholars who argue for inclusivity, cultural humility and respect for diverse epistemologies (Micozzi, 2002; Phillips-Beck et al., 2020). Removing the need for a Kahuna further democratised access and helped adapt Ho'oponopono into diverse healthcare contexts.

In addressing the psychospiritual dimensions often overlooked by biomedicine, Ho'oponopono redefines wellness as more than just physical health. Based on an ontology of unity, where 'everything is one', illness is not understood as an isolated event within a 'self-contained' body but in the context of a broader relational disharmony and spiritual imbalance. Healing in this framework is not just the restoration of physical health but also the reconnection and balancing of relationships within oneself, with family, community and the broader cosmos. This interconnected approach challenges the biomedical reduction of health to physiological data and affirms Indigenous epistemologies as empirically valuable frameworks.

Morrnah's work demonstrated the potential of Hawaiian healing traditions to coexist with biomedical models, paving the way for pluralistic healthcare environments. Her integration of an updated Ho'oponopono into mainstream discourses is an example of how diverse paradigms can work together. Scholars such as Micozzi (2002) and Phillips-Beck et al. (2020) emphasise the importance of inclusivity, cultural humility and respect for diverse epistemologies in creating equitable healthcare systems. By integrating Indigenous practices within mainstream settings, Morrnah advanced a vision of relational and inclusive healthcare.

It Is About the Work!

Morrnah's ideas have been presented at a UN Conference, written in numerous books (Micklei Media, 2021; Rafaelovich et al., 2013a, 2013b, 2013c, 2013d, 2013e, 2013f, 2013g, 2013h; Vitale, 2014), translated in different languages, developed further by different practitioners and taught throughout the world. Despite this, her contributions remain unacknowledged in mainstream holistic and healthcare practices. According to KR, Morrnah always said that 'it's about the work'. But why do women tend to focus on the work instead of promoting themselves?

From a politics of visibility perspective, Simon de Beauvoir discussed how women's work is often devalued unless it gains male recognition or endorsement (Beauvoir, 2008). In this context, women might choose to focus on the intrinsic value of their work instead of self-promotion. At the same time, women have been traditionally socialised to take on caregiving roles (Gilligan, 1982) and Morrnah's jobs as a teacher, nurse and Red Cross driver reflect her alignment with an ethics of care. Prioritising the quality and impact of the work itself over individual recognition is also a reflection of Morrnah's commitment to the ethics of care. As mentioned at the beginning of the chapter, Morrnah was not known by her title but by her first name. This might also reflect the cultural narrative of women expected to be modest and humble which might lead to their downplaying their accomplishments (Bartky, 2015). However, I do not think this is the case for Morrnah. While I am not fully familiar with the cultural and professional contexts within which she worked, from what I have read, her approach seems to be that of a strong woman refusing to buy-in to the self-promotion narrative linked to success.

McRobbie (2008) challenges the notion that one's value is linked to their marketability and explained that some women might consciously reject the imperative to self-promote, choosing instead to focus on the substance of their work as a form of resistance. I cannot say with certainty whether KR and Morrnah would ascribe to any of the above, but KR has mentioned that in any true art, it is about the work itself, while the person comes and goes (K. Rafaelovich, personal communication, 8 August 2024). In her own words and the accounts of her life, Morrnah was not afraid to be a 'radical' while staying true to her calm, peaceful self. Most accounts of Morrnah suggest she was a calm person who mostly shone through her life and her actions rather than her words.

Reimagining Healthcare through Unity and Co-creation

At a time when conventional healthcare systems with hierarchical dynamics, siloed structures and systemic inequities, Morrnah's updated Ho'oponopono offers a transformative framework. Her ontology of unity transcends traditional paradigms by emphasising shared responsibility, co-creative healing and the interconnectedness of all aspects of health. By shifting the focus from individual, self-contained autonomy to relational and holistic understandings of well-being, her work challenges the reductionist models of biomedicine towards more patient-centred approaches.

Morrnah's practice of cleaning subconscious memories reflects an ontology that addresses relational, emotional and spiritual dimensions addressing the current needs for interdisciplinary collaboration and integrated care. This practice bridges Indigenous Hawaiian healing traditions with contemporary healthcare needs, challenging epistemic injustices and systemic exclusions that often marginalise non-Western knowledge systems. Through the concept of the 'cleaning memories' as a practice of transformation, health is re-imagined not just as the absence of disease but as a harmonious balance of the physical, emotional spiritual and relational. From this perspective, healthcare values the lived experiences of patients and integrates diverse epistemologies. Her approach also helps dismantle power dynamics and hierarchies. Morrnah was a revolutionary thinker who radically redefined healing through her transformation of Ho'oponopono from a traditional communal practice to a universally accessible modality.

By resisting conventional notions of visibility and success, her life reflected her commitment to unity, accountability and lived experience. Morrnah's legacy offers a pathway for reimagining healthcare as an inclusive, holistic practice within the interconnected whole of all life.

References

Bartky, S. L. (2015). *Femininity and domination: Studies in the phenomenology of oppression*. Routledge.

Beauvoir, S. (2008). *Το δεύτερο φύλο* (Τ. Κωσταντινάτου, Μτφ.). Αθήνα: Μεταίχμιο.

Bologh, R. W. (1981). Grounding the alienation of self and body: A critical, phenomeoological analysis of the patient in western medicine 1. *Sociology of Health & Illness*, 3(2): 188–206.

Bortoft, H. (1996). *The wholeness of nature: Goethe's way toward a science of conscious participation in nature*. Lindisfarne Books.

Bowman, P. (1982, July 8). Kahuna updates ancient practices: Interview of Morrnah Simeona. *The Honolulu Advertiser*.

Browne, A. J., & Fiske, J. A. (2001). First nations women's encounters with mainstream health care services. *Western Journal of Nursing Research*, 23(2): 126–147.

Cameron, M. (2010). Feminization and marginalization? Women ayurvedic doctors and modernizing health care in Nepal. *Medical Anthropology Quarterly*, 24(1): 42–63.

Cammell, P. (2015). Relationality and existence: Hermeneutic and deconstructive approaches emerging from Heidegger's philosophy. *The Humanistic Psychologist*, 43(3): 235–249.

de Brito Sena, M. A., Damiano, R. F., Lucchetti, G., & Peres, M. F. P. (2021). Defining spirituality in healthcare: A systematic review and conceptual framework. *Frontiers in Psychology*, 12: 756080.

Duncan, G. (2000). Mind-body dualism and the biopsychosocial model of pain: What did Descartes really say? *Journal of Medicine and Philosophy*, 25(4): 485–513.

Foucault, M. (2003). *The birth of the clinic: An archeology of medical perception* (A. M. Sheridan, Trans.). Vintage. (original work published 1963)

Gergen, K. J. (2009). *Relational being: Beyond self and community*. Oxford University Press.

Gergen, K. J. (2015). Toward a relational humanism. *The Journal of Humanistic Counseling*, 54(2): 149–165.

Gilligan, C. (1982). *In a different voice: Psychological theory and women's development*. Harvard University Press.

Gómez-Vírseda, C., De Maeseneer, Y., & Gastmans, C. (2020). Relational autonomy in end-of-life care ethics: A contextualized approach to real-life complexities. *BMC Medical Ethics*, 21: 1–14.

Green, M. H. (2008). Gendering the history of women's healthcare. *Gender & History*, 20(3): 487–518.
Haraway, D. (1988). Situated knowledges: The science question in feminism and the privilege of partial perspective. *Feminist Studies*, 14(3): 575–599.
Hellowell, M., & Schwerdtle, P. N. (2022). Powerful ideas? Decolonisation and the future of global health. *BMJ Global Health*, 7(1): e006924.
Ho, A. (2009). 'They just don't get it!' When family disagrees with expert opinion. *Journal of Medical Ethics*, 35(8): 497–501.
Hogle, L. F. (2002). Claims and disclaimers: Whose expertise counts? *Medical Anthropology*, 21(3–4): 275–306.
Infante, E. M. (1992, February 17). Morrnah Simeona, Kahuna Lapa'au (obituary). *Honolulu Advertiser*. https://www.newspapers.com/article/honolulu-star-advertiser-orbituary/28931516/.
IZI LLC. (n.d.). https://www.self-i-dentity-through-hooponopono.com/, accessed 07 December 2023.
Kelly, J. P. (2024). Expanding the health narrative frame. *Health Communication*, 30: 1–5.
Khalsa, S. (n.d.). *Morrnah Nalamaku Simeona, Hawaiian healer*. https://amazingwomeninhistory.com/morrnah-nalamaku-simeona-hawaiian-healer/.
Kretzer, K., Davis, J., Easa, D., Johnson, J., & Harrigan, R. (2007). Self identity through Ho'oponopono as adjunctive therapy for hypertension management. *Ethnicity & Disease*, 17(4): 624–628.
Lawton, J. (2003). Lay experiences of health and illness: Past research and future agendas. *Sociology of Health & Illness*, 25(3): 23–40.
Marcum, J. A. (2005). Biomechanical and phenomenological models of the body, the meaning of illness and quality of care. *Medicine, Health Care and Philosophy*, 7: 311–320.
Martins, A. P. V. (2020). Women, male doctors, and female historians: a historiographic essay on the history of women, medicine, and gender (D. Grosklaus Whitty, Trans.). *História, Ciências, Saúde-Manguinhos*, 27: 241–264.
McRobbie, A. (2008). *The aftermath of feminism: Gender, culture and social change*. Sage.
Mehta, N. (2011). Mind-body dualism: A critique from a health perspective. *Mens Sana Monographs*, 9(1): 202–209. https://doi.org/10.4103/0973-1229.77436.
Micklei Media. (2021). *The coronation of consciousness: A divine helping hand through the Ho'oponopono of Morrnah Simeona* (3rd ed. English Version). Bernhardswald: Micklei Media.
Micklei Media. (n.d.). *The seeds of success, planted by Morrnah Simeona*. https://pacificaseminars.de/en-hooponopono-english-about-pacificaseminars.htm, accessed 08 November 2024.
Micozzi, M. S. (2002). Culture, anthropology, and the return of 'complementary medicine'. *Medical Anthropology Quarterly*, 16(4): 398–403.
Phillips-Beck, W., Eni, R., Lavoie, J. G., Avery Kinew, K., Kyoon Achan, G., & Katz, A. (2020). Confronting racism within the Canadian healthcare system: Systemic exclusion of first nations from quality and consistent care. *International Journal of Environmental Research and Public Health*, 17(22): 8343.
Rafaelovich, K., Hew Len, I., & Ramsrtum, M. (2013a). *Blue ice: The relationship with the self* (MSKR SITH® Conversations, Book 1). Bingboard Consulting LLC.
Rafaelovich, K., Hew Len, I., & Ramsrtum, M. (2013b). *Blue ice: Memories and relationships* (MSKR SITH® Conversations, Book 2). Bingboard Consulting LLC.

Rafaelovich, K., Hew Len, I., & Ramsrtum, M. (2013c). *Blue ice: Get to the cleaning* (MSKR SITH® Conversations, Book 3). Bingboard Consulting LLC.
Rafaelovich, K., Hew Len, I., & Ramsrtum, M. (2013d). *Blue ice: Partnering with the child* (MSKR SITH® Conversations, Book 4). Bingboard Consulting LLC.
Rafaelovich, K., Hew Len, I., & Ramsrtum, M. (2013e). *Blue ice: How to clean* (MSKR SITH® Conversations, Book 5). Bingboard Consulting LLC.
Rafaelovich, K., Hew Len, I., & Ramsrtum, M. (2013f). *Blue ice: Clean ahead* (MSKR SITH® Conversations, Book 6). Bingboard Consulting LLC.
Rafaelovich, K., Hew Len, I., & Ramsrtum, M. (2013g). *Blue ice: Caring for our body* (MSKR SITH® Conversations, Book 7). Bingboard Consulting LLC.
Rafaelovich, K., Hew Len, I., & Ramsrtum, M. (2013h). *Blue ice: Cleaning with finances* (MSKR SITH® Conversations, Book 8). Bingboard Consulting LLC.
Rocca, E., & Anjum, R. L. (2020). Complexity, reductionism and the biomedical model. In *Rethinking causality, complexity and evidence for the unique patient: A cause health resource for healthcare professionals and the clinical encounter* (pp. 75–94). Springer.
Thakurdas, A. (2008). Ho'oponopono: Universal healing method for mankind. *International Journal of Healing and Caring*, 8(3).
Vitale, J. (2014). *At zero: The quest for miracles through Ho'oponopono*. Wiley.
Waitzkin, H. (1989). A critical theory of medical discourse: Ideology, social control, and the processing of social context in medical encounters. *Journal of Health and Social Behavior*: 220–239.
Wall, J. A., & Callister, R. R. (1995). Ho'oponopono: Some lessons from Hawaiian mediation. *Negotiation Journal*, 11(1): 45–54.
Weber, M. (2009). *From Max Weber: Essays in sociology* (H. H. Gerth, & W. Mills, Trans., 1st ed.). Routledge. https://doi.org/10.4324/9780203452196.

11 Professor Dame Clare Gerada

The 'Doctor's Doctor' Challenging the Institution of the Medical Self

John-Paul Byrne

Introduction

> Doctors are human. Doctors should not have to sacrifice their lives for their profession . . . The days of the doctor being the superhuman, all-giving, sacrificing individual are over. It is now time to have a more realistic contract with our patients and with the health systems in which we work, a contract where the doctor is cared for and can expect the same compassion as the patients they treat.
>
> (Gerada 2018, p. 169)

Medicine is a prestigious and profound profession. It is also a profession under threat from the growing disjuncture between professional expectations and frontline realities (Byrne et al. 2023; Zuger 2004). High rates of burnout, moral injury, depression and suicide (Zapata et al. 2023; Gerada 2018) signify a deteriorating relationship between doctors and their profession that has taken a toll on doctors' mental health: a relationship that Professor Dame Clare Gerada has dedicated her career to. Writing two years before the pandemic-related consolidation of healthcare workers as 'heroes of the frontlines' (Felsenthal 2020), Professor Dame Clare Gerada called for a move beyond the dehumanisation of doctors as superhuman – for the good of the health system, patients and the doctors themselves. Emphasising the power – and potentially dehumanising effect – of medical professional identity, Dame Gerada unpacks the values and expectations of 'the medical self' (Gerada 2021a), asking whether what we ask of doctors' lives and well-being might be too much. This is a question that has never been more resonant in a post-pandemic world of enervated healthcare systems and healthcare professionals that are far too often both the firefighters *and* the fuel.

This chapter will celebrate the work and writing of Professor Dame Clare Gerada as a revolutionary in healthcare management in highlighting and challenging the detrimental power of the medical self-identity which 'can, and often does, get out of hand' (Gerada 2021a). Initially providing a brief

DOI: 10.4324/9781003546610-11

overview of Dame Gerada's background and career, this chapter unpacks her conceptualisation of the 'medical self' as a collective, cognitive institution that both protects and endangers doctors. This approach draws attention to the potentially negative effects of the contestation between the intrinsic pride of being a doctor, and the personal sacrifices required of medicine. It then discusses specific characteristics of the medical self as depicted by Gerada, namely self-sacrifice and stigma, embedding these in wider research evidence and framing them as pathologies of professional identity. The conclusion briefly discusses the lessons from Dame Gerada's work for healthcare management today highlighting the how structural antecedents – both professional and organisational – shape the mental health risks inherent in the medical professional identity mental, while also noting her calls for a new, more realistic social contract for medicine that bridges the gap between expectations and reality. In doing so, the chapter embeds Dame Gerada's writing within broader sociology and management literature to highlight how, in a post-pandemic world, we need to recondition the medical work bargain to one that humanises doctors, removes barriers to mental health support take-up and ensures that doctors are cared *for* so that they can provide sustainable, high-quality care.

From the Doctor's Daughter to the Doctors' Doctor

Professor Dame Clare Gerada is the first woman in nearly 70 years to hold the position of Chair (2011–2014) and President (2021–2023) of the Royal College of General Practitioners (RCGP). A London-based general practitioner (GP) with a long-held interest in addiction and mental health, she is founder and Medical Director of Practitioner Health, a service providing mental health and addiction support to doctors, and patron of Doctors in Distress, a charity seeking to prevent suicide in medicine. In 2000, Clare was appointed a Member of the Order of the British Empire for services to medicine and substance misuse. She was named among the 100 most powerful women in the UK in 2013 by BBC Radio 4's *Women's Hour*. In 2020, she was awarded a damehood in the Queen's Birthday Honours for her services to general practice. Through these positions, and her career generally, Dame Gerada has played a major leadership role as head education standards, promoting the profession of general practice throughout various iterations of National Health Service (NHS) reform, and protecting the profession from privatisation, and from itself.

Born in Nigeria to Maltese parents, Clare arrived in the UK as a 'double-immigrant' – a diversity that she feels enhanced her practice in engaging with local communities (Gerada 2023). Her career began with her father, also a GP, who 'kindled' her love of medicine and general practice, and instilled the importance of giving back to society (Gerada 2021b). From a very early age, patients were a familiar part of Clare's life. The family living room functioned as the surgery waiting room. Clare regularly attended home visits around Peterborough with her father, and unsurprisingly she recalls her toys as full-size skeletons and tendon hammers (Gerada 2021b). Recalling her childhood, it is interesting to see the influence identity had on Clare from a young age as she notes the need to separate herself from the patients in her father's practice by answering the phone with authority (as 'Dr Gerada's daughter'). Hinting at the link between identity, rules and sacrifice that she would explore later in her career, Clare also recalls always being aware that she had to 'behave in the streets because I was "the doctor's daughter"' (Gerada 2021a), and that personal space at home may have been her first personal life sacrifice. This focus on the underlying power of identity and expectations – good and bad – can be seen throughout Dame Gerada's career. From the development of humanising substance abuse services in primary care, to the protection of the general practice profession in leadership positions within the NHS and the RCGP, and finally to the 'medical self' identity and its relationship with doctors' lives, and impact on their mental health.

Drawing on her considerable experience supporting doctors with addiction and mental health issues with Practitioner Health, Clare has written extensively on doctors' work, identity, mental health, and the medical profession, with the most recent book titled, ***Beneath the White Coat: Doctors, Their Minds and Mental Illness*** (Gerada 2021a). This chapter will concentrate on this latter contribution of Dame Gerada as the 'doctor's doctor' caring for doctors with mental health issues and challenging the sacrifices and risks to mental health inherent in the development the 'medical-self' identity. In doing so, I hope to highlight the importance of identity and humanisation, tracing these themes from Dame Gerada's childhood to her writing on professional identity and work in medicine, through to lessons for healthcare management in ensuring positive working lives and environments for doctors today.

Medicine as Cognitive Institution

> For more than a decade I have been leading a confidential service for doctors with mental health and addiction problems (NHS Practitioner Health). What is striking is despite having high levels of mental illness, and working within the medical system, doctors have low rates of presentation to treatment services
>
> (Gerada 2022, p. 7)

Europe's health workforce is in the midst of both a labour *and* mental health crisis (Azzopardi-Muscat et al. 2023) with high rates of burnout, stress, anxiety and depression intensified by the COVID-19 pandemic (Ghahramani et al. 2021; Zapata et al. 2023). Even prior to the pandemic, burnout among doctors in the USA was described as an urgent public health problem affecting clinicians, patients, trainees and healthcare organisations (National Academies of Sciences, Engineering, and Medicine 2019). Research has shown how doctors have higher rates of suicide when compared to the general population – especially female doctors (Gerada 2018). The cover headline for the September 2024 issue of the BMJ illustrates the resonance of this issue: 'Preventing Doctor Suicide: Why we need action now' (Waters 2024). Yet, these high rates of distress are not matched by high numbers of doctors seeking mental health support services (Byrne et al. 2023; Gerada 2022a). For Gerada, the key to unlocking this juxtaposition of doctors' high rates of mental distress and low rates of support service presentations is the 'medical-self' identity (Gerada 2021a, 2022) and how it moulds the experience of being both a doctor and part of the medical profession.

The medical self is an omnipresent identity that intertwines the personal ('I') and the collective ('we') so successfully that medicine becomes 'more than just something I do, but something I am' (Gerada 2021a, p. xii). Being a doctor becomes an all-consuming identity, irrespective of personality or context. The distinctiveness of this identity is reinforced as doctors begin to 'learn a new language, wear new clothes and carry special objects, such as the stethoscope and bleep' while 'below the surface feelings have also developed, namely, power, authority and invincibility' (Gerada 2022a, p. 7). The medical self thus contains extrinsic, relational and intrinsic features that mark itself out as special. These features are normalised via a long, complex professional socialisation process where medical students acquire the formal knowledge and behaviours required of doctors, while also absorbing the unwritten rules, values and expectations of the medicine – usually referred to as the hidden curriculum (Gerada 2021a; Scambler 2009; Becker et al. 1961).

Drawing on the work of the sociologist Erving Goffman, Gerada (2021a) conceptualises the medical self as a collective cognitively – rather than physically – bounded institution characterised by a distinctive and legitimised set of 'norms and narratives'. These norms are collectively reinforced as doctors spend long hours living, working, suffering and learning with each other within the clinical environment (Gerada 2021b). The development of the medical self produces three inconsistent dynamics that must be managed by doctors. First, it creates psychological defence mechanisms, enabling doctors to carry out the job and deal with despair and death. For example, Smith and Kleinman (1989) note the important development of affective neutrality and objectivity during medical school to manage feelings of fear and disgust. Second, the medical self exposes doctors to a unique set of work–life stressors and thus risks to mental health. A wide range of research has highlighted the experience of insurmountable workloads, limited breaks, work–life conflict (Byrne et al. 2023; Shanafelt et al. 2015), alienation (Byrne et al. 2023) and the use of 'medicine-as-vocation' to legitimate organisational neglect (Humphries et al. 2024).

The third dynamic of the medical self ensures the comprehensive internalisation of medicine's rules and expectations (e.g. altruism, authority, invulnerability) which obstructs the seeking of help (Gerada 2021a, 2022). Patients get sick, not doctors – who are protected by their 'magic white coats' (Gerada 2021b). Expanding on this in an interview with Dr Paula Redmond on the *When Work Hurts* podcast, Clare notes that; 'you learn the rules of engagement, which is you don't take time off sick, you support your peers, you do long hours' (Gerada 2022b). Here the institutionalisation of medicine's 'rules of engagement' represents a culture comprised of a subtle interplay of professional expectations, workplace conditions and behaviours and organisational demands. These characteristics – both protective and harmful – are all at play within the medical self.

Dame Gerada's detailed conceptualisation of the medical self provides an interrelated, three-fold contribution to healthcare management. It is grounded in her practical frontline experience providing support to doctors in distress and therefore draws on relevant concerns for modern doctors. Unlike the specialisation-ethos of medicine, Dame Gerada draws on other disciplines to hold a mirror up to medicine – from within the profession. This is an important, legitimating point. Sociology has long held an interest in the complexities and contradictions of medicine (Freidson 1975; Becker et al. 1961). Gerada's work departs from typical analyses of burnout and moral injury in drawing on the work of sociology (she cites the work of Hochschild and Goffman) to help us understand the structural antecedents of doctors' distress. Finally, this conceptual approach – underpinned by her empirical experience supporting doctors – provides a unique contribution to understanding what might be termed the structural pathologies of the medical professional identity.

The Pathologies of a Professional Identity

Pathology is the study of disease and illness; however, the term actually derives from the Greek for the study of suffering. As such, it provides a suitable frame to discuss how features of the medical self may become deleterious to doctor well-being when the accumulation of frontline demands and professional norms and expectations overwhelm personal resources and capacities. In her writing, Gerada (2021) highlights the potentially detrimental power self-sacrifice and stigma can have within the experience of modern medicine.

The 'rules of self-sacrifice' (Gerada 2021a) represent the archetypal unwritten characteristic of medicine. To illustrate this, Gerada (2021a) points to the very first line of the World Medical Association Geneva Declaration which reads; 'I solemnly pledge to dedicate my life to the service of humanity' (World Medical Association 2017). Research on doctors experience of work shows how this pledge is borne out in the expected norms of intensified *and* porous work time (Byrne et al. 2020), work–life imbalance (Humphries et al. 2020; Shanafelt et al. 2015), shrinking social networks (Wessely and Gerada 2013) and impact on their physical and mental well-being (Byrne et al. 2023; Creese et al. 2021). In a remote ethnographic study of hospital doctor's core work needs (autonomy, belonging, competence), Humphries et al. (2024) depict the strain of a professionalised self-sacrifice underpinned by organisational neglect. The authors show how the inherent nature of medicine is used to justify under staffing and a disconnect between the frontline and management resulting in long hours, and doctors coming in to work on days off to ensure patients were seen to. Building on the norm of invulnerability and separateness from patients, (lack of) sick leave also represents one of the tenets of the rules of self-sacrifice. Gerada (2021) notes how difficult it is for doctors to take on a 'sick role' and therefore take sick leave, emphasising how this issue manifests in high rates of presenteeism, reflecting a 'visible manifestation of how central doctors' work is to their identity'. Rosvold and Bjertness' (2001) survey of Norwegian physicians provides an apt example here where they found that 80% of physicians had worked during an illness for which they would have listed their patients as sick. Doctors' paradoxical experience of sick leave during COVID-19 also provides an illustration of the power of this norm with research describing feelings of guilt when taking mandatory COVID-19 sick leave (Creese et al. 2021) compared to the pre-pandemic norm of attending work while ill (Byrne et al. 2020).

Expectations of self-sacrifice were also present in the narratives of the COVID-19 pandemic as doctors (and healthcare workers generally) were declared the heroes of the frontline (Felsenthal 2020). However, while governments and the public globally stood to applaud the bravery and sacrifices of healthcare workers during the pandemic, doctors met this heroic rhetoric with cynicism, citing their pre-pandemic experience of extreme job demands, everyday work–life sacrifices, high stress and inability to provide high-quality care in under-resourced health systems (Creese et al. 2021; Darlow 2020). Here, we see the interplay of two themes of Dame Gerada's work – identity and humanisation. The heroic identity builds on the 'specialness' and 'othering' of the medical self, implying that they are comfortable with risks and sacrifice and don't want or require safe conditions at work. While public and health systems leveraged the otherness of the medical self, the medical counter-narrative sought to re-humanise doctors who feel fear and require care themselves. Here, the COVID-19 experience may provide lessons going forward for the medical profession and healthcare management more broadly in shining a global spotlight on the hitherto overshadowed contestation between the person and the doctor within the medical self.

Stigma refers to negative perceptions of individuals/groups emanating from relations of shame due to deviations from prescribed 'normal' states (Scambler 2009), expectations and behaviours. As such, it refers to the other side of the self-sacrifice coin within the medical self. If the rules of self-sacrifice imply norms of invincibility and invulnerability, it represents a real risk to doctors' reputations and careers if they are to show vulnerability, incompetence or be unwell. By internalising the expectations of the medical self, doctors also internalise what behaviours and beliefs are *not* legitimate. Drawing on her vast experience supporting doctors, Gerada (2022b) points to shame and stigma as two key factors preventing doctors from seeking mental health supports even when unwell – especially where mental health supports are perceived to impinge on fitness to practice standards. This point is supported by a range of literature.

In a qualitative study of GPs seeking treatment for mental distress, Spiers et al. (2017) note how stigma impacted participants extrinsically ('unwritten rule' that GPs don't have mental illness so it is not talked about) and intrinsically as GPs experiencing mental illness felt a sense of failure. This latter form of self-stigmatisation represents a major obstacle to support presentations for doctors (Gerada 2021a). An inability to live up to the rules of the medical self negatively affected doctors' sense of themselves and their ability to take up supports. Henderson et al.'s (2012) qualitative exploration of doctors who had been out of work for six months note the role of self-stigmatisation – fuelled by a belief in the perceived and required invulnerability of doctors – in preventing doctors returning to work. In a realist review of interventions aimed at tackling doctors' and medical students' mental ill-health, Carrieri et al. (2020) found that doctors were more likely to experience mental distress when they feared that seeking supports may jeopardise their career. The authors recommend the normalising of discussions of struggle within medical schools and the profession more broadly. Similarly, Byrne et al.'s (2023) comparative review of COVID-19 policy interventions to support healthcare workers' mental health identified how the Ministry of Health in Lithuania had to remove mental disorders from the conditions influencing medical professional licensing to encourage take-up of psychological supports during the pandemic. These examples illustrate the role of regulatory structures in reinforcing the medical self and empowering perceptions of professional stigma.

Gerada's articulation of the medical self thus asks whether doctors' distress and unhappiness starts with what the profession *internalises* and the job *expects*, and whether it is time to change aspects of this culture. Whether what you *are* as a doctor is also a flawed, vulnerable human. This chapter will now discuss what we can learn from Dame Gerada's work on the medical self to improve healthcare management today.

Humanising the Medical Self: Aligning Professional Expectations and Frontline Reality

> Whether they care to admit it or not, doctors are human. There must be a cultural shift in how they're treated at work and an acceptance that they can be affected by stress and poor mental health
>
> (Amandip Sidhu *in* Waters 2024, p. 307)

Understanding and alleviating doctors' work–life distress is fundamental for the sustainability of medicine, and health systems, globally. As Bodenheimer and Sinsky (2014) noted, seeking to improve patients' experience of care without improving the working lives of doctors and healthcare staff is futile. Dame Gerada has seen this work–life–self distress first-hand, a distress severely escalated by doctors' experience of the pandemic. On the *When Work Hurts* podcast, Clare notes how the Practitioner Health service saw approximately 5,000 doctors seek support between March 2020 and April 2021, compared to 5,000 doctors in the ten years preceding COVID-19 (Gerada 2022b). She notes high rates of anxiety, moral distress and a profession that is 'collectively depressed . . . low self-esteem, you feel worthless and hopeless as a profession' (Gerada 2022b). The prevalence of these conditions and feelings represents a major morale issue at workforce level and can lead to tragic outcomes at the individual level.

Amandip Sidhu (quoted above) set up the UK Charity Doctors in Distress following the death of his brother Jagdip by suicide. In an interview in the BMJ, Amandip reflects on how his brother's job as a cardiologist consumed all of his time and energy, working 70–80 hour weeks and regularly going in on days off (Waters 2024). Making a poignantly similar point to Gerada (2022) above, Amandip describes how his brother was constantly in a high state of anxiety, concerned about patients and potential mistakes, noting; 'He just couldn't let go. He couldn't switch off from being a doctor' (Sidhu *in* Waters 2024, p. 307). This example illustrates the power of an all-consuming professional identity that legitimates both ceaseless demands *and* responsibilities. Writing about doctors and suicide, Gerada (2018) emphasises the importance of not 'losing sight of the person behind the professional', and it is here that we need to anchor a more humanised version of the medical self. Dame Gerada has called for a new, more realistic work contract – one that minimises the sources of distress for doctors, removes the professional and practical barriers to mental health support take-up and ensures doctors are cared for so that they can provide care. However, as Amandip notes in the quote above, this requires a cultural and structural shift that must occur within, and beyond, medicine. Here, Dame Gerada's challenging of the self-sacrifice and invulnerability (and masculinity) of the medical self can offer lessons for healthcare management going forward.

In providing a thorough unpacking of the medical self, and how it shapes doctors' experience of their profession, their work, *and themselves*, Dame Gerada's work demonstrates the power and persistence of the normative structures underpinning medicine. Importantly, this perspective moves beyond individual and organisational frames of burnout and moral injury to show how the antecedents of the mental distress experienced by doctors may originate in medical school, to be reinforced within a strained clinical environment. Where norms of individualism, authority, expertise, invulnerability and self-sacrifice meet frontline working contexts of ceaseless demands, high responsibility, limited control and organisational deafness, the result can be guilt, anxiety, shame and tragedy (Creese et al. 2024; Waters 2024; Gerada 2021a). This perspective calls out the futility of short courses on resilience and mindfulness within a context where doctors are institutionalised into a professional culture of invulnerability self-sacrifice, working every day in under-resourced and under-staffed contexts which limit their ability to deliver high-quality care, and are under so much pressure at work that it is impossible to attend. Gerada makes clear that the risks to doctors' mental health have structural antecedents. As such, these normative structures and dynamics involve multiple stakeholder organisations, and therefore require an inter-sectoral response (Greer et al. 2017), involving medical schools, professional training colleges, unions, and healthcare organisations and departments. An inter-sectoral approach would also see doctors' mental health as a core feature of medical workforce capacity as it has implications for doctors' lives and well-being, the sustainability of healthcare systems and the quality of patient care (Byrne et al. 2023; Firth-Cozens and Greenhalgh 1997). Calling out the negative dynamics of, and multi-stakeholder responsibility for, the medical self represents an important first step in addressing the antecedents of doctors' distress. A further step, advocated for by Dame Gerada (2018), is a new, humanised social contract for medicine.

Dame Gerada's work is a clarion call for a new social contract between medicine and the public, the health system and its own professionals. One that builds on the learning from COVID-19 to work towards two important goals: a realignment of professional expectations and organisational realities and a humanising of doctors that emphasises their vulnerability and fallibility as human beings who require their own care. As Amandip Sidhu notes at the beginning of this section, these goals require a culture change within medicine and subsequently healthcare broadly. A wide range of research has demonstrated the experience of disconnect and alienation emerging from the gap between professional expectations and frontline realities for doctors (Byrne et al. 2023; Zuger 2004). Frontline medicine has changed. Demographic transitions, chronic disease burdens and administrative workloads, alongside developments in medical science, population health and integrated care, have fundamentally altered the quantity and quality of healthcare delivery demands. In a retrospective analysis of 100 million primary care consultations in the UK between 2007 and 2014, Hobbs et al. (2016) find a 'substantial increase' in the patient-facing workload suggesting that primary care could be reaching a 'saturation point'. The authors also worryingly note that their study only focused on direct clinical workload and therefore overlooked the administrative and professional workloads for GPs (Hobbs et al. 2016). Put simply, the medical workload has moved beyond the doctor's control and the normative structures and cultures of medicine need to catch-up with frontline realities. Gerada (2022) notes that the days of the 'omni-competent' doctor are over and health systems need to recognise that an omni-present medical self cannot meet these demands. However, the 'system' here is inter-sectoral in nature and requires medical schools and professional training bodies to call out the protections and risks within the medical self, i.e. where it departs from modern clinical life and what the work of medicine is, and expects, in the 21st century. It also requires healthcare organisations to support rather than abandon the core work needs of doctors (Humphries et al. 2024) so that doctors are staffed appropriately, able to take sick leave without guilt, can access breaks, food and water, and are treated as a key member of the healthcare delivery team rather than as isolated, de-humanised, invulnerable professional. Gerada's (2021) writing is key here in acknowledging and aligning the medical profession as cognitive, the work as intimate and interpersonal, and the self as more than a doctor.

Finally, Gerada's delineation of the factors that keep doctors away from the supports they often require also provides learning for healthcare management. Simply put, the availability of supports (e.g. counselling) does not guarantee their use. Supporting Gerada's (2021) emphasis on the power of the medical self, research findings demonstrate that where a professional identity is so ingrained and pervasive, deviation from expected norms represents a stigmatising risk – intrinsically and extrinsically (Spiers et al. 2017; Henderson et al. 2012). The aftermath of the COVID-19 experience could represent a watershed moment for medicine's perception of itself in normalising narratives of struggle and vulnerability among doctors (Creese et al. 2021). Building on this progress requires a dismantling of not only the professional but also organisational (unprotected time, rota schedules) and regulatory (e.g. fitness to practice implications) barriers to mental health supports (Byrne et al. 2023; Gerada 2021a). Humanising the medical self is thus a complex, inter-sectoral effort that requires a reciprocal understanding of medical and management 'worlds' (Creese et al. 2024) in order to align professional expectations with frontline realities and ensure the sustainability of high-quality medical care.

Conclusion

Medicine is a profoundly important profession that plays a pivotal role in the health of societies across the globe. At the same time, doctors are human. It is in this conjunction of the profound and the humane that the medical self must reside and thrive – for the sake of doctors, patients and healthcare organisations. Professor Dame Clare Gerada's career points to the power of identity and the importance of humanisation within medicine. Her writing on the medical self – the focus of this chapter – calls attention to the structural antecedents of doctors' mental distress, the risks to mental health inherent in the development the medical-self and the need to realign public and professional expectations of doctors with frontline clinical realities. The question we must ask post-pandemic is how sustainable is a healthcare system that relies on individual heroes rather than supporting them?

A new social contract is required; one that humanises doctors, enables the take-up of mental health supports and ensures a non-corrosive relationship between the pride of being a doctor and the sacrifices of medicine. For healthcare management, this means taking a purposefully inter-sectoral approach to acknowledge and address the normative structures underpinning work-life strain in medicine. For example, under-staffing, sick leave guilt and sacrifice of personal time and well-being intertwine and reinforce each other in a race to distress. A coherent, unanimous message across medical schools, professional training colleges, regulatory bodies and healthcare organisations is required to align professional expectations with modern workplace conditions and organisational demands in health and medicine. If we are to maintain one message from Dame Gerada's writing, it is this: we must not lose sight of doctors as human and healthcare as social and the urgent need to renovate the professional and organisational structures of medicine to enable the medical self to blossom.

References

Azzopardi-Muscat, N., Zapata, T., and Kluge, H. (2023) 'Moving from health workforce crisis to health workforce success: The time to act is now'. *The Lancet Regional Health – Europe* 35, 100765. https://doi.org/10.1016/j.lanepe.2023.100765

Becker, H. S., Geer, B., Strauss, A. L., and Hughes, E. C. (1961). *Boys in white: Student culture in medical school.* Chicago, IL: University of Chicago Press.

Bodenheimer, T., and Sinsky, C. (2014) 'From triple to quadruple aim: Care of the patient requires care of the provider'. *The Annals of Family Medicine* 12(6), 573–576. https://doi.org/10.1370/afm.1713

Byrne, J.P., Conway, E., McDermott, A.M., Costello, R.W., Prihodova, L., Matthews, A., and Humphries, N. (2020) 'Between balance and burnout: Contrasting the working-time conditions of Irish-trained hospital doctors in Ireland and Australia'. In Montgomery, A., van der Doef, M., Panagopoulou, E., and Leiter, M.P. (eds)

Connecting healthcare worker well-being, patient safety and organisational change: Aligning perspectives on health, safety and well-being. Cham: Springer. https://doi.org/10.1007/978-3-030-60998-6_6

Byrne, J.P., Humphries, N., McMurray, R., and Scotter, C. (2023) 'COVID-19 and healthcare worker mental well-being: Comparative case studies on interventions in six countries'. *Health Policy* 135, 104863. https://doi.org/10.1016/j.healthpol.2023.104863

Carrieri, D., Mattick, K., Pearson, M., Papoutsi, C., Briscoe, S., Wong, G., and Jackson, M. (2020) 'Optimising strategies to address mental ill-health in doctors and medical students: 'Care under pressure' realist review and implementation guidance'. *BMC Medicine* 18(1), 76–86. https://doi.org/10.1186/s12916-020-01532-x

Creese, J., Byrne, J.P., Conway, E., Barrett, E., Prihodova, L., and Humphries, N. (2021) '"We all really need to just take a breath": Composite narratives of hospital doctors' well-being during the COVID-19 pandemic'. *The International Journal of Environmental Research and Public Health* 18(4), 2051. https://doi.org/10.3390/ijerph18042051

Creese, J., Byrne, J.P., Conway, E., O'Connor, G., and Humphries, N. (2024) '"They say they listen. But do they really listen?": A qualitative study of hospital doctors' experiences of organisational deafness, disconnect and denial'. *Health Services Management Research*. https://doi.org/10.1177/09514848241254929

Darlow, J. (2020) 'Thanks for the support, but I don't want your clapping'. *BMJ Opinion*, April 16. https://blogs.bmj.com/bmj/2020/04/16/jennifer-darlow-thanks-for-the-support-but-i-dont-want-your-clapping/. Accessed on 9 August 2024.

Felsenthal, E. (2020) 'Heroes of the front lines: Front line workers tell their own stories in the new issue of TIME'. *TIME Magazine*. https://time.com/collection/coronavirus-heroes/5816805/coronavirus-front-line-workers-issue/. Accessed on 9 August 2024.

Firth-Cozens, J., and Greenhalgh, J. (1997) 'Doctors perceptions of the links between stress and lowered clinical care'. *Social Science & Medicine* 44(7), 1017–1022. https://doi.org/10.1016/s0277-9536(96)00227-4

Freidson, E. (1975) *The profession of medicine*. New York: Dodd and Mead.

Gerada, C. (2018) 'Doctors and suicide'. *British Journal of General Practice* 68(669), 168–169. https://doi.org/10.3399/bjgp18X695345

Gerada, C. (2021a) *Beneath the white coat: Doctors, their minds and mental illness*. Routledge.

Gerada, C. (2021b) *Royal Society of Medicine (RSM) in conversation live with Dame Clare Gerada*. https://www.youtube.com/watch?v=FAmQjBrYUGQ. Accessed on 25 September 2024.

Gerada, C. (2022a) 'Doctors' identity and barriers to seeking care when unwell'. *The British Journal of Psychiatry* 220, 7–9. https://doi.org/10.1192/bjp.2021.52

Gerada, C. (2022b) '"Who's holding the hope?" A conversation with Dame Clare Gerada by P. Redmond'. *When Work Hurts* podcast, February 14. https://drpaularedmond.com/whos-holding-the-hope-a-conversation-with-dame-clare-gerada. Accessed on 25 September 2024.

Gerada, C. (2023) *Dame Clare Gerada final speech as RCGP president – RCGP conference 2023*. https://www.youtube.com/watch?app=desktop&v=vXIS9kFgoyo. Accessed on 11 September 2024.

Ghahramani, S., Lankarani, K.B., Yousefi, M., Heydari, K., Shahabi, S., and Azmand, S. (2021) 'A systematic review and meta-analysis of burnout among healthcare workers during COVID-19'. *Frontiers in Psychiatry* 12, 758849. https://doi.org/10.3389%2Ffpsyt.2021.758849

Greer, S.L., Vasev, N., and Wismar, M. (2017) 'Fences and ambulances: Governance for intersectoral action on health'. *Health Policy* 121(11), 1101–1104. https://doi.org/10.1016/j.healthpol.2017.09.014

Henderson, M., Brooks, S.K., Del Busso, L., Chalder, T., Harvey, S.B., Hotopf, M., Madan, I., and Hatch, S. (2012) 'Shame! Self-stigmatisation as an obstacle to sick doctors returning to work: A qualitative study'. *BMJ Open* 2(5), e001776, October 15. https://doi.org/10.1136/bmjopen-2012-001776

Hobbs, F.D.R., Bankhead, C., Mukhtar, T., Stevens, S., Perera-Salazar, R., Holt, T., and Salisbury, C., and National Institute for Health Research School for Primary Care Research. (2016) 'Clinical workload in UK primary care: A retrospective analysis of 100 million consultations in England, 2007–14'. *Lancet* 387(10035), 2323–2330, June 4. https://doi.org/10.1016%2FS0140-6736(16)00620-6

Humphries, N., Creese, J., McDermott, A.M., Colleran, G., McDermott, C., and Byrne, J.P. (2024) '"That's just how medicine is": A remote ethnographic study of Ireland's failure to meet the core work needs of its hospital doctors'. *SSM – Qualitative Research in Health* 5, 100392. https://doi.org/10.1016/j.ssmqr.2024.100392

Humphries, N., McDermott, A.M., Creese, J., Matthews, A., Conway, E., and Byrne, J.P. (2020). 'Hospital doctors in Ireland and the struggle for work-life balance'. *European Journal of Public Health* 30, iv32–iv35. https://doi.org/10.1093/eurpub/ckaa130

National Academies of Sciences, Engineering, and Medicine. (2019) *Taking action against clinician burnout: A systems approach to professional well-being*. Washington, DC: The National Academies Press. https://doi.org/10.17226/25521

Rosvold, E.O., and Bjertness, E. (2001) 'Physicians who do not take sick leave: Hazardous heroes?' *Scandinavian Journal of Public Health* 29(1), 71–75. https://doi.org/10.1177/14034948010290010101

Scambler, G. (2009) 'Health-related stigma'. *Sociology of Health & Illness* 31(3), 441–455. https://doi.org/10.1111/j.1467-9566.2009.01161.x

Shanafelt, T.D., Hasan, O., Dyrbye, L.N., Sinsky, C., Satele, D., Sloan, J., and West, C.P. (2015) 'Changes in burnout and satisfaction with work-life balance in physicians and the general US working population between 2011 and 2014'. *Mayo Clinic Proceedings* 90(12), 1600–1613. https://doi.org/10.1016/j.mayocp.2015.08.023

Smith, A.C., and Kleinman, S. (1989) 'Managing emotions in medical school: Students' contacts with the living and the dead'. *Social Psychology Quarterly* 52, 56–69. https://psycnet.apa.org/doi/10.2307/2786904

Spiers, J., Buszewicz, M., Chew-Graham, C.A., Gerada, C., Kessler, D., Leggett, N., Manning, C., Taylor, A.K., Thornton, G., and Riley, R. (2017) 'Barriers, facilitators, and survival strategies for GPs seeking treatment for distress: A qualitative study'. *British Journal of General Practice* 67(663), e700–e708. https://doi.org/10.3399/bjgp17x692573

Waters, A. (2024) 'Doctor suicide: "All I could see were tasks mounting, appointments being booked, and people constantly knocking on my door"'. *BMJ* 386, q1879. https://doi.org/10.1136/bmj.q1879

Wessely, A., and Gerada, C. (2013) 'When doctors need treatment: An anthropological approach to why doctors make bad patients'. *BMJ* 347, f6644. https://doi.org/10.1136/bmj.f6644

World Medical Association. (2017) *Declaration of Geneva, the physician's pledge.* https://www.wma.net/policies-post/wma-declaration-of-geneva/. Accessed on 23 September 2024.

Zapata, T., Azzopardi-Muscat, N., McKee, M., and Kluge, H. (2023) 'Fixing the health workforce crisis in Europe: Retention must be the priority'. *BMJ* 38, 947. http://dx.doi.org/10.1136/bmj.p947

Zuger, A. (2004) 'Dissatisfaction with medical practice'. *New England Journal of Medicine* 350, 69–75. https://www.nejm.org/doi/full/10.1056/NEJMsr031703

12 Conclusion – What Now for Women in Healthcare Management?

Éidín Ní Shé and Robert McMurray

Introduction

> Based on data available in 2021, women comprise almost 70% of the global health and social workforce but it is estimated they hold only 25% of senior roles.
>
> (WHO, 2021)

This edited collection focus was on shining a brighter light on the contributions of women in health and social care management. As educators in healthcare management, we have struggled to find exemplars of diverse women who have managed and changed health and social in their local contexts. The World Health Organization's (WHO) data cited above illustrates that the pipeline of women in the workforce is not an issue but the evidence notes within health and social care the "why" women don't take up managerial roles (Baduge et al., 2024; Bear, 2021; Karakcheyeva et al., 2024; Zeinali et al., 2021). All too often, there is an internalised belief from women that the traits of a leader and manger do not describe them. This discourages them from leadership positions while a hostile work culture where sexist micro-aggressions and cliques still occur compound the problem (Bismark et al., 2015; Ham et al., 2011). Health and social care systems could be seen as gender neutral, technical systems, but in reality, they are complex adaptive systems connected with power and political relations (Kruk et al., 2018). They must be understood via the lens in which they are shaped via their socio-political contexts reinforcing and reflecting their social norms (Percival et al., 2018). Now more than ever this understanding must be our lens for change.

Readers of this collection can conclude, as we do as editors, that the chapters presented by the authors in this book are in no way comprehensive of the work women have done and continue to do to manage within their local health and social are systems. However, it does shine a light for the first time of the experience and reflections from both historical and contemporary

DOI: 10.4324/9781003546610-12

women that can be used for future learning. The title of this edited collection links women in health management as ***global revolutionaries***. In our research for this chapter on characteristics of female revolutionaries, much historical resources are available (Erkkila, 1987; Redmond & McAuliffe, 2024). Nikolayenko (2020) outlines how women's involvement in a revolution can follow three different strategies: patriarchal, emancipatory and hybrid. The patriarchal model assumes that motherhood is a key driver of women's activism. The emancipatory model is a catalyst for women's activism enabling access to formal leadership positions. The hybrid model includes a variety of motivations for women's engagement. It identifies the diversity of women's roles and acknowledges various degrees of success in gender equality in different contexts (Nikolayenko, 2020). The women showcased in this book draw on these strategies with work presented from Kenya, Hawaii, Türkiye, Nigeria, USA, Ireland and the UK, and from disciplines that span medicine, social work, mental health, health promotion, occupational therapy, midwifery, pharmacology and traditional healing. Each of the chapters illustrates how the women worked within their contexts to become revolutionaries. Many have been hidden from plain sight due to their gender, values, religious and/or political identity or to the perceived lack of importance due to the 'feminisation' of some of their work.

Being the First

There is overwhelming consensus in the literature that women are underrepresented in health and social care management (Mousa et al., 2021; Proimos et al., 2024). We still see contemporary articles on women being the 'first' in areas of health and social care in different settings (O'Mahony, 2025; Omari, 2024). Chapters presented in this collection show how many of the women highlighted were the 'first'. Yıldırım and Ali Icbay's chapter on Safiye Ali outline what she had to do to become the 'the first female physician licensed to practice in the Turkish Republic'. Training to become a doctor in Germany, Dr Ali returned to find new opportunities with the establishment of the Turkish Republic becoming the first female doctor. She held the line on being paid the same fee as her male colleagues but also advocated that those who could not afford to pay could access her services for free. Her work shifted the focus from a clinical lens to a broader recognition of the social determinants of health resulting in her focus of social justice and advocacy that had a significant impact in the lives of women and children. She transferred her clinical work to political, becoming one of the first women to run for parliament. Within the Nikolayenko (2020) model of female involvement in revolutions, Dr Ali clearly followed the hybrid strategy, leaning into ideas of motherhood and family within the new republic and at the same time advancing pay equity and the role of women in national leadership, political and education insisting the women had every right to be there.

Walsh's chapter on Elizabeth Abimbola Awoliyi, Nigeria's first female medical doctor, obstetrician and gynaecologist, captures and celebrates many 'first' achievements. Similar to Ali's trajectory Dr Awoliyi travelled to Ireland to study medicine at the Royal College of Surgeons and graduated in 1938. As Walsh outlined she was 'not only in the minority in terms of her gender, but also in terms of her ethnicity'. Similar to Dr Ali, the recognition of the social determinants of health was the fore of Dr Awoliyi's work and advocacy. As an active leader of women's rights, she worked across sectors to empower women in Nigeria. She also mentored and empowered many female doctors through her pioneering work in public health education and via her appointment as the Senior Specialist Gynaecologist and Obstetrician by the Federal Ministry of Health in Nigeria. She advocated through her roles and is aligned to Nikolayenko's (2020) patriarchal strategy by becoming the architects of maternal public health in Nigeria.

Hidden Women due to the Feminisation of Work

The book chapters presented offer deep insight into the lives of women, many of whom have been invisible (Redmond & McAuliffe, 2024). Williams' chapter on Maida Herman Solomon provides an insight into her pioneering social work and career focused on activisms and education. Williams concludes that much of Solomon's contributions have been hidden so far due to the 'feminisation of social work'. Many female social workers continue to experience this as illustrated from a recent study from Spain that concluded that that there was increased burnout and workload among female professionals, a general under-representation of women in managerial positions and a perception that their work are undervalued (Romero-Martín et al., 2025). COVID-19 focused our attention on the critical importance of our health and social care workforce. It also brought to the fore that women experience a 24% pay gap compared to men across health and social care (WHO, 2022).

Moving Away from the 'Superhuman'

High levels of personal and work-related burnout were found among female health workers during COVID-19 (Adamis et al., 2023; Morgan et al., 2022). Byrne outlines in his chapter on Professor Dame Clare Gerada's contribution by highlighting the medical self and holding a mirror to high rates of burnout and depression of doctors. Gerada was also the 'first' woman to hold the position of Chair and President (2021–2023) of the Royal College of General Practitioners (RCGP) in the UK. Gerada, born in Nigeria to Maltese parents, came to the UK as an immigrant where she worked in primary care as a general practitioner in London. Byrne maps the link between managing the 'superhuman' identity perceived of doctors, and Gerada's focus and work on recognising the need to support doctors' mental health by establishing 'Practitioner Health', a service providing mental health support to doctors. The need to refocus from the learnings of COVID-19 is stressed in Byrne's chapter by not only encouraging doctors to avail of the mental health supports that are available but also stressing the need for society as a collective to enable an inter-sectoral approach and 'humanise doctors'.

Advocacy on Issues Still Relevant Today

Mwendwa in her chapter presents on the work of Edwina Jeruto Kwallah in Kenya. Kwallah comes from the Maasai and Kalenjin communities and has spent her career implementing interventions on child protection and gender-based violence working primarily with women and girls. Kenya is one of the regions of sub-Saharan Africa. Mwendwa notes that child marriage and female genital mutilation continue to be practised 'particularly among pastoralist and nomadic communities including the Samburu, Maasai, Pokot, Rendille and Somali ethnic groups in Kenya'. Kwallah leads an Irish-funded non-governmental organisation called Cara Projects. The organisation has been providing a safe space for over 600 children, since 2008, to acquire formal education, accessed counselling, medical attention, legal aid and re-integration into society. Edwina has taken risks to support these children by educating her communities, including men. She has developed trust and alliances to continue the critical work of Cara. Mwendwa concludes that much of the leadership and support work that Edwina Jeruto Kwallah delivers is unseen. As a women leader working within her own community to support and empower, she deserves recognition. The chapter clearly celebrates Kwallah's work and provides a template for us all on how to undertake change in collaboration with local communities.

Around 800 women die each day from preventable causes related to pregnancy and childbirth (Musaddiq, 2023). The contemporary literature continues to stress the importance of having midwifes from diverse ethnic background as a mechanism to enhance safety and person-centred care that is based on cultural safety (Mantula et al., 2023; Preziosi et al., 2025). Ada Shillman became known as 'mother of the community' in Jewish Dublin in the late 1880s. She stepped into her role as a community midwife out of necessity as presented by the authors Curtin, Carroll and Keegan. A mother of eight children, with her husband unwell, she became the sole breadwinner. Training to become a midwife in 1888, the authors' review of the records suggests 'this was not normal with the overwhelming majority of registrants being Irish and of Roman Catholic or Church of Ireland denomination'. While the Jewish community grew at the time, Jewish mothers avoided the maternity services as they deemed them not appropriate for customs. Shillman established midwifery practices providing specific culturally appropriate care for Jewish families and also introduced means-testing to support all who came to her service.

In 2026, Ireland will finally have moved into a new national children's hospital (*Irelands New Children's Hospital*, n.d.; McAleese et al., 2021). McAuliffe's chapter on Drs Kathleen Lynn, Elizabeth Tennant, Katherine Maguire, Ella Webb and Dorothy Stopford Price highlights their contribution in establishing in 1919 St Ultan's Hospital, a secular hospital for sick infants. These women came together as community activists, as they were concerned by excessive infant and maternal motility rates. A recent academic paper advocates for the need for framing the gender disparity in senior management and participation as 'men's overrepresentation' rather than 'women's under-representation' (Liaquat et al., 2025). Much can be learned from the practice of operations at St Ultan's Hospital. McAuliffe outlines how the established hospital was entirely managed by women and actively favoured the hiring of female staff over men. There was a recognition that 'many female doctors were deprived of professional opportunities enjoyed by their male counterparts' and thus the focus was creating a 'radical secular female space' until its closure in the 1980s. The collective efforts of Drs Kathleen Lynn, Elizabeth Tennant, Katherine Maguire, Ella Webb and Dorothy Stopford Price should be a learning opportunity for us all as they worked together towards a new way of working and delivery of a service that was responsive to community needs.

New Approaches

Much of our focus in modern health systems is on advancing and supporting person-centred care (Auld et al., 2024; Candelaria et al., 2024). There is a recognition that in this 'third era for medicine' patients can be partners resulting in better outcomes (Berwick, 2016). Pettigrew, Cahill and O'Mahoney's chapter on Ann Beckett outlines how at the age of 14 she had her leg amputated following an infection. This physical disability had a profound impact on her path to becoming an occupational therapist. The chapter outlined how it impacted her ways of working and how she engaged with patients. Beckett, as outlined in the chapter, also enabled psychological safety within her team as a key requirement for collective leadership approaches (Edmondson & Bransby, 2023). Beckett enabled a culture where staff felt 'valued and valuable' where the teams were sociable together and first names were used. Much of the contemporary literature around collective leadership advances these types of approaches to support team working (De Brún & McAuliffe, 2020; O'Donnell et al., 2021). Supportive and safe team working are prerequisites for the delivery of patient centred care.

Much of the content we teach and research we undertake today within contemporary healthcare management is focused on new power approaches. Co-production has been advocated as an approach to enable local solutions to enable more women in managerial roles (Proimos et al., 2024; Saville et al., 2024). Tzouramani's chapter focuses on the work of on Morrnah Nalamaku Simeona, a Hawaiian Indigenous Kahuna Lapa'au woman, whose practice of Ho'oponopono stresses the importance of the 'interconnectedness of individuals, communities and the natural environment'. Much of this focus can be found in the 'One Health' initiatives that stress the importance of collaborative and multidisciplinary approaches and recognise that human health is intricately linked to those of other animals and the environment (Panel (OHHLEP) et al., 2022). Simeona recognised the active role that patients can play in their care and she reframes healing as a process that empowers the patients. Tzouramani's chapter notes how Simeona worked towards integrating Indigenous knowledge systems into healthcare in different settings and provided that it could co-exist with the biomedical model. Similarly, the chapter by Norton and Brogan's provides insight into the implementation of the CHIME Framework into the Irish mental health recover movement that consists of five components – Connectedness, Hope and optimism, Identify, Meaning and Purpose and Empowerment. Shifting from a biomedical model to a personal recovery model acknowledges the role of the person using services as the author of their own recovery (Fox, 2025). The authors using an autoethnography approach reflect on how Brogan enabled the shift to CHIME within the Irish context. Notably the authors reflect on the importance that Brogan had on co-production with service users and elevating their insights so that mental health services could learn for the 'betterment of the service as a whole'.

Where to? Moving Beyond Recognising We Have a Problem

Writing this conclusion chapter in March 2025, we are mindful that we are observing a retreat of diversity, equity and inclusion initiatives within large organisations such as Facebook and McDonalds and within the Federal government of the United States of America (Gallogly, 2025). Scaling-back efforts like pay audit transparency reporting, diverse recruitment and equitable promotion practices will further impact opportunities for women to enter senior managerial roles within the health and social care workforce. Targeting women who stepped up to become mentors and role models under diversity programmes is now a reality for many working in federal human and health services in the United States of America (Lovelace & Edwards, 2025). This is in many ways a chilling thought and will have long-term impacts on women in healthcare management. We are at a crossroads and there is a need to pause, be honest and understand why these changes are being championed by a large cohort of men and women (McCarthy, 2025). We also have to be honest, recognise and reflect on the evidence that women in healthcare management can 'sometimes impede other women's advancement . . . this challenges assumptions that women naturally support each other's career progression and adds complexity to the understanding of internalised gender biases' (Lux et al., 2025).

For those of us working in higher education, we must review, reflect and act on what adaptions are required in our curriculum and training. It also reinforces the importance of this edited volume so we can learn and include women's experiences and perspective for future learning and to create an enabling culture (Boyd, 2019; Ní Shé et al., 2018).

Unless organisations, states, educators and policymakers are willing to learn from previous women's experiences of leading and managing we will continue to observe a 'snake and ladder' process of women in management (Magee & Penfold, 2022). The recent evidence is overwhelming that female leaders have positive effects on financial performance, innovation, ethical practice, health, organisational culture and other women's career outcomes (Chung et al., 2023; Clark, 2025; Kalbarczyk et al., 2025). The focus on the need to demonstrate and reinforce this again and again in 2025 must be shattered and instead the focus must be on action. Much of the chapters showcased how women, out of necessity, developed and organised services for areas of neglected health (e.g. women's health, health prevention, rural populations), tackling contentious health issues (e.g. female genital mutilation, management of mental disorders) and managing the care of health providers themselves (e.g. providing space for women to practice, managing the mental well-being of healthcare workers). The women shown in this collection have worked around the world to innovate, deliver and manage services that addressed unmet needs. They have shined a light on the needs of the vulnerable who appear to have been invisible to more androcentric healthcare. They also organised to do something about it. Healthcare management requires people who can adapt and respond to an ever-evolving system. Many of these women clearly adapted and went beyond health management to influence education, political and societal change. Creating the space for this enabling culture must be the responsibility of everyone. Capturing the evidence on what women do must be prioritised for future learning and we hope this is the start of a diverse collection of their experiences.

References

Adamis, D., Minihan, E., Hannan, N., Doherty, A. M., & McNicholas, F. (2023). Burnout in mental health services in Ireland during the COVID-19 pandemic. *BJPsych Open*, *9*(6), e177. https://doi.org/10.1192/bjo.2023.552

Allen, G. (n.d.). The case for DEI reinvention, not retreat. *Forbes*. Retrieved 4 February2025,fromhttps://www.forbes.com/sites/gemmaallen/2025/01/27/dei-crisis-looms-the-case-for-reinvention-not-retreat/

Auld, K., Devaparanam, I., Roberts, S., & McInerney, J. (2024). Lived experiences of healthcare: Putting the person in person centred care in the medical radiation sciences. *Radiography*, *30*(3), 856–861. https://doi.org/10.1016/j.radi.2024.03.012

Baduge, M. S. D. S. P., Garth, B., Boyd, L., Ward, K., Joseph, K., Proimos, J., & Teede, H. J. (2024). Barriers to advancing women nurses in healthcare leadership: A systematic review and meta-synthesis. *eClinicalMedicine*, *67*. https://doi.org/10.1016/j.eclinm.2023.102354

Bear, J. B. (2021). Forget the 'mommy track': Temporal flexibility increases promotion aspirations for women and reduces gender gaps. *Psychology of Women Quarterly*, *45*(3), 294–307. https://doi.org/10.1177/03616843211003070

Berwick, D. M. (2016). Era 3 for medicine and health care. *JAMA*, *315*(13), 1329–1330. https://doi.org/10.1001/jama.2016.1509

Bismark, M., Morris, J., Thomas, L., Loh, E., Phelps, G., & Dickinson, H. (2015). Reasons and remedies for under-representation of women in medical leadership roles: A qualitative study from Australia. *BMJ Open*, *5*(11), e009384. https://doi.org/10.1136/bmjopen-2015-009384

Boyd, S. (2019). From 'great women' to an inclusive curriculum: How should women's history be included at key stage 3? *Teaching History*, *175*, 16–23.

Candelaria, D., Tyagi, V., Gallagher, R., Hendriks, J., & McCormack, B. (2024). Person-centredness in cardiovascular care: The need for a whole-systems perspective. *European Journal of Cardiovascular Nursing*, *23*(8), e161–e163. https://doi.org/10.1093/eurjcn/zvae052

Chung, E., El-Harakeh, A., Weinberg, J. L., Azeez, O., Ortigoza, A., Johnson, A., Harrison, M., & Kalbarczyk, A. (2023). A scoping review on resources, tools, and programs to support women's leadership in global health: What is available, what works, and how do we know? *Annals of Global Health*, *89*(1), 27. https://doi.org/10.5334/aogh.3921

Clark, J. (2025). The case for women's leadership in global health. *BMJ (Clinical Research Ed.)*, *388*, r190. https://doi.org/10.1136/bmj.r190

De Brún, A., & McAuliffe, E. (2020). Identifying the context, mechanisms and outcomes underlying collective leadership in teams: Building a realist programme theory. *BMC Health Services Research*, *20*(1), 261. https://doi.org/10.1186/s12913-020-05129-1

Edmondson, A. C., & Bransby, D. P. (2023). Psychological safety comes of age: Observed themes in an established literature. *Annual Review of Organizational Psychology and Organizational Behavior*, *10*, 55–78. https://doi.org/10.1146/annurev-orgpsych-120920-055217

Erkkila, B. (1987). Revolutionary women. *Tulsa Studies in Women's Literature*, *6*(2), 189–223. https://doi.org/10.2307/464269

Fox, J. (2025). Autoethnographic reflections on mental distress and medication management: Conceptualising biomedical and recovery models of mental health. *Community Mental Health Journal*, *61*(2), 213–220. https://doi.org/10.1007/s10597-024-01230-5

Gallogly, N. (2025, January 22). The D.E.I. retreat has some notable holdouts. *The New York Times.* https://www.nytimes.com/2025/01/22/business/dei-programs-initiatives-costco-microsoft.html

Ham, C., Clark, J., Spurgeon, P., Dickinson, H., & Armit, K. (2011). Doctors who become chief executives in the NHS: From keen amateurs to skilled professionals. *Journal of the Royal Society of Medicine, 104*(3), 113–119. https://doi.org/10.1258/jrsm.2011.110042

Irelands New Children's Hospital. (n.d.). Retrieved 24 February 2025, from https://newchildrenshospital.ie/

Kalbarczyk, A., Banchoff, K., Perry, K. E., Nielsen, C. P., Malhotra, A., & Morgan, R. (2025). A scoping review on the impact of women's global leadership: Evidence to inform health leadership. *BMJ Global Health, 10*(2). https://doi.org/10.1136/bmjgh-2024-015982

Karakcheyeva, V., Willis-Johnson, H., Corr, P. G., & Frame, L. A. (2024). The well-being of women in healthcare professions: A comprehensive review. *Global Advances in Integrative Medicine and Health, 13*, 27536130241232929. https://doi.org/10.1177/27536130241232929

Kruk, M. E., Gage, A. D., Arsenault, C., Jordan, K., Leslie, H. H., Roder-DeWan, S., Adeyi, O., Barker, P., Daelmans, B., Doubova, S. V., English, M., Elorrio, E. G., Guanais, F., Gureje, O., Hirschhorn, L. R., Jiang, L., Kelley, E., Lemango, E. T., Liljestrand, J., . . . Pate, M. (2018). High-quality health systems in the sustainable development goals era: Time for a revolution. *The Lancet. Global Health, 6*, e1196–e1252. https://doi.org/10.1016/S2214-109X(18)30386-3

Liaquat, U., Heilman, M. E., Godsil, R. D., & Balcetis, E. (2025). Women underrepresented or men overrepresented? Framing influences women's affective and behavioral responses to gender gap in political leadership. *Journal of Experimental Social Psychology, 117*, 104709. https://doi.org/10.1016/j.jesp.2024.104709

Lovelace, B., & Edwards, E. (2025, February 5). Federal health workers terrified after 'DEI' website publishes list of 'targets'. *NBC News.* https://www.nbcnews.com/health/health-news/federal-health-workers-terrified-dei-website-publishes-list-targets-rcna190711

Lux, A. A., Salehi, N., Hurley, D., & Emanuel, E. (2025). Dismantling pervasive gender stereotypes in healthcare leadership contexts with an ecological systems theory approach. *Journal of Management & Organization*, 1–32. https://doi.org/10.1017/jmo.2024.79

Magee, L., & Penfold, R. (2022). Game of snakes and ladders: Barriers and enablers for aspiring women leaders in healthcare. *BMJ Leader, 6*(1). https://doi.org/10.1136/leader-2020-000221

Mantula, F., Chamisa, J. A., Nunu, W. N., & Nyanhongo, P. S. (2023). Women's perspectives on cultural sensitivity of midwives during intrapartum care at a maternity ward in a national referral hospital in Zimbabwe. *SAGE Open Nursing, 9.* https://doi.org/10.1177/23779608231160476

McAleese, T., Brent, L., O'Toole, P., Synnott, K., Quinn, N., Deasy, C., & Sheehan, E. (2021). Paediatric major trauma in the setting of the Irish trauma network. *Injury, 52*(8), 2233–2243. https://doi.org/10.1016/j.injury.2021.05.032

McCarthy, J. (2025, February 14). Justine McCarthy: Amid all of the toxic masculinity, no one mentions the toxic femininity that supports it. *The Irish Times.* https://www.irishtimes.com/opinion/2025/02/14/when-the-institutions-of-the-land-imply-women-are-inferior-the-risk-is-you-start-to-believe-them/

Morgan, R., Tan, H.-L., Oveisi, N., Memmott, C., Korzuchowski, A., Hawkins, K., & Smith, J. (2022). Women healthcare workers' experiences during COVID-19 and other crises: A scoping review. *International Journal of Nursing Studies Advances*, *4*, 100066. https://doi.org/10.1016/j.ijnsa.2022.100066

Mousa, M., Boyle, J., Skouteris, H., Mullins, A. K., Currie, G., Riach, K., & Teede, H. J. (2021). Advancing women in healthcare leadership: A systematic review and meta-synthesis of multi-sector evidence on organisational interventions. *eClinicalMedicine*, *39*. https://doi.org/10.1016/j.eclinm.2021.101084

Musaddiq, T. (2023). The impact of community midwives on maternal healthcare utilization. *Health Economics*, *32*(3), 697–714. https://doi.org/10.1002/hec.4640

Nikolayenko, O. (2020, April). *Invisible revolutionaries: Women's participation in the revolution of dignity* [Text]. City University of New York. https://doi.org/10.5129/001041520X15699553017268

Ní Shé, É., Burton, L. J., & Danaher, P. A. (Eds.). (2018). *Social capital and enterprise in the modern state*. Springer International Publishing. https://doi.org/10.1007/978-3-319-68115-3

O'Donnell, D., O'Shea, M., Donnelly, S., Ní Shé, É., O'Donoghue, G., Bourke, N., Brennan, J., Claffey, A., Cosgrave, S., Lang, D., Maloney, P., McAuliffe, E., McGuigan, C., McMahon, N., O'Shea, D., Quinn, S., Reilly, P., & Whitty, H. (2021). *Getting started in developing core competences for interprofessional collaboration within integrated care teams for older people: A framework for the national integrated care programme for older people*. University College Dublin. https://www.icpop.org/publications

O'Mahony, S. (2025, February 12). 'It is super rewarding' – Ireland's first female consultant neurosurgeon on the patients that keep her going every day. *Irish Independent*. https://www.independent.ie/entertainment/television/tv-news/it-is-super-rewarding-irelands-first-female-consultant-neurosurgeon-on-the-patients-that-keep-her-going-every-day/a503989909.html

Omari, R. Y. (2024). Shattering the surgical glass ceiling: Women surgeons in the Middle East. *British Journal of Surgery*, *111*(1), znad396. https://doi.org/10.1093/bjs/znad396

Panel (OHHLEP), O. H. H.-L. E., Adisasmito, W. B., Almuhairi, S., Behravesh, C. B., Bilivogui, P., Bukachi, S. A., Casas, N., Becerra, N. C., Charron, D. F., Chaudhary, A., Zanella, J. R. C., Cunningham, A. A., Dar, O., Debnath, N., Dungu, B., Farag, E., Gao, G. F., Hayman, D. T. S., Khaitsa, M., . . . Zhou, L. (2022). One health: A new definition for a sustainable and healthy future. *PLOS Pathogens*, *18*(6), e1010537. https://doi.org/10.1371/journal.ppat.1010537

Percival, V., Dusabe-Richards, E., Wurie, H., Namakula, J., Ssali, S., & Theobald, S. (2018). Are health systems interventions gender blind? Examining health system reconstruction in conflict affected states. *Globalization and Health*, *14*(1), 90. https://doi.org/10.1186/s12992-018-0401-6

Preziosi, J., Portaleone, S., Colagiovanni, E., Tedesco, G., Rizzi, F., Rega, M. L., Danza, M., Lanzone, A., & Anderson, G. (2025). Predictors of cultural competence among healthcare professional in maternity department: A systematic review. *Midwifery*, *142*, 104285. https://doi.org/10.1016/j.midw.2025.104285

Proimos, J., Boyle, J. A., Garth, B., Loh, E., & Teede, H. J. (2024). The role of medical colleges and member organisations in advancing women in health care leadership. *Medical Journal of Australia*, *220*(7), 346–351. https://doi.org/10.5694/mja2.52244

Redmond, J., & McAuliffe, M. (Eds.). (2024). *The politics of gender and sexuality in modern Ireland*. Fourt Courts Press. https://www.fourcourtspress.ie/books/2024/the-politics-of-gender-and-sexuality-in-modern-ireland

Romero-Martín, S., Elboj-Saso, C., & Íñiguez-Berrozpe, T. (2025). Feminization and burnout among female social workers. *Journal of Social Work*, 14680173241312764. https://doi.org/10.1177/14680173241312764

Saville, N. M., Uppal, R., Odunga, S. A., Kedia, S., Odero, H. O., Tanaka, S., Kiwuwa-Muyingo, S., Eleh, L., Venkatesh, S., Zeinali, Z., Koay, A., Buse, K., Verma, R., & Hawkes, S. (2024). Pathways to leadership: What accounts for women's (in)equitable career paths in the health sectors in India and Kenya? A scoping review. *BMJ Global Health*, *9*(7). https://doi.org/10.1136/bmjgh-2023-014745

WHO. (2021). *Closing the leadership gap: Gender equity and leadership in the global health and care workforce* (1st ed.). Policy Action Paper, June. World Health Organization.

WHO. (2022). *The gender pay gap in the health and care sector a global analysis in the time of COVID-19*. https://www.who.int/publications/i/item/9789240052895

Zeinali, Z., Muraya, K., Molyneux, S., & Morgan, R. (2021). The use of intersectional analysis in assessing women's leadership progress in the health workforce in LMICs: A review. *International Journal of Health Policy and Management*, *11*(8), 1262–1273. https://doi.org/10.34172/ijhpm.2021.06

Index

Page numbers in **bold** refer tables on the corresponding page. Page numbers followed by n refer notes.